D1563032

Mods, Rockers, and the
Music of the British Invasion

MODS, ROCKERS, AND THE MUSIC OF THE BRITISH INVASION

James E. Perone

Westport, Connecticut
London

Library of Congress Cataloging-in-Publication Data

Perone, James E.
    Mods, rockers, and the music of the British invasion / James E.
Perone.
        p. cm.
    Includes bibliographical references, discography and index.
    ISBN 978–0–275–99860–8 (alk. paper)
    1. Rock music—Great Britain—History and criticism.   I. Title.
    ML3534.6.G7P47   2009
    781.660941'09045—dc22   2008029355

British Library Cataloguing in Publication Data is available.

Library of Congress Catalog Card Number: 2008029355
ISBN: 978–0–275–99860–8

First published in 2009

Praeger Publishers, 88 Post Road West, Westport, CT 06881
An imprint of Greenwood Publishing Group, Inc.
www.praeger.com

Printed in the United States of America

The paper used in this book complies with the
Permanent Paper Standard issued by the National
Information Standards Organization (Z39.48–1984).

10 9 8 7 6 5 4 3 2 1

Contents

Acknowledgments

This book could not have been written without the valuable assistance of a number of people. I wish first to thank Karen Perone for offering moral and technical support throughout this and all of my book projects for Greenwood Press and Praeger Publishers, and for offering much-needed input at every stage of every project.

Over the course of writing several books, the entire staff of the Greenwood Publishing Group has been most helpful and cooperative. I wish to extend special thanks to editor Daniel Harmon for his assistance in putting this book together.

I also wish to send a special shout of thanks out to Ron Mandelbaum and the entire staff of Photofest for the photographs that appear in this book.

I also wish to thank three British rock and roll performers who were there to see and to contribute to the development of a distinctive British approach to the genre in the late 1950s and nearly 1960s. Tony Sheridan, Ron Ryan, and Mick Ryan all took time out of their schedules to answer my questions and share insights. Ron, in particular, spent a total of a couple of hours talking with me via telephone about a wide range of relevant topics. Thanks, too, to Peter Dintino, who arranged the telephone linkups between Ron and myself.

I wish to extend a sincere word of thanks to the Mount Union College Faculty Development Committee, to Dr. Patricia Draves, dean of the college, and to the college's board of trustees for approving my spring 2008 sabbatical leave so that I could work on this project.

And, finally, a special word of thanks to Mary Cotofan for her work in helping me in the editorial stages of several Praeger Publishers projects I have undertaken. Mary and her copy editors do yeoman work with all the technical details that I manage to have left unaddressed at the manuscript stage.

Despite my own best efforts and the assistance of those named above there are bound to be errors in this book: they are solely my responsibility.

1

Introduction:
The Mods versus the Rockers

In a memorable scene from the Beatles' 1964 film *A Hard Day's Night,* a reporter asks Ringo Starr if he is a Mod or a Rocker. The drummer responds that, in fact, he is neither: he is "a Mocker." While Starr's response clearly is framed as a joke, there is an element of truth in it. One thing that added to the Beatles' appeal was their ability to balance the old (the Rockers) and the new (the Mods). And, with their subtle antiauthoritarianism and sense of the absurd, they really were in a literal sense mockers of sorts. But who were the Mods and the Rockers, and how do they serve as a metaphor for the development of rock and roll in Great Britain from the 1950s through the British Invasion? That is the purpose of this book: to use the Mods and the Rockers as a metaphor for the progression of British rock from the Elvis Presley imitators of the mid-1950s to the work of the Beatles, the Dave Clark Five, the Who, the Kinks, Gerry and the Pacemakers, the Searchers, the Rolling Stones, Billy J. Kramer and the Dakotas, the Zombies, and all the other British groups that ruled the U.S. record charts in 1964–1966. Before we can use the Mods and Rockers as a metaphor, however, we must delve into just who these groups were and what they stood for.

THE MODS AND THE ROCKERS

On Easter weekend 1964, a long Bank Holiday, two rival British youth gangs, the Mods and the Rockers, met up in various resort locations in England, and violence broke out. The riots on Brighton beach and elsewhere attracted the attention of the press in

The Who's 1979 film *Quadrophenia* depicted the infamous battles between rival youth gangs the Mods and the Rockers that took place Easter Weekend, 1964. These battles form a metaphor for the development of British Invasion rock, which was born out of 1950s Rocker aesthetics and by 1964 had turned more consciously Mod in approach. Courtesy of Photofest.

the United Kingdom and abroad. There seems to be little evidence that there was widespread documented physical animosity between the two groups before the riots that erupted in 1964.[1] However, the Mods and the Rockers represented two very different approaches taken by disenfranchised British youth.

The Rockers were associated with motorcycles, and in particular with the larger, heavy and powerful Triumph motorcycles of the late 1950s. They favored black leather, much like American motorcycle gang members of the era. Their musical tastes ran to white American rock and rollers such as Elvis Presley, Gene Vincent, and Eddie Cochran. Vincent and Cochran, in particular, captured the attention of British teens with their 1960 concert tour of the United Kingdom, the infamous tour in which Vincent was injured and Cochran was killed in an automobile accident. As we shall see, early British rock musicians focused on the rockabilly of Bill Haley and His Comets, Elvis Presley, Vincent, Cochran, and Buddy Holly. In many respects it was the breaking free of overt imitation of these musical references and the incorporation of direct influences from African American blues and R&B that laid the foundations for the development of a uniquely British rock and roll that took Britain by storm in 1962 and 1963, and came to the shores of the United States in 1964 and 1965. In other words, the story of the development of British Invasion rock can be seen as a move away from the Rocker aesthetic.

By contrast, the Mods made a conscious attempt to appear new (hence, "Mod," or modern) by favoring Italian motor scooters and wearing suits. Musically, Mods favored modern jazz, Jamaican music, and African American R&B. In the early 1960s, the lines between the Mods and the Rockers were clearly drawn: the Mods thought of themselves as more sophisticated, more stylish, and more in touch with the times than the Rockers were. The Rockers, however, viewed the Mods as effeminate snobs.

Any discussion of Mods and Rockers must also include discussion of the Teddy Boys and Teddy Girls. This segment of the British youth subculture developed after World War II—it predates the Mods and Rockers—and its male members initially were identified by the Edwardian suits they wore. It has been widely acknowledged that in Britain, "they were the first group whose style was self-created."[2]

Curiously, the Teddy Boys (and Girls) are seen as the spiritual ancestors of both the Mods and the Rockers. Visually, with their so-called D.A. (or, less euphemistically, "duck's arse") haircuts, they resembled early American rock and roll stars. They also resembled American film icons such as Marlon Brando—particularly as he appeared in the 1953 biker film *The Wild One*—and James Dean as he appeared in the 1955 film *Rebel Without a Cause*. The Teddy Boys and Girls, then, took American popular culture and adopted and adapted it to their own needs in order to define their subculture. Certainly, the emphasis on the outsider and the interest in American motorcycle gangs directly influenced the Rockers of the late 1950s and the early 1960s. The Teddy Boys, however, adopted the new Edwardian-styled fashions that British clothing companies were pushing to young people. Their manner of dress, then, influenced the Mods.

The curious and somewhat confusing mix of various gang-like youth subcultures in the late 1950s in Britain plays a role in the youth-exploitation film *Beat Girl*. In this 1960 movie—which starred Christopher Lee, Oliver Reed, Gillian Hills, Adam Faith, and Noëlle Adam—one can see elements of the developing Mod culture (the jazz-loving, coffee-bar teen group represented by Faith's, Hills's, and Reed's characters) and a touch of the developing Rocker culture (in the form of a large, American-style car that is used in one sequence from the film, and hair styles worn by some of the minor young male characters). Near the end of the film, a group of Teddy Boys destroy Faith's sports car. It is interesting to note that the nascent Mods and Rockers of the film seem not to be in conflict with each other, or at least not nearly as much as the "Teds" (as Faith's character, Dave, calls them) are in conflict with these newer groups. While *Beat Girl* can in no way be construed as a serious sociological study of the conflicts between youth gangs in late-1950s Britain, it does capture the need for self-identification that ran through all of these groups. It also shows that this self-identification was manifested in clothing, musical style, and lingo (the principal youth characters use language that comes straight out of American beatnik stereotypes). I submit that image and fashion also played a role in drawing young people in the United Kingdom and in the United States to particular rock performers. In fact, the bands that succeeded most fully in the British Invasion possessed important visual hooks that made them instantly identifiable, even without a single note of music being heard.

While we will not detail the Mods, Rockers, and Teds per se—they are being used primarily as a metaphor for the changing aesthetics in British youth culture from the 1950s to the early 1960s—it is important to note that sociologists have determined that despite their outward differences (hair, dress, mode of transportation, and so on) the groups share several crucial links. For one thing, members of the youth gangs of the 1950s and early 1960s tended to be working class. And, although some members of the gangs described themselves as middle class, very rarely were Britain's upper social and economic classes represented in the Teds, Mods, or Rockers.[3] Likewise, we shall see that skiffle and rock musicians that sprang up within British youth culture in the 1950s and early 1960s also tended to come from the working class.

As we shall see, by the time of the British Invasion, the bands that made a commercial and sociological impact in the United States either leaned heavily in the Mod direction or were interesting hybrids that took their influences from the music favored in the late 1950s and early 1960s by both the Mods and Rockers and made it into something that was essentially different from the source material. So, although the classic seaside resort battles between the Mods and the Rockers took place in the spring of 1964, the musical battle had already been decided in favor of the Mods.

One aspect of the development of British Invasion rock that the reader must keep in mind is the devastation that Great Britain endured in World War II. Nearly every biography or autobiography of British rock musicians who were born in the late 1930s or the first few years of the 1940s touch on—or even focus on—the results of the war. Not only did the war create indelible images on the psyche of the young people who were children during the German bombardment of the United Kingdom, but the destruction of factories, schools, and housing areas created harsh economic conditions that lasted for years. As George Harrison stated in the documentary film *The Beatles Anthology,* "You couldn't get a cup of sugar, never mind a rock 'n' roll record."[4]

Not only were the economic effects of World War II felt during the childhood of the musicians that were part of the British Invasion, they continued to be felt for some time. Burned out buildings, bombed shipyards, and other physical manifestations of the war persisted, and they symbolize the terrible economic and poor living conditions in which working-class families found themselves well after the war was over. It is almost as though the harsh living conditions and poverty of the Great Depression in the United States, which spawned what Tom Brokaw calls "the Greatest Generation"[5] (the younger side of Strauss and Howe's "G.I. Generation"[6]), returned in Britain in the 1940s and early 1950s, thus creating a generation of young people who had fundamental differences from their American counterparts (the Baby Boomers).

Another reality of the United Kingdom that Americans tend not to appreciate fully is the British class structure. While there is not sufficient space to detail this, it needs to be noted that economic and social class distinctions were much more clearly defined in the Britain of the 1940s and 1950s (when the British Invasion musicians were growing up) than within the white population of the United States. In the United States, the greatest divide was that associated with race. In Great Britain—a nation with a more homogenous racial and ethnic makeup in the 1940s and 1950s than the United States—the great divide was of social and economic class.

Bill Wyman (formerly of the Rolling Stones) touches on this in the foreword to his book *Bill Wyman's Blues Odyssey: A Journey to Music's Heart & Soul,* in which he writes, "I was born in Southeast London just prior to the outbreak of World War II. Although my father worked, we were far from well off; life was a struggle. Years later, I found that many black musicians grew up in the Southern states of the US in difficult circumstances, something of a shared experience." Although Wyman acknowledges that he had to endure none of the racism that blacks had to endure in the United States, he goes on to tell of doing well enough on his examinations to be able to attend a good school, but of feeling like an outsider at school because of his cockney accent and background.[7] The intensity of the class system is confirmed by Chris Stamp, one-time manager and producer of the Who, who stated that the working class in London in the 1950s found themselves in a "similar socio-economic situation to the blacks in America."[8] Ron Ryan (the Walkers, the Riot Squad, and early songwriter for the Dave Clark Five), who was from a working-class part of London and did not have the advantage of attending the best schools, says of the British class system of the 1940s and 1950s, "I think the only way to describe it to an American is to make the coalition with kids like me and the Blacks before the 1960s in the USA. We went to run-down schools, and got very rough treatment from teachers in the main. Some were very brutal."[9]

By and large, the musicians that made up the British Invasion came from working-class families—they did not come from the upper classes of British society. The working-class nature of skiffle and early rock and roll (the music could be played to a large extent on homemade instruments) was seen as a way out of poverty. Once the young male musicians realized that they could earn money from their music—as well as use music as a way to impress girls—they made this connection between music and circumventing the established class system. The musicians strove to better themselves economically and musically, with the two goals working hand in hand. The connections that working class youths, particularly in London, felt with American blacks also transferred to an appreciation of and kinship with American blues music.

Perhaps because they were not very commercially appealing subjects for pop songs, economic and social class did not come up all that often in the early British rock repertoire. In fact, the song with the clearest references to the harsh realities of life for working-class British youths was "We Gotta Get out of This Place," which although made famous by the Animals, from the industrial city of Newcastle-upon-Tyne, was actually written by American Brill Building songwriters Barry Mann and Cynthia Weil. Here and there, however, there are veiled references to class distinction in British society. Gerry and the Pacemakers' self-penned "Ferry Cross the Mersey," for example, seems to suggest that in Liverpool social class and family lineage is not as important as in other parts of the country. Gerry Marsden writes and sings that in Merseyside, "they don't care what your name is, boy; they'll never turn you away." Despite the fact, though, that they did not often deal explicitly with poverty and the discrimination inherent in the British social class system in song, the desire to break free of the constraints of social and economic class was one of the important forces driving the teens growing up in the 1950s to take to music.

Essentially the story of the development of British Invasion rock, then, is the story of skiffle in the early and mid-1950s leading to heavily rockabilly-influenced music in the late 1950s, with R&B and electric blues entering the mix moving into the 1960s. To a large extent, British rock and roll moved from direct imitation of American rockabilly structures, and instrumental and vocal styles, to a more thorough integration and modification of R&B-based styles.

Although economics and class played a role in driving the young musicians who would become part of the British Invasion of the United States in 1964 and 1965, it was what these musicians inherited from American music and from the British stars of the 1950s, and especially how they took those resources and adapted them, that ultimately made an impact in America. Let us now turn to the early forays into American roots music in the form of skiffle and early rock and roll as we lead up to 1964.

2

Skiffle and 1950s Teen Idols and Rockers

SKIFFLE

As early as the 1920s, the term "skiffle" was used to denote a form of African American folk music, performed on such homemade instruments as a corrugated washboard scraped with a metal thimble or a bass constructed with a broomstick and a single string attached to a washtub, wooden box, or tea chest. Skiffle was a folk style that was associated at the time with rent parties in black communities in southern cities such as Memphis and eventually in the great northern urban center, Chicago. In the United States, skiffle as an entertainment form was largely supplanted by blues music, particularly electric blues music. This especially was true as larger groups of people met in larger urban centers for rent parties: eventually, amplified instruments were used so that the musicians could be heard.

Some British traditional jazz groups of the early 1950s included a self-contained skiffle group that entertained while the rest of the members of the group took a break. A member of Chris Barber's Jazz Band, singer/guitarist Lonnie Donegan, recorded a version of "Rock Island Line" in 1954. The arrangement essentially copied that of the American folk and blues musician Lead Belly, who had performed and recorded the song in the 1930s. The origins of the song are difficult to trace, but it appears to be considerably older, and may originally have been part of the double entendre, antislavery repertoire, being at once a song about (1) the Chicago, Rock Island, and Pacific Railroad and (2) the Underground Railroad. The Underground Railroad interpretation is supported by the fact that Rock Island, Illinois, had a relatively strong antislavery movement, and that versions of the song that circulated during the era of audio recording mention the rail line extending into the deep South, areas that in fact never were served by the Chicago, Rock Island, and Pacific Railroad.

In any event, Donegan's recording of this American folk song was a smash hit in Britain and started a skiffle craze. According to London singer, guitarist, and songwriter Ron Ryan, the attraction of skiffle to British teenagers was that it was homemade music and the guitarist only needed to know two chords. In other words, working class teens with limited financial resources and limited musical skills could make this music. Ryan, who was a member of the Walkers and the Riot Squad, reports than "every street in London had a skiffle band" between 1955 and 1957 as a result of the Donegan recording of "The Rock Island Line" and the skiffle craze it started.[1] Incidentally, the 1950s skiffle craze was largely a British phenomenon: American youth were already enthralled with rock and roll in the 1954 to 1957 period and apparently found little attraction in skiffle, although there are some ties between some of the repertoire favored by British skiffle groups and what would become popular around the end of the 1950s in the United States with the folk revival.

If one examines the biographies of nearly every British rock musician who was born between the late 1930s and the early 1940s, one can see the impact of skiffle. John Lennon, Paul McCartney, and George Harrison were members of a skiffle band called the Quarry Men, which morphed into the Beatles by 1960; Tommy Steele was a member of the Cavemen—later the Steelmen—which started out as a skiffle group; Ringo Starr was a member of both the Eddie Clayton Skiffle Group and the Darktown Skiffle Group before joining Rory Storm and the Hurricanes, then playing in Tony Sheridan's backing band, and then joining the Beatles; Billy Fury founded the Formby Sniffle Gloup (a play on words in place of the more customary name by which the group might have been known: the Formby Skiffle Group); Cliff Richard—when he was still using his given name, Harry Webb—also performed in a skiffle band before he formed the Drifters[2] (later, the Shadows); and three members of the most famous lineup of the Shadows— Hank Marvin, Tony Meehan, and Jet Harris—briefly performed with the Vipers Skiffle Group. Even some of the younger British rock musicians, such as Jimmy Page, performed in skiffle groups as teens. Roger Daltrey, lead singer of the Who, goes so far as to suggest that Lonnie Donegan and homemade skiffle music was *the* thing that suggested to him that he could become a musician.[3]

One of the interesting features of the repertoire of the skiffle groups is the extent to which they both turned to then-out-of-fashion traditional American country music, such as the Carter Family's "Worried Man Blues," and traditional African American work songs and Anglo American folk music. In some respects, then, the 1955–1957 skiffle groups anticipated the late 50s and early 60s folk revival in America, the scene that saw renewed interest in established folk performers such as Pete Seeger, as well as the emergence of the Kingston Trio, Joan Baez, Buffy Sainte-Marie, the Highwaymen, Bob Dylan, and others.

Even a cursory glance at the repertoire covered by the Vipers Skiffle Group on their 1957 album *Coffee Bar Session* (Parlophone 1050, 1957; reissued on compact disc as Bear Family BCDE 15954, 1996) shows the extent to which that band focused on traditional American folk and folk-revival music. The album includes Woody Guthrie's "This Land Is Your Land," Pete Seeger's "If I Had a Hammer," as well as "The John B. Sails," the folk song that Dave Guard reworked as "Sloop John B." for the Kingston Trio at the close of the 1950s and that Brian Wilson further reworked in the mid-1960s as a hit single for the Beach Boys. In fact, one of the more interesting but not generally acknowledged facts about the British rock bands of the early 1960s was the extent to which they initiated the merger of folk and rock, well before the better-known work of the American group, the Byrds. For example, on their 1963 debut album, *Meet the Searchers,* the Liverpool-based Searchers included Pete Seeger's "Where Have All the Flowers Gone." While the Searchers' version of the song—as well as Tommy Steele's contemporaneous version—is clearly influenced by the 1962 hit version by the Kingston Trio, the Searchers' recording, especially, includes enough of a rock feel for it to be considered an early incarnation of folk-rock. An even better-known example of pioneering work by a British band in merging folk and rock is the famous 1964 recording of the nineteenth-century American folk song "The House of the Rising Sun," by the Animals. The Animals' recording is thoroughly rock in its orientation and made it to No. 1 in the U.S. *Billboard* pop singles charts nearly a year before the supposed invention of the merger of American folk with British Invasion–style rock in the Byrds' 1965 hit "Mr. Tambourine Man."

While it is difficult to find overt references to skiffle in the electric guitar–based music of the later British Invasion bands, the fascination with American roots music continued to be felt in these bands. From time to time, too, the direct influence of 1950s British skiffle could be felt. The Beatles' recording of "Maggie Mae" (on *Let It Be*)—a song that is based on the 1856 song "Darling Nellie Gray" by American composer Benjamin R. Hanby—dates from January 1969 and resembles the best-known previous U.K. version of "Maggie Mae," a 1957 hit for the Vipers Skiffle Group.

Incidentally, in 1999, former Beatle Paul McCartney recorded "No Other Baby," a song that the Vipers released as a single near the end of the skiffle craze in 1958. In the liner notes for his *Run Devil Run* album, McCartney states, "I've no idea how this one got so embedded in my memory. . . . I never had the record, still haven't."[4] Ironically, in 1958 the Vipers were working with record producer George Martin, who would produce nearly all of the Beatles' recordings. Perhaps because he was recalling a record he heard 40 years before, McCartney actually changes the opening melodic figure of "No Other Baby." The Vipers' version of the song opens with a melodic phrase (transposed to C major and omitting the repetitions of the opening pitch) G, A, B, A, G. In contrast, McCartney sings G, A, B-flat, A, G. The flatted-seventh scale-step (B-flat) gives the song a bluesier feel. Interestingly, the McCartney version of the opening melody mirrors the opening melodic phrase of Johnny Kidd and the Pirates' 1959 song "Please Don't Touch." Perhaps McCartney's memory of the Vipers' recording was obscured by the Johnny Kidd recording.

The work of the Vipers Skiffle Group is particularly important in three respects. First, lead singer Wally Whyton sounds distinctly British in his pronunciations, not that this characteristic is necessarily all that far removed from Lonnie Donegan's work. It is a notable distinction, though, from the approach that most of the British teen idols that came out of skiffle took: save for Tommy Steele, the late 1950s and early 1960s British solo rock singers tended to sound as though they are trying to sound as American as possible—sometimes affecting American rockabilly accents, inflections, and vocal mannerisms. The Vipers Skiffle Group was also important in extending the skiffle repertoire more into the territory of rockabilly and early American rock and roll. Certainly, their recording of the song "Jim Dandy" illustrates the clear links between American rockabilly and British skiffle. The Vipers was also important as the breeding ground for Cliff Richard's backing groups, the Drifters and the Shadows.

In addition to American roots music in the form of skiffle, other forms also were early influences on British teens in the 1950s, including country music. Ron Ryan states that the 1920s and 1930s recordings by the so-called Singing Brakeman, Jimmie Rodgers, influenced him,[5] and Billy Fury acknowledged the influence of Hank Williams, because Williams and other country-western honky-tonk singers sang about real life.[6] John Lennon, who is quoted as saying that he heard American country music before he ever heard rock and roll (which, in fact, is not at all surprising or illuminating considering that for at least the first decade of Lennon's life there was no such thing as rock and roll), also acknowledged the importance of Hank Williams.[7] George Harrison listed Jimmie Rodgers and Slim Whitman as influences.[8] The jump between skiffle and the rockabilly of such American country–influenced musicians as Bill Haley and His Comets and Elvis Presley (before he moved from rockabilly to pop) was not too great. Some of the early British rock and roll musicians who came out of skiffle groups initially gravitated toward a rockabilly style, including Tommy Steele, Marty Wilde, Billy Fury, and (to a lesser extent) Cliff Richard.

As Elvis Presley became more of a corporate commodity late in the skiffle era, young British skiffle bands turned to other, more contemporary, and stylistically purer rockabilly influences. For example, 15-year-old Paul McCartney first made a favorable impression on the slightly older John Lennon—leader of a skiffle group called the Quarry Men—when he demonstrated in July 1957 that he could play and knew all the lyrics to Eddie Cochran's rockabilly song "Twenty Flight Rock." Lennon asked McCartney to join the Quarry Men, a band that, with the addition of McCartney's even younger friend, George Harrison, and a succession of drummers, became the Beatles. Incidentally, when McCartney first saw the Quarry Men performing, Lennon was singing the 1956 Del-Vikings hit "Come Go with Me," a song more closely related to street corner doo-wop than the kind of material usually associated with skiffle. This suggests that skiffle was not so much an end as it was a jumping off point into other American popular and roots music styles.

Also in 1957, another Liverpool band, Lance Fortune and the Firecrests, recorded several covers of American rockabilly and pop songs, including "Come Go with Me" and Buddy Holly's hit "That'll Be the Day." Holly's influence on post-skiffle-era British musicians will be discussed in the next chapter, because it was felt most intensely after Holly toured Great Britain in 1958. However, Fortune's recording of the song is worth noting as a skiffle-style adaptation of rockabilly. Fortune and the Firecrests' version of "That'll Be the Day," which is available on the collection *Unearthed Merseybeat, Vol. 3*, dispenses with the driving drums and finger-picked guitar pattern of Buddy Holly and the Crickets' original version; therefore, it has more of the homemade feel of skiffle. Fortune (who was born Chris Morris), however, directly imitates the vocal mannerisms of Holly, and the backing vocal parts come right out of the work of the Crickets.

According to Ron Ryan, a skiffle musician during this period, the next logical step for his group and for other London-area musicians was to turn to African American blues.[9] In his book *Stone Alone*, former Rolling Stones bass guitarist Bill Wyman also identifies skiffle as one of the principal gateways into rural American blues in the mid-1950s. In fact, the lines between white country music, rural blues, and the more stylized songs of black songwriters such as Lead Belly are somewhat blurred, depending on what specific songs one chooses as examples. A move from skiffle toward rural blues would, in fact, not be a great leap. In fact, some early to mid-1950s R&B would not be all that far removed from the more country-style music covered by some skiffle bands. A great example of the linkage between R&B, skiffle, and what emerged as a uniquely British approach to rock and roll can be found in what is purported to be the first rock and roll recording from Liverpool, Johnny Guitar's and Paul Murphy's 1957 cover of Little Richard's "She's Got It." At the same time as Lonnie Donegan and other British skiffle musicians, and Tommy Steele, the first British teen idol, were recording hit records, American country, pop, rock and roll, and R&B records also appeared on the British charts. Little Richard's 1956 recording of "She's Got It," for example, hit No. 15 on the British charts. Johnny Byrne—known as Johnny Guitar—and Paul Murphy made an amateur recording of the song in 1957. On this recording, which is available in the collection *Unearthed*

Merseybeat, Vol. 1, the basic rhythmic feel, melody, and harmony of the original are intact. Guitar and Murphy improvise with Little Richard's lyrics somewhat (as if working without the benefit of a lyrics sheet), and accompany their singing with what sound like purely acoustic guitars.[10] The acoustic sound, along with strumming patterns that would not be out of place in country or rockabilly, make for a fascinating mix: the performance includes elements of white American country/rockabilly and black American R&B, but with a homemade skiffle quality. Incidentally, Johnny Guitar and Paul Murphy later performed with Rory Storm and the Hurricanes, one of the leading Liverpool rock bands that at the time of their peak popularity in Liverpool and in Hamburg, Germany, included Ringo Starr on drums.

While Lonnie Donegan initially popularized skiffle as a sort of sidebar to performances with Chris Barber's Jazz Band, with a focus on rural American folk, blues, and country material, the examples of "Twenty Flight Rock," "That'll Be the Day," "She's Got It," and the work of the Vipers Skiffle Group illustrate that the homemade skiffle performance style provided young musicians with a gateway into American country, rockabilly, rural blues, southern R&B, and, by extension, commercial rock and roll. Listening to a cross section of recordings—official releases and amateur recordings of early British skiffle stars through the young musicians late in the skiffle craze—suggests that perhaps the main criteria for choice of repertoire were that the songs be American, rhythmically interesting, harmonically simple, and southern/rural/roots oriented. A splintering of this amalgamation of influences into more strictly defined types marked the next several years in the development of British rock and roll (somewhat akin to the Teddy Boys' influence leading to the opposing forces, the Mods and the Rockers). Curiously, the years between 1960 and the full-scale British Invasion then found these then disparate styles joined back together in a variety of combinations to give British Invasion rock its unique sound. While the play out of this scenario is evident through listening to the music from the skiffle years through 1964, musicians who were first inspired by skiffle and then became part of the British Invasion scene also confirm it. For example, while Bill Wyman describes skiffle as a gateway into authentic rural American blues, he also describes how he and the other members of what would become the Rolling Stones in 1963 came from different directions—Brian Jones from jazz and purist blues, Mick Jagger principally from blues, Charlie Watts from traditional jazz, and himself from rock and roll and commercial blues—and merged them into a unique style. Wyman also discusses members of the pre-fame Rolling Stones, Brian Jones principally, studiously analyzing the inner workings of American blues.[11] British musician Ron Ryan confirms this as a British cultural trait. In a telephone interview, Ryan stated that what "the Brits are really good at is sectioning something, taking it apart to see how it works, and then reassembling it in a new way."[12] Whether consciously or unconsciously, then, this seems to be the way in which British pop music developed after the end of the skiffle craze. This post-skiffle deconstruction, analysis, and reassembly took several years to accomplish. In the meantime, the British entertainment industry took note of the popularity of early white rockabilly musicians such as Bill Haley and Elvis Presley and provided several young British singers a pathway from skiffle into national popularity.

1950s BRITISH TEEN IDOLS

Although most Americans are not aware of the fact, there was a rock and roll scene in the United Kingdom well before the British Invasion of America in 1964. In this section, we will examine some of the work of the most successful British rock musicians to emerge in the 1950s, including Tommy Steele, Cliff Richard, Billy Fury, Marty Wilde, and Adam Faith. These are singers that primarily came out of the skiffle craze and were packaged as rockabilly teen idols, in a manner that owed much to the Elvis Presley model.

Born in Bermondsey, South London, in 1936 as Thomas Hicks, Tommy Steele emerged as the first British rock and roll musician in 1956. Hicks worked on the Cunard ship lines for four years beginning when he was 15. During that time he learned to play guitar and began entertaining his shipmates. He performed on American military bases on his shore leaves, and tried to listen to as many American country and rock and roll recordings as he could. In 1956 he put together a band called the Cavemen. Hicks and the Cavemen, who were performing in London's Soho, came to the attention of the impresario Larry Parnes. Although Parnes is often credited with renaming his 19-year-old discovery "Steele," there is evidence that the name came from a variant of Hicks's paternal grandfather's original, non-Anglicized name. However, it should be noted that Parnes's later discoveries received such descriptive names as Fury, Gentle, Pride, Fame, and Wilde. The Cavemen became the Steelmen.

Steele's 1956 recordings, such as "Rock with the Caveman," "Rock around the Town," and "Elevator Rock," all owe a very clear debt of gratitude to the 1954 and 1955 work of Bill Haley and His Comets. The Steele recordings feature electric guitar, tenor saxophone, piano, and a vocal style that curiously combines the rhythmic feel of Haley's singing with a pronounced cockney accent. The overt British-ness of Steele's pronunciations clearly differentiates his work from that of Cliff Richard, Marty Wilde, and Billy Fury—the other prominent British rock musicians of the 1950s seemed almost to sing with American (and particularly Southern American) or neutral accents. Vocally, then, Steele sounds less derivative of American rockabilly than in particular Wilde and Fury. Cockney accent aside though, Steele's early recordings feature the instrumentation and instrumental rhythmic feel of Haley's brand of Western swing-style rockabilly. Steele and his fellow writers' use of humor in "Rock with the Caveman" is especially effective (although a touch on the misogynistic side), and tenor sax player Ronnie Scott's quote of the opening of Charlie Parker's bebop jazz classic "Ornithology" can also bring a chuckle to those who are in the know.

One of the other more intriguing features of "Rock with the Caveman" is the play cowriters Steele, Lionel Bart, and Mike Pratt undertake with musical form. Each verse of the song begins with a four-measure phrase sung by Steele with little instrumental accompaniment. Incidentally, this is reminiscent of the opening of the famous Bill Haley recording of "(We're Gonna) Rock Around the Clock," not to mention Carl Perkins's self-penned "Blue Suede Shoes." In "Rock with the Caveman," though, the verses also end with a similar phrase. Because of the way in which the text flows from the first to the second verse, it is unclear the first time one hears the song whether the first verse actually ends with a four-measure more-or-less a cappella phrase, or if the second verse begins with an eight-bar phrase. It can sound a bit clunky structurally, if one fully expects the more straightforward structure of a rockabilly classic such as "(We're Gonna) Rock around the Clock," or it can sound highly distinctive, if the listener can experience the song without any preconceived notions about what rockabilly is "supposed" to sound like.

Another early Steele recording, "Doomsday Rock," is more theatrical. This theatricality—as well as the humor that runs through all of his rock and roll recordings—points the way to Tommy Steele's later work in musical theatre. Significantly, Steele wrote or cowrote most of the rock and roll songs he recorded in the 1950s. In retrospect, these 1956 songs and recordings are derivative of Haley and Presley; however, because of Steele's theatricality and cockney accent, there is no mistaking the fact that he is a thoroughly British performer.

It is interesting to note that Lionel Bart was one of Steele's cowriters on "Rock with the Caveman" and "Doomsday Rock." Bart, who was born Lionel Begleiter in London in 1930, was older that most of the rest of the personalities associated with early British rock and roll; however, he wrote songs for or collaborated as a songwriter with several singers, all of whom showed an interest in and talent for acting, including Tommy Steele, Marty Wilde, and Adam Faith. During the period he was associated with these early British rockers, Bart was also associated with Joan Littlewood's Theatre Workshop, a troupe notable for, among other things, promoting the use of authentic cockney accents on the London stage. Bart is best remembered for his 1960 hit musical *Oliver!*

Tommy Steele's biggest early hit was his cover of Guy Mitchell's version of "Singin' the Blues." Mitchell's recording was the hit version of the song in the United States; however, in the United Kingdom, Steele's recording successfully competed against the American version. After 1956, Steele's albums increasingly included show tunes, pop songs, and comedy numbers. Despite his move away from rock and roll and toward the world of film and the stage, it should be noted that his 1963 British music hall–style recording of "Flash, Bang, Wallop!" closely resembles the kind of material that record producer Mickie Most selected for Herman's Hermits to record in 1964 and 1965—such as "I'm Henry the VIII, I Am"—to try to appeal to the American record-buying public during the initial wave of the British Invasion. The British music hall style of "Flash, Bang, Wallop!" also found its way into the work of Manchester-born singer David Jones, who became a star in the United States as a member of the Monkees.

Steele's other post-1956 work was not entirely about show tunes and middle-of-the-road pop. His 1958 cover of the Ritchie Valens song "Come On, Let's Go" not only made it to No. 10 on the British pop charts, it also displays a convincing rock and roll sound. The recording's producer, Joe Meek, places the drums and bass well forward in the mix. This, along with the edginess and slight distortion in the lead guitar provides the track with a rocking drive not entirely commonplace in 1958 British rock and roll.

The next major star of British rock and roll to emerge after Tommy Steele was Cliff Richard. Born Harry Rodger Webb in British India, in 1940, Richard has had a career that has lasted into the twenty-first century. With sales of over a quarter of a billion records,[13] and over 120 recordings (including singles, extended play discs, and albums) that have made the British Top 20, Richard perhaps is the most successful pop musician in British history. Certainly, his record sales in Britain exceed those of the Beatles and Elvis Presley. Much of Cliff Richard's early rock and roll–oriented work was accompanied by the Shadows, a band that became stars in their own right and that helped to define the instrumental sound of a distinctly British rock and roll perhaps more thoroughly than the instrumental groups that backed other British singers who emerged in the 1950s.

The young Harry Webb's family moved from India to England when India gained its independence in 1947. Like so many British teenagers in the mid-1950s, Webb took up skiffle music. By 1958, Webb's band, the Drifters—later Cliff Richard and the Drifters, and later still Cliff Richard and the Shadows—was performing rock and roll. Richard secured a recording contract in summer 1958. Although studio musicians backed Richard on his earliest recordings—the Drifters themselves initially were not offered a recording contract—his debut recording session included the song "Move It," which was written by Drifters guitarist Ian Samwell. Incidentally, Ian Samwell continued to influence the development of British rock and roll into the British Invasion era in his work as a record producer.

Although "Move It" originally was relegated to the B-side of Richard's first single— a cover of Bobby Helms's "School Boy Crush" was the A-side—"Move It" became the hit song. "Move It" was so significant that many writers and British rock musicians regard it as the first true British rock record.[14] One of the first things that is apparent about "Move It" is the electric guitar tone color, which owes less of a debt to American country and rockabilly music than much of what other British rock musicians were recording

Pictured here in the 1970s, Cliff Richard is one of Great Britain's most commercially successful and enduring pop singers ever. Richard's late 1950s recording "Move It" is widely acknowledged as Britain's first important rock and roll single. Courtesy of Photofest.

in 1958. In fact, in 1958 the sound of American rock guitar was changing, especially in the hands of Chuck Berry, Duane Eddy, and Link Wray, not to mention the new popular singer-songwriter-guitarists such as Ritchie Valens and Buddy Holly. The sound that session guitarist Ernie Shear creates on "Move It," does not have the twang of Eddy or the distortion of Wray; however, it does fit in with a contemporary American rock and roll sound and actually is forward looking enough that it anticipates the tone color and style of surf guitar. This is important to note, since lead guitarists for Marty Wilde and Billy Fury, who made their recording debuts within the next year, continued to exhibit strong deliberate ties to Scotty Moore's work on Elvis Presley's rockabilly recordings of 1954 and 1955. In this respect, then, the Cliff Richard recording is forward looking, while the work of Richard's contemporaries Wilde and Fury is deliberately retro in nature.

The rhythm guitar figure in the introduction of "Move It" is also innovative. The figure includes an accent pattern that divides the eight even eighth-notes into a 3+3+2 pattern. While this rhythmic pattern was common in Afro-Caribbean music of the time, it was not common in the rock music associated with Elvis Presley—and Cliff Richard was widely hailed as Britain's Elvis. This accent pattern is probably most familiar to fans of early American rock and roll as is heard in the first measure of the famous two-measure accompaniment figure from the song "Bo Diddley" by the R&B performer of the same name. Thus, even though it may be in an oblique way, Cliff Richard's recording of "Move It" is quite progressive in that most British rock of the late 1950s directly imitated American rockabilly from Bill Haley, through Elvis Presley, to Gene Vincent and Eddie Cochran, and seemed almost consciously to avoid the direct influence of African American sources. Incidentally, when the 3+3+2 subdivision did occur in rockabilly, such as in Eddie Cochran's highly influential "Twenty Flight Rock," it was in the context of a swing rhythmic feel. "Move It," and "Bo Diddley," feature an even (or straight) eighth-note feel.

Lyrically, "Move It" falls into the same category as Chuck Berry's 1957 hit "Rock and Roll Music"; it is a defense of the rock genre in the face of adult disapproval and speculation that it is just a short-term fad. Cliff Richard delivers the lyrics with a bit of the Presley sneer, but he has a distinctive enough approach that Richard's recording of "Move It" sounds less derivative of Presley than some other early British rock. Richard represents a clear step forward from the work of Tommy Steele in the area of vocal rhythmic approach with regards to creating a thoroughly rock-oriented approach. Steele's earliest rock-oriented recordings found him moving from a rhythmically flexible style to a style in which the snappiness of his swing rhythms sounds occasionally stilted. Richard's approach on "Move It" is more precise and rhythmically energetic, with more accentuation on syncopated rhythms than is evident in Steele's work.

While they may not have been direct imitations of the entire package—Ian Samwell's words, music, and arrangement and Cliff Richard and company's performance—that defined "Move It" at the time, the entire feel of the composition and performance can be heard in some later American country-rock songs in the 1970s and 1980s. This is not to suggest that "Move It" necessarily influenced American artists of more than a decade later (such as Eddie Rabbit), but it does suggest the rock and roll authenticity of the recording.

Ultimately, Cliff Richard became a sensation in the United Kingdom and in several other countries around the world—but not in the United States—as a wide-ranging pop performer. In part, this seems to have been because of a conscious management decision to try to broaden Richard's appeal; however, Richard's move away from straight-ahead rock and roll also was caused in part by his conversion to Christianity in 1964. Richard rejected his earlier bad-boy image and recorded a mixture of Christian inspirational and pop music. In the 1970s, however, Richard moved again toward more of a rock-oriented approach in his work. This means that his true rock-oriented work is limited to some of his pre-British Invasion recordings and just a small part of the work he would do well after the initial British Invasion. Because of his broader work as a pop singer, Richard was somewhat insulated from the impact of bands such as the Beatles, the Searchers, the Rolling Stones, the Animals, and a whole host of others in 1962–1965. He was practically alone among the British rock and roll musicians who first emerged in the late 1950s to find his career still intact after the emergence of the bands that ruled the British record charts in the early to mid-1960s. This is important to note, because it speaks volumes about musical style and less about the age of the musicians than might first be apparent. For example, John Lennon, Cliff Richard, Ringo Starr, Adam Faith, and Billy Fury were all born in 1940. Richard became a star in 1958 and (somewhat like Elvis Presley) moved from rock to a more generalized pop sound; Fury became a teen star in 1959 but found his career on the downslide after the emergence of bands such as the Beatles rendered his too-close ties to old-school British rock and roll (and its overt connections to American rockabilly) obsolete; Faith started out as performing music more akin to teen idol pop but adapted his style to reflect the new rock sound to some success; Lennon and Starr became stars in 1962, mostly because of the appeal of their band to younger audience members as a result of the new, modern music style they performed. To put it another way, Starr and Lennon were not younger than Richard, Fury, and Faith, but by 1963 and 1964 their music was.

Born in Blackheath in 1939 and raised in Greenwich, South London, and several other locations throughout England, Reginald Leonard Smith rose to fame as Marty Wilde.[15] Initially, Smith learned to play the ukulele but switched to guitar because the it had become the stringed instrument of choice during Britain's skiffle craze. Eventually, Smith led a group called Reg Smith and the Hound Dogs. Impresario Larry Parnes visited a London club at which Smith was playing a gig in 1958 and signed the young singer-guitarist. Technically, Marty Wilde can claim to be the second British rock and roller after Tommy Steele; his first recording was released shortly before Cliff Richard's debut recording, but Wilde's first single was not a hit. Wilde's first commercially successful hit record (a cover of "Endless Sleep") came very shortly after Richard's success with "Move It."

Ultimately, Marty Wilde's greatest success as a recording artist lasted only from 1958 through 1960. Because Larry Parnes so successfully identified potential teen idols whose appeal largely would be to teenaged girls, Marty Wilde lost some of his fan appeal when he married fellow singer Joyce Baker. Wilde also tended to be most successful commercially with his cover versions of popular American hits, but this also did not lend itself to record chart longevity, particularly as the original American recordings became increasingly available. And, vocally, Marty Wilde tended to sound the most imitative of Elvis Presley and some of the late-1950s American teen idols than other British rock and roll singers of the era. In the early 1960s, as his chart success waned, Wilde, like Tommy

Steele, turned increasingly to pop music and enjoyed some success as a singer-actor in musical theatre. Interestingly, he turned to glam rock in the early 1970s but is best known today for his work of 1958–1960, which he continued to perform on stage into the twenty-first century.

Wilde's recordings of covers such as "Teenager in Love," "Donna," "Sea of Love," "Blue Moon of Kentucky," "Splish Splash," "Honeycomb," and "High School Confidential" capture the spirit and the vocal styles of the American singers who recorded the famous versions of the songs, including Ritchie Valens, Dion and the Belmonts, Jerry Lee Lewis, Elvis Presley, Bobby Darin, and others. In Britain, at least, some of Marty Wilde's cover recordings of 1958 and 1959 out-sold the originals. In retrospect, Wilde's ability to record convincing versions of songs by such a diverse group of American performers was a double-edged sword. On one hand, it enabled Marty Wilde to enjoy two years of chart success. On the other hand, it probably made Wilde more of a musical chameleon than a performer with a well-defined style.

Despite the similarity of Wilde's vocal approach to the Americans who sang the original version of these songs, and his use of a small, rockabilly style backup band, there were some new instrumental sounds that Wilde's recordings introduced to British rock. For one thing, Wilde's band included an electric bass guitar, an instrument that even in American rock bands of the period had not completely supplanted the double bass. Curiously, Wilde's cover of Elvis Presley's version of the Bill Monroe bluegrass song "Blue Moon of Kentucky" generally sounds like a copy of the Presley version—the lead guitarist's solo is heavily influenced by Scotty Moore's work with Presley back in 1954, and Wilde assumes a distinctly Presley-influenced singing style—however, the roots and fifths of the chords clearly are played by an electric bass, and the not the acoustic instrument used by Bill Black on the 1954 Presley recording. The style of the electric bass playing on "Blue Moon of Kentucky" and "High School Confidential" is still based on the extensive use of the roots and fifths of the chords that one would find in rockabilly upright bass playing; however, the greater volume and intensity of the attack of the notes on the electric instrument hints at the direction in which rock in general was moving by the end of the 1950s.

Perhaps the most musically interesting recordings of Marty Wilde's brief period near the top of the British charts, however, were of songs he either wrote or cowrote, including "Wild Cat" and "Bad Boy." "Wild Cat," on which Wilde collaborated with Lionel Bart, bears a 1957 copyright and was the B-side of Wilde's debut single. The recording opens with a tenor sax figure that quotes the opening of Bill Haley and His Comets' 1954 recording of "Shake, Rattle and Roll." Structurally and harmonically, the verse sections of "Wild Cat" are standard rockabilly fare. Wilde and Bart, however, turn to an atypical chord progression for the brief bridge section. This gives the song a distinctiveness that transcends the harmonic clichés of textbook rockabilly; however, it does not flow as naturally as Wilde's even more adventurous harmonic writing would on "Bad Boy." "Wild Cat" is also notable for Big Jim Sullivan's guitar solo. Sullivan's florid single-line style playing exhibits the virtuosity of American country-style lead guitarists of the 1950s.

At its opening, Marty Wilde's self-penned song "Bad Boy" sounds as if it is going to be a typical, or even stereotypical, country-style song. Wilde's lyrics concern a relationship between his character and a girl with whom he is in love. The girl's family and others think of Wilde's character as a "bad boy," but he makes the point that he is just misunderstood. The guitar picking and root-fifth bass line would not be out of place at all in an American rockabilly ballad that leaned in the direction of country-pop music. What really sets the piece apart, not only from the American country music on which it is based but also from most material in the rock and roll world of the late 1950s, is Wilde's harmonic vocabulary. The song is based on a traditional AABA musical form. The eight-measure "A" sections of a typical country ballad of this time period might feature a chord progression such as I, I, IV, IV, V, V, I, I, with each Roman numeral representing the scale degree of the root note of each major chord.[16] In a bold move, however, Wilde replaces the expected V chord with the bIII ("flat III") chord (C, E, G); thus, the progression for the "A" sections is I, I, IV, IV, bIII, bIII, I, I. The sound is completely unconventional and lends a feeling of distinctiveness to "Bad Boy" that is missing from the bulk of the songs Wilde recorded.

There were a few other singer-songwriters who were expanding the harmonic vocabulary of 1950s rock and roll in 1958 and 1959. Perhaps the best-known example is Buddy Holly's unconventional use of the bVII chord in his 1959 ballad "Well . . . All Right." Holly's harmonic vocabulary in the piece essentially mixes naturally occurring triads (three-note chords) that are found both in the major and the Mixolydian scale of the song's key center. Marty Wilde's use of bIII in "Bad Boy" does the same sort of thing but mixes naturally occurring triads from the parallel tonic major and tonic minor. It does not necessarily flow as naturally as Holly's bVII chord, but the idea of mixing the two tonic modes is similar in effect.

In the bridge section of "Bad Boy" Wilde mixes the parallel major and natural minor scale forms. Here, the eight-measure chord progression is IV, IV, I, I, IV, IV, bVI, V, with the bVI chord (F major) being the harmony that is borrowed from the A natural-minor scale.

Perhaps partially as a result of its harmonic distinctiveness, "Bad Boy" was one of the few songs written by a British rock and roll musician in the 1950s that was covered by other artists. The critically acclaimed but commercially largely unsuccessful 1970s British band Nirvana (not to be confused with the American grunge band of the same name) recorded Wilde's composition, as did rockabilly revivalist Robert Gordon. "Bad Boy" is also notable as Marty Wilde's only recording to make the singles charts in the United States; however, it was not a huge breakthrough for British rock, as it stopped just short of the *Billboard* Top 40.

Although Marty Wilde turned to musical theatre and recorded only sporadically after the early 1960s, he continued to write songs, including British chart successes for Lulu, the Status Quo, and others. His own attempt to revive his career as a 1970s glam rocker never quite took off, but throughout the 1980s he made important contributions as a songwriter and record producer to the career of his daughter, the popular new wave singer Kim Wilde. Marty Wilde continues to perform his old hits in oldies shows into the twenty-first century.

Born Ronald William Wycherley in Liverpool in 1940, Billy Fury became Larry Parnes's next big star, with a more substantial and longer-lasting career in the British rock world than Marty Wilde. Like just about every other British rock star of the late 1950s and early 1960s, Wycherley was a member of a skiffle group during the 1954–1957 skiffle craze. In his case, it was the Formby Sniffle Gloup, which was named for a tugboat on which Wycherley worked. In retrospect, Wycherley's wordplay—Formby Sniffle Gloup, as opposed to the Formby Skiffle Group—anticipates the kind of wordplay in which fellow Liverpublian John Lennon later engaged in his books *In His Own Write* and *A Spaniard in the Works*. Unlike most of his contemporaries, Fury was also a fairly prolific rock and roll songwriter. Fury's discovery by Parnes was the stuff of legend. According to the oft-repeated story, Wycherley approached Parnes at an October 1, 1958 concert and tried to interest the impresario in some of his songs for recording by Wilde. Apparently, Parnes pushed the young Wycherley up onto the stage to sing his songs in front of the assembled audience. He was a hit, was signed by Parnes, and was rechristened Billy Fury.

Fury's recording career began quickly after his legendary unannounced appearance before Larry Parnes. His first hit single, "Maybe Tomorrow"/"Gonna Type a Letter" was released in January 1959 and reached No. 18 on the British pop charts, the highest chart ranking of any Billy Fury single until his cover of Tony Orlando's "Halfway to Paradise" hit No. 4 in 1961.

Billy Fury's first album, *The Sound of Fury*, was issued in 1960. Significantly, all the songs on *The Sound of Fury*, as the majority of the singles that Fury had released since late 1958, were self-penned. Taken as a whole, the 10 songs on this album and the singles Fury recorded in 1961 and 1962 illustrate the changes that were taking place during this period. Most importantly, one can hear hints of the changes that came with the ascension of bands such as the Beatles, the Dave Clark Five, and Brian Poole and the Tremeloes in 1962–1964—changes that symbolically fit in with the battles between the Rockers and the Mods.

Born in Liverpool, Billy Fury's brand of rock and roll evolved from heavily Elvis Presley–influenced rockabilly to a British beat group style by the time of the British Invasion. Despite Fury's lack of commercial success in the United States, he was a major rock and roll star in Britain before the emergence of groups such as the Beatles, the Dave Clark Five, and the Rolling Stones. Courtesy of Photofest.

Perhaps one of the first things that the listener will notice about the album is found in the credits on the back cover. The accompanying instrumentalists are given as: Reg Guest, piano; Joe Brown, electric guitar; Alan Weighell, electric bass; Bill Stark, bass; and Andy White, drums. The need for two bass players—one on acoustic and one on electric—was necessitated by the desire to recreate the sound of the slap bass of early 1950s rockabilly. Forty years after the release of *The Sound of Fury*, Joe Brown recalled that no English bass players at the time were adept at true American-style slap bass (in which the acoustic bass plays the bass line and simultaneously provides percussion sound in the absence of drums), so Weighell played the pitches on his electric bass, while Stark simultaneously slapped his instrument for purely percussive effect.[17] For his part, Brown virtually recreates the lead guitar figures that typified Scotty Moore's work on Elvis Presley's early recordings for Sun Records and RCA. On *The Sound of Fury*, a group called the Four Jays provides backing vocals, the same role the Jordanaires played on Presley's recordings beginning in 1956. Billy Fury himself takes on some of the vocal characteristics of early Presley recordings. Considering the fact that Presley was serving in the U.S. Army from 1958 to 1960 and therefore was not as visible as he had been earlier, and that the Presley material released at the end of the 1950s and in 1960 turned increasingly toward pop and ballads and away from rock and roll, *The Sound of Fury* is deliberately retro. It recreates the feel and the attitude of 1954–1956 era rockabilly. Significantly, though, Fury included no covers; he wrote all the material either under his own name (Billy Fury) or using the pseudonym Wilbur Wilberforce.

While I will not detail all of the cuts on *The Sound of Fury,* I will discuss several of the songs. It is particularly interesting to see how Fury and the backing instrumentalists and vocalists recreate the spirit of a half-decade-old style while simultaneously including hints at the changes that were about to take place in British rock music.

The album begins with "That's Love." This song typifies old-school rockabilly perhaps better than any of the others on the album. Fury's phrase structure, vocal melody, chord progressions, and the instrumental and backing vocal arrangement all fit comfortably within the context of what Elvis Presley and his backing band were recording at Sun Studios and in their early work for RCA. It is particularly interesting to compare this song with Marty Wilde's compositions from approximately the same time period. Unlike Wilde, who incorporates some uncommon harmonic relationships—including modally borrowed chords and chords whose roots move by the interval of a third (as opposed to the more common root motion by fourths and fifths)—Fury's "That's Love" uses the diatonic (entirely within a single scale) I, IV, and V chords in the key of E major for the verses. The bridge begins on the subdominant—standard fare for country songs of the 1950s—and uses the same three chords as the verses. The melody is entirely diatonic, with conjunct motion and just a few relatively small chordal skips. Fury avoids the overtly British-sounding pronunciations of Tommy Steele and Adam Faith, thereby further tying "That's Love" to American rockabilly. Joe Brown plays electric guitar fill figures that are stylistic copies of the work of Scotty Moore, Reg Guest's piano playing incorporates figures that might be considered clichés of American country music of the 1950s, and Andy White's drums are light and placed in the background of the mix. If one were trying to create an entirely new composition and recording that captured the sound of early rockabilly, one could scarcely do better than "That's Love."

The album's second track, "My Advice," is more interesting musically than "That's Love." Here, Fury combines aspects of rockabilly with a touch of the new R&B-based sound that was just finding its way into British rock and roll. In particular, the accents in the introduction spell out the 3+3+2 division of a measure of music that was heard in the forward-looking introduction of Cliff Richard's recording of "Move It." This rhythmic feel, though, was probably most associated at the time with American R&B in the form of the song "Bo Diddley," as well as in Latin music of the day. The lead electric guitar figure that Joe Brown plays in the introduction incorporates string bends that sound more like they come from the world of the blues than from country music.

It is also interesting to note that the instrumental introduction of "My Advice" is based on an even eighth-note feel, while the song proper incorporates a swing feel. While a shift back and forth between a swing feel and a straight eighth-note feel was uncommon in earlier rockabilly, it was in the air around the time of *The Sound of Fury*. For example, Eddie Cochran's January 1960 recording of "Cut Across Shorty" moves from a shuffle/swing feel in the verses to straight eighth notes in the chorus. Incidentally, historian Colin Escott notes that the Crickets, Buddy Holly's old group, backed up Cochran on the recording session.[18] Buddy Holly, and the post-Holly lineup of the Crickets, continued to influence British bands into the early 1960s.

The shifts between straight eighth notes and a swing feel, the bluesy lead guitar figures in the introduction, and the harder-edged rhythmic feel of the introduction all represent the progressive sounds in "My Advice." Once the song proper begins, Fury uses a standard American rockabilly vocal approach, the guitar figures revert back to the standard rockabilly stylebook, and the drums lighten up. The Four Jays sing the Jordanaires-style backing vocal figures that pervade the rest of the album. In fact, the whole gestalt of the piece (minus the introductory figure) suggests a cross-Atlantic cousin of the 1957 Elvis Presley hit "(Let Me Be Your) Teddy Bear."

Another example of Billy Fury mixing elements of the old and the new can be found in the song "Since You've Been Gone." The opening of the song is slow in tempo; however, a quicker rock rhythmic feel begins at approximately the 1:27 mark (slightly over halfway through the piece). What makes the song particularly interesting is Fury's inclusion of a chord progression in the bridge section that features major triads that descend by whole steps: A, G, F. The F major chord then drops a half-step to the song's dominant-seventh chord, E7. The use of the bVII (G) and bVI (F) chords (especially in succession) is unusual for early rockabilly style. By the late 1950s, however, Buddy Holly was making extensive use of the bVII chord in his groundbreaking song "Well . . . All Right." The use of poly-modality (incorporating both the normal, major seventh scale-step [G-sharp in case of a song in the key of A major], and the lowered seventh scale-step [G] as important, fully consonant chord tones [the G# as the third of the V7, and the G as the root of the bVII]) increasingly defined rock harmonic practice in the 1960s. Around the same time as Billy Fury's use of the bVII chord, Johnny Kidd and the Pirates did the same sort of thing, and the modal mixture of the two different versions of the seventh scale step became a staple of the writing of the Kinks' Ray Davies and the Who's Pete Townshend within a few years, and even found its way into the music of the more pop-oriented bands of the British Invasion (e.g., Freddie and the Dreamers' "I'm Telling You Now"). The bVII chord continued to form an important part of the harmonic vocabulary of British bands in the heavy metal era (e.g., Black Sabbath's "War Pigs"). To the extent, then, that this harmonic practice soon became almost a signifier of British rock, and remained one into the heavy metal era, Billy Fury's, Marty Wilde's, and Johnny Kidd's use of it in 1960 represent an important step toward the definition of a British style of rock.

The *Sound of Fury* track "Turn My Back on You" is notable for its use of imitation slap bass and the studio echo that defined the sound of early Sun Records rockabilly. Fury even uses extra syllables—"a-turn-a my back on-a you"—that also recall stereotypes of rockabilly. With "That's Love" as a medium-tempo example, and "Turn My Back on You" as an up-tempo example, Billy Fury ironically is marked as both an unabashed Elvis imitator and as the greatest pure rockabilly singer-songwriter in Britain.

"You Don't Know" is another one of the particularly interesting songs on *The Sound of Fury*. Fury's lyrics, in which he plays the role of a man who is desperately in love with a woman who is unable to recognize his feelings or to love him back, represent nothing new. In fact, a fair number of Fury's compositions find him playing the role of the jilted lover or the man who is in love with a woman who can never love him back. The harmonic progression of the verses of "You Don't Know," which sticks pretty much squarely with what some musicians call the "oldies progression" (I, vi, IV, V) of songs such as "Heart and Soul" and a plethora of 1950s ballads, also is nothing new. In the bridge, Fury uses only the IV and the V chords. Fury's melody is simple in structure and only covers the range of a perfect fifth, from scale-step 6 below tonic (e.g., B, in this D major song), to the third scale-step above tonic (F-sharp). And this includes both the melodic phrases of the verse and the bridge. Despite the fact that this entire description tends to make "You Don't Know" sound an awful lot like a cookie cutter cliché of 1950s heartache and simplicity, the song succeeds. In large part, this is because of the simplicity—and therefore the apparent sincerity—of the instrumental setting and Fury's understated singing. It stands in sharp contrast to the glossy, heavily orchestrated ballads recorded by Cliff Richard and Adam Faith around this time, and the sort of ballad arrangements Billy Fury himself would go on to record in the near future.

On the occasion of the 40th anniversary of the release of Billy Fury's debut album, guitarist Joe Brown was quoted as saying, "Well, the *Sound of Fury* has become quite a classic, you know, amongst the old Teddy Boys and that, and real rock fans love that small ten inch album."[19] Yes, for the most part, the music of *The Sound of Fury* reflects the Teddy Boy/Rocker aesthetics of the time: the compositions, arrangements, and vocal and instrumental styles are all based on the 1954–1956 rockabilly of Elvis Presley and his backing band of Scotty Moore, Bill Black, and D. J. Fontana. There is also a little of the influence of later American rockabilly artists Buddy Holly, Carl Perkins, Gene Vincent, and Eddie Cochran in evidence.

As the 1950s came to a close, Elvis Presley set a paradigm for maintaining a popular music career beyond the teen rock idol stage: he turned to pop and to ballads. The first wave of British rock and roll stars, Cliff Richard, Tommy Steele, and Marty Wilde, did not exactly follow Presley's lead, although Richard's move to pop came close. Steele and Wilde also turned to pop and ballads; however, they also moved in the direction of musical theatre. Even Billy Fury, at the insistence of Decca Records, turned increasingly to pop ballads and covers after *The Sound of Fury*. It is, however, far too easy and misleading to dismiss Fury's post-1960 work as a turn from rock. Fury continued to record self-penned rock songs. Let us take a look at one particular post–*Sound of Fury* song, "Don't Jump," from 1962, as an example of the fundamental change that was taking place in British rock in 1960–1963.

"Don't Jump" was released on an extended-play disc (EP) in January 1962. Once again, Fury portrays the jilted lover, except in this case his character is being enticed to jump to his death by the sirens of mythology. Ultimately, though, he heeds the chant of the backing male vocalists, "Don't jump, Billy boy, don't jump," and decides "no woman's worth the trouble." The instrumental backing, which in late 1961 is possibly by the Blue Flames, includes powerful drums and lead guitar figures that move closer to electric blues than did earlier Fury recordings. The drum part, especially the driving sixteenth-note figures that occur several times, gives the recording a significantly heavier feel than any of Fury's *Sound of Fury*–era recordings. In fact, the drum playing is in the same mold as that in Little Eva's 1962 dance hit "The Loco-Motion," as well as British singer Doug Sheldon's cover of "Your Ma Said You Cried in Your Sleep Last Night" and the percussion-heavy style of the Dave Clark Five.

Billy Fury continued to enjoy chart hits in Britain into the mid-1960s, although the hits became fewer and farther between. He also appeared in movies and as a concert attraction. Decca Records issued Billy Fury singles in the United States at the time of the British Invasion—such as a single consisting of "Hippy Hippy Shake" and "Glad All Over." However, Fury never caught on in the United States like his Liverpool colleagues the Beatles, the Searchers, and Gerry and the Pacemakers. Unfortunately, Fury's 1963–1964 rock recordings pale in comparison to those of his contemporaries. For example, the 1964 cover of "Glad All Over" lacks the energy and sonic intensity of the Dave Clark Five's hit recording of the same year. And, insofar as a crucial part of the appeal of the Dave Clark Five's version of the song was the arrangement and Clark's use of deliberately over-the-top studio reverb, the clean production and lack of echo and reverb on the Fury recording produces nothing more than a pleasant cover of the tune and not a serious competitor to the original recording. Fury's version is not dissimilar to the approach taken by Brian Poole and the Tremeloes on their recordings from the same period: they are technically well worked out, peppy, but ultimately not as powerful or as memorable as the work of the musicians who succeeded in making the transition to popularity in the United States. Add to that the fact that the roller rink style of the organ playing on the Fury recording of "Glad All Over" calls to mind Chris Montez's 1962 hit "Let's Dance," something that was two years away from sounding novel. "Hippy Hippy Shake" is more successful, although again it is not as distinctive as the Swinging Blue Jeans' hit version, or even as successful as the Beatles' cover that they recorded for broadcast on the BBC in summer 1963. Again, the musicianship of the instrumentalists is impeccable, especially the lead guitarist and bass guitarist. It just does not possess that intangible personality of the performances by the Swinging Blue Jeans and the Beatles. Another Fury recording from the same time period, a reworking of the mid-1950s Eddie Fontaine rockabilly song "Nothin' Shakin' (But the Leaves on the Trees)," actually is more interesting. Fury's fellow Liverpublians, the Beatles, who performed the song as part of their stage act in 1962 (it appears on the *Live! at the Star-Club* recordings that singer-bandleader King Size Taylor made of the Beatles in Hamburg in 1962), included it on their Parlophone audition tape (also in 1962), and recorded it for the BBC in July 1963. What the Beatles did not do, however, that Fury, his arrangers, and backing musicians do on their recording of "Nothin' Shakin'" is to change the song from a rockabilly song to a beat group number.

One curiosity of these British Invasion—era recordings of Billy Fury can be heard in the vocal arrangements. On some of these songs, the producers present Fury singing the melody as it is harmonized through studio overdubbing. Some British Invasion—era bands, notably the Hollies and the Beatles, had adopted the two-part harmony style of the Everly Brothers. Especially in the case of the Hollies, this was broadened into a three-part block harmony style on some 1964–1965 recordings. Therefore, the vocal arrangements on these Billy Fury recordings sounds current in light of what the new successful bands were doing. The problem is that the Hollies, the Beatles, the Searchers, and other bands that routinely used vocal harmony on their recordings were just that: bands. They were not presented as soloist-with-backing-ensemble structures. For Billy Fury to be presented in a group context suggests that the star-plus-backing group paradigm of Fury, Steele, Wilde, and the other solo singing stars that emerged between 1956 and 1960 was waning by the time of the British Invasion. Stars such as Fury and the others were so fully established within that older paradigm that, even if they covered the latest au courant hits, such as Fury did on occasion in 1963 and 1964, they could never fully fit into the new group paradigm that defined the bands that achieved success in the actual British Invasion of the United States in 1964 and 1965.

Ultimately, the rheumatic fever Billy Fury suffered as a child caused his health to decline in the mid-1960s. From then until his death in 1983, Fury's work in music was sporadic. He was highly active during the 1970s and up to his death in 1983, however, as an environmentalist. Billy Fury was commemorated as Liverpool's first rock star by the unveiling and showing of a life-size bronze statue of the singer-songwriter in a typically dramatic pose at the Museum of Liverpool Life in 2003. Today, the statue stands outside the Piermaster's House at the Albert Dock in Liverpool.

Incidentally, an important part of the story of Billy Fury's significance is the legacy of the fine musicians who backed him up in the studio and on stage. Two members of the backing group on *The Sound of Fury*, drummer Andy White and lead guitarist Joe Brown, had significant careers after *The Sound of Fury*. White, who hailed from Scotland, played on recording sessions by a wide variety of pop artists but probably gained his greatest fame for one particular session on September 11, 1962. Record producer George Martin hired White to play drums on that date for the Beatles' second recording session for EMI. Martin had not been impressed with the band's new drummer, Ringo Starr, at the Beatles first session, which had taken place a week earlier. So it is Andy White playing drums on "P.S. I Love You" and on the original American single release of "Love Me Do" (the recording of "Love Me Do" from the earlier session was the one released in the United Kingdom). Lead guitarist on *The Sound of Fury*, Joe Brown, was also active as a session musician, but also led his own rockabilly band in the early 1960s. After *The Sound of Fury*, Billy Fury was backed by the Blue Flames, which under the name Georgie Fame and the Blue Flames, was an important British R&B group in the early to mid-1960s. When Fury's manager, Larry Parnes, fired the Blue Flames, allegedly for being too jazz-oriented, the band that later gained fame as the Tornados for their worldwide instrumental hit "Telstar" backed Fury.

Born Terence Nelhams in Acton, West London in 1940, Adam Faith became the last significant teen idol before the emergence of groups right around 1960. Like just about every other eventual British pop star of the late 1950s and early 1960s, Nelhams was a fan of Lonnie Donegan during the skiffle craze. In 1957, Nelhams worked as a film cutter in the London movie industry by day while managing and singing with a skiffle band—the Worried Men—in the evenings. After a successful appearance by the Worried Men on the BBC's live music television program *Six-Five Special*, the show's producer, Jack Good, secured a recording contract for Nelhams, and gave him the stage name Adam Faith.

Although Faith's first recordings were not commercially successful, he made it to No. 1 on the British pop charts in 1959 with the song "What Do You Want?" The Johnny Worth composition and the pizzicato string–heavy arrangement closely resembles Buddy Holly's "It Doesn't Matter Anymore." Although Faith denied Holly's influence on his vocal approach on the record,[20] melodically, rhythmically, and orchestrationally, the two recordings clearly are close cousins. And, despite Faith's contention that it was British singer/keyboardist Roy Young who influenced Faith's vocal work on the track, Faith's singing style calls to mind Holly famous "hiccups" more than anything else. Despite what might be labeled the "Hollyisms" of Faith's singing, however, his overtly British accent calls to mind the work of Tommy Steele. Most of Faith's other successful singles in the 1959–1962 period also fall much closer to what American pop teen idols, such as

Fabian, were recording than they do to rock and roll, and vocally and orchestrationally several, especially "Poor Me" and "Someone Else's Baby," are near clones of "What Do You Want?"

One infamous Faith recording that exhibits a slightly harder edge is the 1960 John Barry/Trevor Peacock song "Made You," which was included in Barry's soundtrack for the film *Beat Girl*. For its single release, "Made You" was paired with an arrangement of "When Johnny Comes Marching Home." Officially, the single was a double A-side, and "When Johnny Comes Marching Home" hit No. 11 on the British pop charts, while "Made You" reached No. 5. This was despite the fact that the BBC banned "Made You" because of its (for the time) sexually explicit lyrics. Even on this more rock-oriented recording, which features virtuoso rockabilly lead electric guitar by Joe Brown, the arrangement includes somewhat syrupy orchestral strings. Incidentally, the truncated version of the song that was featured in the film *Beat Girl* is edgier and more effective.

The pop side of Adam Faith's work perhaps is most evident in his No. 4 hit from late 1960, "Lonely Pup (In a Christmas Shop)." This record pushed Faith even more into the realm of middle-of-the-road pop than "What Do You Want?" Faith was quite candid on a number of subjects in interviews—his December 1960 appearance on the live interview television program *Face to Face*, for example, found the singer acknowledging his enjoyment of premarital sex—and he was quick to express his real feelings about the kind of records he made back in the late 1950s and early 1960s. For example, journalist Spencer Leigh, who interviewed Faith in 1983, wrote the following in his 2003 obituary of Faith: "When I interviewed him at the time, he was dismissive of his records. Asked to sign a compilation of his hits, he shook his head and said, 'Who buys this crap?' He added, 'The best British rock 'n' roll record was 'Move It!' Do you think I even came close to that?'"[21]

To Faith's and his managers' credit, he was the one British teen idol who emerged in the 1950s but still adapted in a significant way to Merseybeat and the new British rock style that took the United Kingdom by storm in 1962 and 1963. Instead of instrumentalists from the John Barry Seven and the John Barry Orchestra, the year 1962 found Faith working with a new group, called the Roulettes. This band consisted of bass guitarist John Rodgers (who died in 1964 and was replaced by John Rogan), drummer Bob Henrit, lead guitarist Russ Ballard, and rhythm guitarist Peter Thorpe. This new assemblage enjoyed several entries into the British charts before parting ways in 1965. One of the songs recorded by the group, "It's Alright," was originally released in the United Kingdom as a B-side. For U.S. release in 1965, the single's sides were flipped and "It's Alright" became Faith's only Top 40 single in America.

The significant thing about "It's Alright" and Faith's other recordings with the Roulettes is that they fit squarely into the British Invasion sound. In particular, the vocal harmonies are reminiscent of the Beatles and the Searchers, and drummer Bob Henrit matches the energy of the more virtuosic of the British rock drummers of the era. Incidentally, Henrit's work probably is best experienced on the song "The First Time." In contrast, Cliff Richard's two pre-1970 *Billboard* Top 40 hits in the United States, "Living Doll" (1959) and "It's All in the Game" (1964), are teen idol–style pop songs and most decidedly not rock songs. (Marty Wilde and Billy Fury never made the *Billboard* Top 40 in the U.S.)

Faith and the Roulettes parted company in 1965, and Faith turned increasingly to the business world. He also worked as a record producer (producing Roger Daltrey's first solo album) and as a manager (Leo Sayer was one of his clients). The Roulettes formed the basis of the unusually named group Unit 4+2, which enjoyed a 1965 hit in the United Kingdom in the single "Concrete and Clay." The U.S. release of the song made it to No. 28 on the *Billboard* pop charts. Two members of the Roulettes, Bob Henrit and Russ Ballard, later were members of the band Argent, thereby successfully making the transition to late 1960s rock. In 1983, Henrit took over the drum spot in the Kinks.

I have focused discussion on the British teen idols associated with Larry Parnes because they were the best-selling young pop singers in Britain in the late 1950s and early 1960s. There were, however, other notable British rock performers during this period. Vince Taylor—born Brian Holden in 1939—is particularly interesting. Holden moved with his family from England to the United States in 1946. Eventually, he made his way back to London and became a rock star. By the 1960s, Taylor's career was already marked by various personal problems. He might have remained one of the asterisks in the history of British rock and roll were it not for his song "Brand New Cadillac." This twelve-bar blues was issued as the B-side of the single "Pledgin' My Love" in 1959. The form of the piece is notable, because most of the rock and roll material recorded in Britain at the time was not in blues form. Despite the fact that "Brand New Cadillac" was a B-side, it was destined to become Vince Taylor's best-remembered work, because it was covered to great effect by the Clash on their famous 1979 album *London Calling*. Ex-Stray Cat and noted swing and rockabilly revivalist Brian Setzer covered the song in 1994. In the early 1960s, Vince Taylor frequently performed in black leather, and was backed by the Playboys. Interestingly, Taylor continued to appear in Rocker-style black leather even as his repertoire turned increasingly to R&B music. Thus, he remained, at least in his clothing and wild image, tied to the 1950s.

The story of the development of British rock and roll is not just the story of the singing stars. Producers, session musicians, promoters, and others also played important roles. Although more individuals could be detailed, let us examine the contributions of three: Jack Good, John Barry, and Larry Parnes.

Jack Good (born 1931) was the producer behind the BBC television program *Six-Five Special*. On this 1957–1958 show, Good brought the emerging skiffle and rock performers of the era into British living rooms. It was Terence Nelhams's appearance on *Six-Five Special* with the Worried Men that convinced Good to promote Nelhams—renamed Adam Faith. However, it was the television program *Oh Boy!*, which Good developed at the ITV network, that propelled homegrown rock and roll in Britain in a more significant way. It was at Good's insistence that "Move It" was designated the A-side of Cliff Richard's first single. Good apparently believed that "Move It," with its lyrics that promoted rock and roll music and with the solid rock and roll vocal and instrumental performance, captured the spirit of the youth-oriented music *Oh Boy!* sent out over the television airwaves: "Move It" became the theme song for the program. Eventually, Jack Good moved to the United States and was the driving force behind the ABC television program *Shindig!* A wide variety of musical acts appeared during *Shindig*'s 1964–1966 run. Perhaps most notable, however, were the performances of major British acts—including the Beatles, the Rolling Stones, the Yardbirds, the Hollies, Donovan, Manfred Mann, the Who, and others—and a number of American bands that were directly influenced by the British Invasion—such as the Byrds and the Turtles.

Probably best known today as the film composer responsible for the soundtracks to movies such as *The Lion in Winter, Dances with Wolves, Out of Africa, Midnight Cowboy, Born Free,* and nearly a dozen of the popular James Bond films, composer/arranger/bandleader John Barry (born John Barry Prendergast in 1933) also played a prominent role in the early development of British rock and roll. Barry's early work was in jazz, but by 1957 and 1958 his group, the John Barry Seven, was a virtuoso instrumental ensemble that featured the electric guitar of Vic Flick and performed rock and roll with a jazz grounding. In addition to leading the group and playing trumpet, Barry also sang. The John Barry Seven briefly backed Tommy Steele and made a successful appearance on Jack Good's *Six-Five Special.* When Good created *Oh Boy!*, the John Barry Seven became one of the house bands. As such, Barry's group backed up all the major British pop stars of the late 1950s; however, they became especially closely associated with Adam Faith. Faith's recordings featured some songs composed by Barry, Barry's arrangements, and Barry's band and orchestra. The John Barry Seven enjoyed some success on its own as a recording group, especially on instrumentals. Barry's score and his group's instrumental backing work in the film *Beat Girl* (1960) captured the growing interest in modern jazz that became one of the early signifiers of the Mods.

Although Barry himself turned increasingly to film soundtrack music in the 1960s, some members of the John Barry Seven continued to have an impact on popular music throughout the decade. Lead guitarist Vic Flick, for example, backed Cliff Richard, Tom Jones, and other singers. Flick became most famous, however, for his performance of the electric guitar solo in the theme music for the James Bond movies, beginning with *Dr. No.* One can hear strong hints of Flick's heavily reverbed, low-register lead guitar style from the

Bond movie theme in his work with John Barry in the theme music for the 1960 film *Beat Girl.* Incidentally, Flick's work also can be heard with a studio ensemble, the George Martin Orchestra, on the soundtrack of the Beatles' film *A Hard Day's Night:* Flick plays the lead guitar part on the instrumental arrangement of "This Boy." John Barry Seven drummer Bobby Graham became a premiere session musician. By 1965, Graham played on top hits by Peter and Gordon, Brian Poole and the Tremeloes, the Kinks, Tom Jones, and others. Pianist Roy Young made his way to Hamburg in the early 1960s, and played piano and organ in Tony Sheridan's backing band. He also sat in with the Beatles at some of their gigs at the Star-Club. Young later joined Cliff Bennett and the Rebel Rousers, and continued to perform with his own band and as a studio musician: he appears, for example, on David Bowie's *Low* album. While few British Invasion–era rock musicians ever acknowledge John Barry's arrangements or his band as an influence for its sound, the contributions of former band members such as Roy Young, Vic Flick, and Bobby Graham in other groups and as session musicians make the John Barry Seven an important part of the history of the development of British rock.

As the promoter who was responsible for discovering and/or managing the careers of Billy Fury, Tommy Steele, Dickie Pride, Vince Eager, Joe Brown, Johnny Gentle, Marty Wilde, Georgie Fame, and others, Larry Parnes (1930–1989) exerted a great impact on the development of British rock and roll. Most of the artists associated with Parnes came out of the skiffle craze and turned to rockabilly-inspired rock and roll once they began their recording careers. Apparently following the lead of Elvis Presley's manager, Colonel Tom Parker, Parnes had his artists turn increasingly to ballads and middle-of-the-road pop beginning around 1960. The jazz-based vocalist/organist Georgie Fame was one notable exception. One thing all the Parnes artists shared, however, was good looks, as evidenced by the fact that several made successful transitions to film and the stage. It was no secret that Parnes was gay. Writer and former NPR commentator Steven D. Stark discusses gender and sexuality in detail in his book *Meet the Beatles.* Stark quotes manager, writer, and producer Simon Napier-Bell as writing that gay promoters such as Parnes and Brian Epstein could tell what teenage girls would like in their teen idols, because they discovered and promoted boys "they fancied themselves."[22] While only a few of Parnes's artists survived the onslaught of the bands that emerged in Britain in 1962 through 1964, they provided an important first step in the process of developing a uniquely British approach to rock and roll. They may not have been cutting-edge rock artists, but they did prove that, at least within Britain, British pop musicians could successfully compete with American artists on the record charts.

I would contend that, regardless of what kind of material they eventually embraced, Cliff Richard, Marty Wilde, Tommy Steele, and Billy Fury were all musicians who in their rock and roll recordings were most closely aligned with the aesthetics of the Rockers, the progressive features of Richard's recording of "Move It" and some of the harmonic daring of Wilde and Fury notwithstanding. All were viewed at least at some point of their early careers as Elvis Presley imitators, or at least as derivative of Presley. Early in his career, Presley fit in comfortably with the images of actors James Dean (*Rebel Without a Cause*) and Marlon Brando (*The Wild One*). They, along with later 1950s American rockabilly artists, such as Eddie Cochran and Gene Vincent, appeared as macho, dangerous to a certain extent—exactly the biker image the Rockers affected. Because of their association with rockabilly, the early British rock stars who did not successfully move to pop music or musical theatre, as Cliff Richard and Tommy Steele did, were forever linked with the 1950s. This especially would seem to be the case with the recording career of Marty Wilde. Billy Fury did not entirely make the transition to the kind of British rock that took America by storm in 1964 and 1965. While the R&B that he moved toward in a song such as "Don't Jump" moved closer to the Mod aesthetic than other British rock musicians who had emerged in the 1950s, Fury was still fundamentally perceived as a rocker. In fact, the vast majority of publicity photos of Fury find him striking dramatic poses as a singer and/or guitarist that come directly out of the image-building publicity that was given to Presley early in his career and to Gene Vincent and Eddie Cochran in the 1958–1960 period. It also appears that one of the other factors that kept a performer such as a Billy Fury tied to the 1950s was the fact that he was a soloist; to a large extent, unless one were a female vocalist, the British stars who achieved fame in the United States and Canada as part of the British Invasion were members of groups.

It is necessary to keep in mind the role of the intersection of style, fashion, and self-definition and self-identification in the mix of factors that kept these exact contemporaries of Ringo Starr and John Lennon from continuing their pop chart domination beyond the point when the Beatles and other groups started their domination of the record charts. Various studies of youth gangs stress their importance as a form of self-identification. For example, Hunter S. Thompson's insider study of the Hell's Angels motorcycle gang[23] and Stanley Cohen's more academically framed study of the battles between the Mods and Rockers,[24] both of which deal with the 1964–1965 period and what led to the state of gangs at that time, detail the sense of belonging and self identification that came with gang membership. The sense of connection was so complete that one simply did not easily move into and out of the gangs, let alone move between rival gangs. Likewise, the identification of a recording artist with a particular genre class (e.g., rockabilly-focused Rocker or R&B-focused Mod) was not easily changed, particularly once the artist's career had been defined by consumers.

The next generation of British rock musicians that was just starting to develop professionally in the late 1950s and early 1960s generally did not acknowledge a debt of gratitude to Steele, Richard, Wilde, and Fury. For example, *The Beatles Anthology*, a huge collection of material taken from interviews with John Lennon, Paul McCartney, George Harrison, and Ringo Starr, includes very few references to the first wave of British rock stars. What references there are generally either deal with the Beatles unsuccessful audition to back Billy Fury on a 1961 concert tour or deride the members of this first wave of stars as singers who did not write their own songs and who (at least in Ringo Starr's assessment) were far too willing to perform and record whatever was handed to them by managers and producers.[25] The fact that Billy Fury wrote every song on *The Sound of Fury,* as well as a few of his later single releases, and that Tommy Steele and Marty Wilde did at least a small amount of writing, calls into question the accuracy of Starr's assessment of the early British rock stars. The fact remains, however, that this is how the next wave of musicians perceived Fury, Steele, Wilde, and Richard. When asked about his perception of these musicians, Ron Ryan, who worked as a writer for the Dave Clark Five and had his own bands throughout the 1960s, responded quite directly, "Well, they were all just imitating Elvis, weren't they?"[26] Other male British entertainment figures who belonged to the generation that included members of the Beatles, the Who, and most of the Rolling Stones had a similar reaction to the British teen idols as Ron Ryan did. For example, Monty Python member Michael Palin (born 1943) is quoted as saying, "There were British artists like Billy Fury and Cliff Richard, but it was largely American pop music that we were in to."[27] Comments such as this suggest that while the artists covered in this chapter were successful recording and concert artists, they just were not particularly influential. The next wave of British rock musicians would continue to turn to American popular music for inspiration, but not as fully to Bill Haley and Elvis Presley as the Billy Furys and Marty Wildes had done: they looked to younger American rock stars, such as Gene Vincent and Buddy Holly, and, significantly, they looked to African American performers and styles such as blues and R&B. This was a crucial step in the development of British rock music, for it made the music one step closer to American roots music.

3

1960–1963: From the Rocker Aesthetic to the Mod Aesthetic

There is no magical cutoff date on which old-style, rockabilly-based British rock and roll ceased to exist and a new style of British rock music suddenly appeared. One thing that reading the story of the careers and recordings of the teen idols that followed Tommy Steele shows is that there was considerable overlap between Cliff Richard, Marty Wilde, Billy Fury, and Adam Faith. Within the group of musicians that will be discussed in this chapter, too, there is considerable overlap between dates and musical styles. In general, though, the first several years of the 1960s found British rock moving away from rockabilly and toward music with a stronger R&B and blues focus. This movement toward emulating the styles of black American artists represented a Mod trend. One of the major changes one can see in the British artists detailed in this chapter—even those who made virtually no impact in the United States as part of the British Invasion—is that unlike Faith, Fury, Richard, Wilde, Steele, and the other male solo singers who emerged between 1956 and 1959, these artists are cited as direct influences on the likes of the Beatles, the Who, Gerry and the Pacemakers, and others. The reader will also notice that the British artists who are the transitional figures that lead up to the British Invasion are, for the most part, groups (e.g., Johnny Kidd and the Pirates, Brian Poole and the Tremeloes, the Tornados, and so on). Although Cliff Richard was associated with the Shadows nearly from the beginning of his career, he must be considered a solo singing star to a large extent, particularly because even before the 1950s were over he was recording pop songs that often included studio orchestral instruments and other non–rock band sounds. However, because Richard and the Shadows did sometimes operate in the studio and in concerts as a unit without the addition of a studio orchestra, they also represent a move in the direction of groups and away from the solo male singing star paradigm of the 1950s. Keep in mind, too, that Adam Faith and Billy Fury also moved toward more of a soloist-plus-group context in their work beyond approximately 1962. The emphasis on groups as we move toward the British Invasion of America is significant because of what groups symbolize. The bands that eventually dominated American pop music charts and radio airwaves generally had strong group and strong individual personalities. Therefore, the prototypical British Invasion band celebrated both individualism and a sense of collective whole. As we shall see in this chapter, that was not necessarily true in what I will label "transitional" groups.

AMERICAN INFLUENCES

Let us begin our look at the changes that took place in British music in the late 1950s and early 1960s by considering some of the American artists who toured the United Kingdom as the 1950s came to a close, including Muddy Waters, Buddy Holly and the Crickets, Eddie Cochran, and Gene Vincent. This will be followed by a brief look at some of the American artists who, while not necessarily heard live in concert by young British musicians, still exerted significant influence on rock music in Britain.

Blues singer-songwriter-guitarist Muddy Waters helped to inspire some white British musicians to expand their exploration of American roots music in the direction of rural blues and electric blues. From a purely technical standpoint, the move from skiffle to rural blues involved not all that much change for young British musicians in the late 1950s: for one thing, while some of the songs performed by skiffle bands used one or two chords, a fully formed twelve-bar blues can be played by a guitarist who can play three chords. And some of the songs that skiffle groups performed came out of the black rural tradition anyway. The electric guitars and instrumental improvisation, as well as some of the vocal performance practice of electric blues, though, needed some encouragement. Muddy Waters's tour of Britain in 1958 became a gateway into authentic American blues music—a form that was not as easy to find in British record stores in the late 1950s as were some other American vernacular music forms.

Curiously, sometimes the influence of Waters and other blues musicians is easier to detect in the monikers chosen by British bands than in the music itself. For example, Waters's song "Mannish Boy" lent its name to one of David Bowie's earliest bands. The most famous example of the influence of Muddy Waters on a British band in its choice of name, however, is the Rolling Stones, named for the 1948 Waters recording "Rollin' Stone." The influence of Waters in the music itself is a little more difficult to detect, because although American blues songs formed part of the repertoire of some British bands, they were not necessarily the bands' biggest hits. Generally, the early blues recordings of what would become well-known, commercially successful bands tended to be overshadowed by their self-penned Top 40 material, at least in terms of the mass public knowledge of the bands. For example, ask members of the general public how many have heard the Rolling Stones' cover of "I Just Want to Make Love to You" versus how many have heard "Satisfaction" or "Get Off My Cloud." For blues aficionados or for serious study of the musical development of the blues-oriented British Invasion bands, however, these early recordings are crucial.

Of the songs associated with Muddy Waters, one of the more interesting for study is the aforementioned "I Just Want to Make Love to You." Bassist, songwriter, and record producer Willie Dixon composed the song in 1954, the year in which Waters recorded it. While one could debate whether or not "I Just Want to Make Love to You" was the greatest blues composition covered by British bands, the fact is that a relatively large number of bands included it as part of both their live and recorded repertoire. While the Rolling Stones' recording of 1964 might be the best-known British cover, Johnny Kidd and the Pirates, the Kinks, the Yardbirds, and others also recorded the song.

One of the things that is particularly interesting about the covers of this song is that each group puts its own stamp on the song to a greater extent than some of the other blues songs that were covered. For example, up-tempo songs, such as "I've Got My Mojo Working," tended to be performed in similar tempo and style to the original. Certainly, Alexis Korner and Blues Incorporated's 1962 recording from the influential album *R&B from the Marquee* captures the tempo, mood, and improvisational, polyphonic spirit of Waters' original recording.[1] While Manfred Mann's 1964 recording of "I've Got My Mojo Working" smoothes out the swing rhythms of Waters's and Blues Incorporated's versions, and simplifies some of the polyphony of the various instruments that is heard in the other versions, it is not radically different enough from the original or from various British covers that it is likely to immediately strike the listener as an entirely different approach.

Such is not the case with some of Waters's slower recordings, such as "I Just Want to Make Love to You." For example, the original Waters recording has a tempo of approximately 76 beats per minutes. There is a feeling of sparseness to the recording that hearkens back to the rural roots of the blues. Johnny Kidd and the Pirates, who recorded the song in approximately 1964 for their never-released album, take the song at a moderately paced 96 beats per minute. Kidd and the Pirates, whose attachments to American country music were tenuous at best, still capture the rural, Southern feel of the Waters' version with a single-line electric guitar riff that at least hints at country music. The Rolling Stones' 1964 recording, which found its way onto their first album, includes extensive slide guitar work from Brian Jones, something that comes directly out of the blues tradition that he, more than any other member of the Rolling Stones, championed. However, the Stones take the song at a significantly faster 126 beats per minute. This tempo change helps the song to bridge the gap between rural blues and rock. It is very much in keeping with what British electric blues bands in general, though, were doing with the slower American blues songs they covered. For example, Alexis Korner and Blues Incorporated's 1962 version of Howlin' Wolf's "Built for Comfort" is significantly faster than the original. In the cases of the Rolling Stones' version of "I Just Want to Make Love to You" and Blues Incorporated's version of "Built for Comfort," it seems almost as though "I've Got My Mojo Working" becomes a stylistic paradigm for British blues. Indeed, "Mojo" is often cited as one of the most important influences on both American and British white electric blues. It should also be noted that it would make sense for the Rolling Stones to adopt some of the characteristics of Blues Incorporated in upping the tempo on slow blues tunes: several of the Rolling Stones performed with Blues Incorporated before forming their own group.

These are, however, just a few examples of how British musicians between approximately 1961 and 1964 felt the influence of Muddy Waters. Waters certainly was not alone among the blues musicians who influenced the development of British rock music. It should be noted, though, that the American blues musicians who are mentioned most frequently by British rock musicians, and whose recordings and original compositions were most frequently covered by British musicians of the early 1960s were those who held two things in common: (1) they linked Southern rural blues and Chicago-style electric blues and (2) they tended to be blues musicians who at some time prior to the early 1960s toured the United Kingdom and/or Europe.

Possibly, the reason for the first trait is that it gave at least the feeling—if not the reality—of greater authenticity, greater adherence to the roots music nature of blues to follow the lead of a blues musician whose style had direct links to the acoustic, Southern, rural tradition. From a practical standpoint, study of a broad historical range of recordings by these crossover blues singers and players could provide insight in how one moved between the two styles. Would that not be valuable if a budding rock musician were, say, trying to adapt an early rural blues song to the new style? The second point possibly relates to the fact that authentic blues (as opposed to more commercial forms of R&B) was a niche music even in land in which it was born, and it was even more difficult to come by on recordings in the late 1950s and early 1960s in the United Kingdom. Stories are often told of British musicians obtaining blues recordings from American military bases, on trips to Europe, from American sailors in British port cities, and so on—the music was just not found in large quantities in British record shops. One could reasonably suppose that the blues recordings that were available probably were those of artists who had actually performed in Britain and/or Europe, because name recognition would be more likely to create a demand.

But Muddy Waters himself was not alone in satisfying the two traits of the most influential American blues figures. A number of British rock guitarists mention the importance of Big Bill Broonzy. For example, George Harrison mentions his appreciation of Broonzy's work in the documentary film *The Beatles Anthology*.[2] As a sidebar to his biographical sketch of Broonzy in *Bill Wyman's Blues Odyssey*, Wyman writes, "Big Bill has been an inspiration to many and his influences are still felt today. He was a mentor, a great performer, and an ambassador for the blues."[3] In a 1999 interview, Dave Davies of the Kinks discussed his early musical development, saying that early on he and his brother Ray would "do this sort of Chet Atkins thing," but "then an important thing happened: our brother-in-law, Mike, introduced us to Big Bill Broonzy. I'd never heard anything like it. I was awestruck; I just could not believe the power, the soulfulness of it."[4] Broonzy was, like Muddy Waters, a musician who bridged the gap between the rural blues of Robert Johnson and Chicago-style electric blues. Broonzy toured Europe in 1951 (therefore, over a half-decade before Muddy Waters), and generally is credited with being one of the most important American blues musicians in bringing knowledge and appreciation of the genre to the European continent. It seems that the influences on the emerging British rock musicians came from blues artists that toured either the United Kingdom or Europe, even if those British musicians never actually heard the live performances by the blues artists. It could be reasonably supposed that the name recognition that U.K. and European touring brought to Big Bill Broonzy and later Muddy Waters led to young British singer-guitarists turning first to those American musicians when it came time to seek out blues recordings. And, again, it would also make reasonable sense that record shops might be more apt to stock recordings by "name" blues musicians—the "name" having come from the fact that they were among the few American blues musicians who actually appeared across the Atlantic.

It should be noted that Broonzy played both electric and acoustic guitar at various points in his career, and it seems that both made some impact on British guitarists. The context of Davies's reference suggests the impact of Broonzy's distorted electric guitar sound (he goes on to discuss how the sound of blues artists such as Broonzy and others encouraged him to experiment with amplifiers to get similar effects). Hints of Broonzy's approach to acoustic guitar (perhaps more florid and interesting than his electric guitar work) can be heard in George Harrison's acoustic guitar work on "For You Blue," on the Beatles' *Let It Be* album. Although that 1969 recording is outside the time period covered in this book, I mention it because it suggests the continuing impact of American blues singer-guitarists on British rock music as the 1960s progressed.

In a recording career that lasted approximately 18 months, Buddy Holly not only wrote and recorded songs that are still remembered in the twenty-first century, he also inspired numerous emerging rock musicians, both in the United States and in Britain. Originally, the group known variously as the Crickets, or Buddy Holly and the Crickets, came about as a way of masking Holly's direct involvement in recording projects while he was under contract to a rival company. Holly and the Crickets toured Great Britain in 1958, and their concerts attracted the interest of British musicians who were early in the process of moving from skiffle to rock and roll. Holly, with his fairly plain looks and thick-framed glasses, looked like an average guy—in sharp contrast to the American and British teen idols who were mass marketed by the music industry in the wake of Elvis Presley's success. Holly wrote much of his own material and played lead and rhythm guitar in an engaging and novel manner. He gave the rhythm guitar greater emphasis than was customary in earlier rockabilly, and many of his recorded solos were based on chordal playing, in contrast to the work of earlier rockabilly lead guitar players. With the Crickets providing backing vocals, they were a self-contained rock band that established a prototype for many of the rock bands that followed, especially in Britain. Not only was the month-long concert tour of Britain influential on young musicians who either heard the concerts or toured as opening acts for Buddy Holly and the Crickets, the band's recordings were popular in the United Kingdom.

Even after Buddy Holly left the Crickets in late 1958, moved to New York City, tried to establish a career as a solo act, and ultimately died an untimely death in February 1959, the Crickets continued to influence British bands. Generally, the group was not commercially successful in the United States following Holly's departure, although in 1962 they recaptured at least a little of their former commercial luster. One 1962 single, in particular, a recording of Gerry Goffin and Carole King's "Don't Ever Change" was quite popular in Britain. While this single never made the singles charts in the United States, it topped out at No. 5 in Britain on the *New Musical Express* charts. The Beatles recorded the song on August 1, 1963 for later broadcast on the BBC. The Beatles' arrangement, tempo, and singing and playing style copies that of the Crickets, except that the tempo is slightly faster and the Beatles cover the piano part of the original version on electric guitar. In fact, the Beatles' cover is so true to the original that Ringo Starr copies the drum fills in the introduction and verses. Brian Poole and the Tremeloes also recorded "Don't Ever Change," as the opening part of a medley that also included "The Loco-Motion" and "Let's Twist Again." The Tremeloes' 1963 version of "Don't Ever Change" (originally on the album *Big Big Hits of '62*), while truncated because of the time limitations of the medley format, is also a close reproduction of the Crickets' recording, except, again, with a slightly brighter tempo and with electric guitar covering the piano fills.

The influence of Buddy Holly and the Crickets, though, goes well beyond repertoire. For one thing, Holly, with his thick-rimmed glasses, proved that one need not be conventionally handsome in order to be a commercial success in the music industry of the late 1950s. At least one budding British rock music, Hank Marvin of the Shadows, aped Holly's look by wearing similar thick-rimmed glasses on stage and in publicity photos.

It was Holly's progressive work as a songwriter and as a guitarist, however, that most influenced emerging British rock musicians. The aforementioned Hank Marvin not only wore the same style glasses as Holly, he also played a Fender Stratocaster guitar, just like Buddy Holly. Mike Pender, of the Searchers, has been quoted as saying, "Everything I learned, everything I played, was based on Holly."[5] Indeed, the jangling style of rhythm guitar playing Holly pioneered can be heard in much of Pender's 1963–1965 work with the Searchers. In particular, Holly's style of soloing by using chords—sort of a rhythm guitar approach to lead guitar—comes through on numerous cuts by the Searchers. Also, the classic lineup of Buddy Holly and the Crickets—two guitars, bass, and drums—influenced not only some British rock bands, but also post-Holly American rock bands.

One of the most influential and yet one of the most tragic tours in rock history took place in 1960 when Eddie Cochran and Gene Vincent traveled from the United States to Great Britain. Like Buddy Holly, Cochran and Vincent represented a new, more R&B-oriented approach to rockabilly than what was heard in the instrumental work on Bill Haley and Elvis Presley recordings. Still, though, Cochran and Vincent, with their leather clothing and hairstyles looked the part of Rockers (as opposed to Mods). Perhaps because Colonel Tom Parker refined Presley's image in an attempt to widen the singer's audience, these new Rockers seemed at the time to be wilder, more youth-oriented, and more dangerous than what Presley had become by the end of the 1950s. Cochran songs such as "Summertime Blues" and "Twenty Flight Rock," and Vincent songs such as "Be Bop a Lula" and "Blue Jean Bop," were covered by British rock musicians for years. Not only were some of these artists' songs performed by the newly emerging British rock musicians, the rhythmic vitality, showmanship, and Cochran's and Vincent's (and Holly's, for that matter) abilities to write, sing, and play guitar also suggested that the future lay in developing a complete package. In other words, they were the antithesis of the solo singer, teen idol paradigm.

In addition, Eddie Cochran's 1958 hit "Summertime Blues" includes an example of what would become a staple of British rock drummers in the early 1960s, the "2-and, 4" rhythmic pattern. In this pattern, drum hits, handclaps, or some other accentuation is played on beat 2, mid-way between beats 2 and 3 (the "and" of 2), and on beat 4. Here, the figure is in the handclaps. Although it became almost a cliché of the Merseybeat (Liverpool) bands, it is something that certainly was in the air in from 1960 through the 1964 British Invasion elsewhere. For example, Roy Orbison's 1960 hit "Only the Lonely" includes the figure as an almost-constant part of the drum part. The figure also plays a prominent role in Orbison's most successful single, the 1964 recording "Oh, Pretty Woman." In fact, it could be argued that the Orbison and Bill Dees composition "Oh, Pretty Woman" is perhaps the best American record of the period to capture the most distinctive hooks of British Invasion rock: the opening guitar riff (which sounds suspiciously like an inspiration for several Rolling Stones songs of the following year), and the prototypical drum pattern that is heard in the bridge of the song. Incidentally, it is well worth taking a close listen to the Beatles' performance of the Larry Williams song "Dizzy Miss Lizzie," as recorded on August 30, 1965 and released on the album *The Beatles at the Hollywood Bowl:* while Paul McCartney and John Lennon stick to the Larry Williams accompaniment riffs they played on their studio cover of the song, George Harrison changes up in the second verse and creates a new riff by mashing the end of the "Oh, Pretty Woman" riff (the descending part) onto the beginning of the "Dizzy Miss Lizzie" riff. Orbison and the Beatles toured Europe—the Beatles sometimes opening for Orbison, and Orbison sometimes opening for the Beatles—in 1963, and Orbison reportedly encouraged the Beatles to tour the United States. Perhaps Harrison's quote was a subliminal "thank you" to Orbison, or at least an inside joke.

The drum figure that seemed to define at least in part the Liverpool sound had also been a prominent part of John Barry's jazz/rock and roll score for the 1960 film *Beat Girl*. The drums make especially heavy use of the figure in the title theme music. It is worth noting that Barry's theme music was tied to young, jazz-loving characters that, while clearly modeled on the stereotypes of American beatniks, bear some resemblance to what would become known as Mods in a couple of years. The drum pattern was also a prominent rhythmic figure in the instrumental surf music, as well as in surf songs. Note, for example, that the figure can be heard in "Let's Go Trippin'" (1961) and "Miserlou" (1962) by surf rock pioneer Dick Dale. The Beach Boys' first single, "Surfin'," which was recorded in October 1961, also prominently includes the figure in Dennis Wilson's drums, as does the better-known song "Surfin' Safari," which dates from June 1962.[6] Despite its frequent use in American surf music of the period—and its importance in defining the Liverpool sound in Britain—the British instrumental group that came the closest to an American surf sound, the Shadows, rarely used the figure in their originals.

In order to hear how the Merseybeat groups took older material and fundamentally changed the drum part by adding the famous drum figure, it is worth comparing Chuck Berry's original recording of his composition "Roll Over Beethoven," from 1956, with the Beatles' 1963 recording for the BBC (available on the album *Live at the BBC*) and on the 1963 studio album *With the Beatles*. Berry's drummer maintains a swing feel throughout the piece, and for the most part plays the snare drum only directly on beats 2 and 4. On the Beatles' BBC recording, Ringo Starr maintains the basic swing feel, but accentuates the off-beat after 2. On the studio recording, Starr plays with a straight eighth-note feel and, behind the introductory guitar solo and during the bridge ("Well, if you feel it and like it. . ."), he plays the archetypical "2-and, 4" pattern.

Another illuminating, although much less well-known, example can be found in a rare Gerry and the Pacemakers recording of Ray Charles's "What'd I Say." On the famous 1959 recording, Charles's drummer plays a "2, 4-and" pattern throughout much of the song. On what sounds like an acetate demo recording (available on the album *Unearthed Merseybeat, Vol. 1,* Viper Records, 2003) that dates from 1961,[7] Freddie Marsden of the Pacemakers changes the snare and tom-tom pattern of the original into a "2-and, 4-and" pattern on the cymbals.

Because Little Richard was also such an important influence on British rock musicians of the early 1960s—particularly Paul McCartney, who sang lead on the Beatles studio, radio, and live covers of such Little Richard songs as "Lucille," "Long Tall Sally," and Richard's arrangement of "Kansas City" (which mashes his own composition "Hey, Hey, Hey" onto "Kansas City")—it is also interesting to examine British covers of Little Richard to see how the beat was modified. For example, on the original version of Little Richard's "Lucille" (1957) the drummer places equal emphasis on beats 2 and 4 in the snare drum in the verses; however, on the Beatles' September 7, 1963 recording of "Lucille" for the BBC, Ringo Starr incorporates the "2-and, 4" pattern, with a heavy emphasis on the "and" after beat 2. Another example is the session drummer (possibly Bobby Graham, who was the United Kingdom's busiest studio drummer) on Peter and Gordon's 1964 cover of "Lucille," who uses the "2-and, 4" snare drum pattern during the guitar solo.

Other American rock artists of the 1950s also influenced the newly emerging British bands. Of primary importance were Chuck Berry, Little Richard, the Everly Brothers, and Carl Perkins. While none of these musicians toured the United Kingdom until later than Waters, Holly, Cochran, and Vincent, they exerted their influence through their recordings.

Although Chuck Berry wrote and recorded songs in a variety of styles, forms, and tempi, it was mostly the 12-bar blues and 16-bar blues form rock and roll songs that had the greatest direct impact on the British bands that eventually made up the British Invasion. "Rock and Roll Music," "Roll over Beethoven," and "Carol," just to name three, were all covered by more than one famous British band. Songs such as these, as well as "Memphis, Tennessee," "Little Queenie," "Too Much Monkey Business," and others were all part of the live and recorded repertoire of British Invasion bands. Berry's influence as a guitarist can be heard most clearly in the lead and rhythm guitar work of Keith Richards, although Berry's solos were so much a part of the entire gestalt of his songs that George Harrison, Dave Davies, Tony Hicks, and other lead guitarists copied his solos and/or style not only on covers of actual Berry compositions, but also on new songs that were written in the Berry style.

Born Richard Penniman, singer-songwriter-pianist Little Richard's career in R&B and rock and roll extends back into the late 1940s. While Chuck Berry wrote songs that expressed a youthful appreciation of the rock and roll idiom ("Rock and Roll Music" and "Roll over Beethoven") and songs that commented more directly on teenage life ("School Days") than did the work of Little Richard, Penniman brought a raw, screaming excitement to rock and roll that exceeded anything that came before. Little Richard's boogie woogie and gospel-based rock and roll piano playing directly influenced not only Americans such as Jerry Lee Lewis, but also budding British rock musicians such as Roy Young, Mike Smith, and others. Richard's high-energy songs and vocal style, heard to great effect on "Lucille," "Tutti Fruitti," and "Long Tall Sally," were covered by a number of British Invasion bands, perhaps most famously by the Beatles. For example, much of Paul McCartney's vocal approach to fast rock and roll songs can be traced back to Little Richard. This is true not just on covers, such as the Beatles' recording of "Long Tall Sally," but also on Beatles originals, such as "I'm Down," the 1965 song McCartney penned as a replacement for "Long Tall Sally" as a concert closer.

Singer-songwriter-guitarist Carl Perkins was another American influence on the British rock musicians who emerged after the teen idol era. The Beatles, for example, covered a number of Perkins songs in live performances and on their studio recordings. While at least two of these, "Matchbox" and "Honey Don't," were routinely sung by Ringo Starr, Perkins was a favorite of Beatle George Harrison, who sang lead on covers of "Everybody's Trying to Be My Baby" and "Glad All Over" (not to be confused with the later Dave Clark Five song of the same name). While Perkins did not write the latter song, he recorded it, and Harrison's version, which was part of the Beatles' live repertoire, and which they recorded for broadcast on the BBC, owes a great deal to Perkins' singing and guitar playing. The Beatles also recorded "Lend Me Your Comb," another song associated with Perkins, for the BBC.

The history of the song "Matchbox" illustrates perhaps one of the most important features of Carl Perkins's work in the 1950s. The blues pioneer Blind Lemon Jefferson originally wrote and recorded "Matchbox" back in the 1920s. Perkins rewrote the song and adapted it to the rockabilly style. In fact, Carl Perkins was the rockabilly artist with the closest stylistic ties to African American blues. This is important because much of the story of the transition from the Bill Haley imitators of the late 1950s to mature British Invasion rock is the story of British musicians moving from receiving the influence of African American music second and third hand to receiving it first hand. Because of his closer stylistic ties to blues music, the direct influence of Perkins as a singer, songwriter, and guitarist represents a transitional step for the British musicians that made their impact in the early 1960s.

Phil and Don Everly, collectively known as the Everly Brothers also exerted influence on British Invasion bands in the early 1960s. The Everly Brothers first performed as children on their father's radio program in the 1940s. Although their first record release was not a success, their second single, "Bye Bye Love," was a smash hit in 1957. The Everly Brothers continued a run of Top 10 American hits, including "Wake up Little Susie," "All I Have to Do Is Dream," "Bird Dog," "Let It Be Me," "Cathy's Clown," "When Will I Be Loved," and others. In addition to the chart success they enjoyed in the United States, the Everly Brothers also dominated the British charts. In fact, the high regard in which the British and European public held their music is confirmed by the fact that although the Everly Brothers' chart success in the United States ended in 1962, they continued to enjoy hit singles in Europe and the United Kingdom even into the years of the British Invasion.

As far as their direct influence on the development of British rock goes, the most important and obvious contribution of the Everly Brothers was in their approach to vocal harmony. The most notable feature of the Everlys' approach is that the two often sang in unison rhythms at the harmonic interval of a third. Although their speaking voices are quite distinctive, the brothers achieved a blended tone color when singing. While the Everly Brothers recorded some cover versions of other performers' songs, a fair amount of their hit material was either written by one or both of the brothers, or was written for them. The Everlys and those who specifically wrote for them often actively took advantage of their ability to blend their voices and composed in such a way that the melody and the harmony become one. In other words, unless one already knew the tune—e.g., on the Everly Brothers cover recording of Little Richard's "Lucille"—it would be difficult to determine whether the "harmony" part was a third below the "true" melody or a third above the "true" melody.

Among the British acts that emerged in the early 1960s, the Everly Brothers were more highly influential on northern bands, and in particular on the Hollies and the Beatles. When asked how London rock musicians reacted to the Everly Brothers, Ron Ryan replied "very nice harmonies, but in London we thought the Everly Bros. were a bit 'lightweight.'"[8] But, while London musicians were more attuned to African American blues and harder-rocking white artists such as Bill Haley and Gene Vincent, the Everly Brothers became just another of the components that went into making a uniquely British rock style for some northern bands.

The Everlys' influence on the Hollies is most obvious, because the Hollies actively covered Everly Brothers recordings. For example, the Hollies version of Little Richard's composition "Lucille," from the January 1964 album *Stay with the Hollies,* is significantly more indebted to the Everly Brothers' 1960 recording than to Little Richard's version. Allan Clarke and Graham Nash pretty much copy the Everly Brothers' two-part, close harmony. Likewise, the Hollies' cover of Chuck Berry's composition "Memphis," from the same album, has Clarke and Nash incorporating the same close harmony. The arrangement on "Memphis" is perhaps even more indicative of the extent of the Everly

Brothers' influence on the Hollies: on "Lucille" they copy the Everly Brothers' recording, while on "Memphis," a song not necessarily associated with the Everlys, the Hollies create their own Everly Brothers–influenced vocal arrangement. Within a short time, on the songs in which they harmonized in pretty much unison rhythm, the Hollies expanded the texture to three voices.

The Beatles' debt to the Everly Brothers perhaps is not so obvious, especially since their versions of songs the Everly Brothers recorded take their lead more from the originals than from the Everlys' versions. This is evident in the Beatles' performance of "Lucille" on the BBC. Here, Paul McCartney sings as a soloist and he fully appropriates Little Richard's singing style. However, the Beatles did perform "So How Come (No One Loves Me)," a song associated with the Everly Brothers, as part of their live sets and committed the song to tape as part of their recording auditions. On the surviving recordings of the Beatles performing this song, the vocal harmonies are derived from the Everly Brothers recording. Incidentally, the Beatles were not the only Liverpool group to record "So How Come (No One Loves Me)": the Merseybeats also covered the Everly Brothers' version of the song, as well as "All I Have to Do Is Dream." In terms of the Beatles' own compositions, the two-part harmony—sung by John Lennon and Paul McCartney—on the verse of "Please Please Me," the band's first No. 1 U.K. single, closely resembles the Everly Brothers' work on "Cathy's Clown." And, although the songs do not mimic the Everly Brothers style nearly as much as the opening phrase of "Please Please Me," there are strong hints of Everly Brothers harmony style in "From Me to You" and "Love Me Do." In several of the interview segments in *The Beatles Anthology,* the Beatles acknowledge that the Everly Brothers were one of the groups they listened to and watched. This influence came from the music as well as from the way in which Phil and Don Everly sang into the same microphone with their guitars pressed forward.[9] It is also important to note that the Everly Brothers wrote several of their hit songs, either individually or collectively, including "Cathy's Clown." This must also have encouraged British songwriters such as Lennon and McCartney. Although the Beatles were just as apt to use other textures, such as solo singer, or the girl group (lead vocal plus two backing singers) texture, the influence of the two-voice, who's-got-the-melody style of the Everly Brothers continued to be felt in their original compositions and arrangements throughout the 1960s. For example, the 1969 song "Two of Us" (on *Let It Be*) finds Lennon and McCartney singing in what is not all that far removed from Everly Brothers–inspired two-part harmony.

The Everly Brothers' use of acoustic guitars in ballads, pop, and even harder-rocking songs that they recorded also may have influenced British Invasion bands. Several groups, such as the Beatles and Gerry and Pacemakers, used acoustic guitar as the rhythm instrument from time to time in a variety of song types. Although the influence of the Everly Brothers in this area is not as definitive as it is in the harmony style of the Beatles, the

Hollies, and others, the acoustic rhythm guitar makes the Everly Brothers stand out in late 1950s and early 1960s rock. While it may not necessarily follow that there is a direct correlation between this aspect of the Everly Brother's distinctive texture and British bands, it is notable that the British bands that exhibited the least amount of influence from the Everlys in the vocal harmony department also were the groups that tended rarely to use acoustic guitar as the rhythm instrument.

At the start of the 1960s, British rock musicians began to take notice of the Motown sound that was finding its way onto Berry Gordy, Jr.'s labels Tamla, Motown, and the others that he incorporated under the Motown umbrella. Gordy's music empire began modestly enough: after his discharge from the Army in 1953 he opened a music store that went out of business. Gordy then worked on the assembly lines at the Ford Motor Company and as a semiprofessional boxer. While working at Ford, Gordy began writing songs. His first hit, "Reet Petite," was recorded by Jackie Wilson in 1957. In 1958, Gordy founded Jobete Music, and in 1959 he enjoyed his first major success as a producer and songwriter with "You Got What It Takes." By the time of the British Invasion, "You Got What It Takes" was in the repertoire of a number of British rock bands. Gordy founded Tamla Records in 1960, and built a music empire that by 1964 was the largest independent record company in the world.

Throughout this time period, Gordy's acts appealed to a wide audience demographic. While the vast majority of the early Motown writers, singers, producers, and instrumentalists were black, the key to Gordy's success was the ability of his producers to put together a product that would be at least as commercially successful on the pop charts (which tended to measure sales, airplay, and jukebox plays for a predominantly white audience) as on the R&B charts.

An electric blues scene developed in Britain in 1961 and 1962, which eventually led to the success of blues-oriented rock bands such as the Rolling Stones, the Animals, and the Yardbirds. However, the R&B music of Berry Gordy's Motown appealed to a broader range of bands. For example, while the Rolling Stones covered a number of blues songs by the likes of Willie Dixon, Muddy Waters, and Robert Johnson, and the Beatles did not, both groups covered songs that came out of Gordy's Motown organization. In fact, the first major hit released on any of the Motown labels, "Money," was recorded in 1963 by the Rolling Stones, the Beatles, the Searchers, and others, and the song was in the live repertoire of countless other British bands. The Beatles' second U.K. album, the 1963 release *With the Beatles,* included covers of three Motown songs: "Money," "You Really Got a Hold on Me," and "Please Mister Postman." Several British bands covered Gordy's "Do You Love Me," which originally had been an R&B hit for the Contours, and 1963 versions by the Dave Clark Five and Brian Poole and the Tremeloes both made the British Top 40. The Dave Clark Five version later found commercial success in the U.S.

At the same time that Berry Gordy, Jr. was making inroads in the American music industry and coming to the attention of emerging British rock bands, a parallel was developing in New York City: the Brill Building and girl group scene.[10] In the late 1950s and early 1960s, several music publishing and associated record companies were housed in and near the Brill Building (1619 Broadway in Manhattan). By and large, these companies shared traits with the Tin Pan Alley–era (1880s–1940s) New York City popular music establishment: a sizeable proportion of the songwriters were young and Jewish, and the companies had a firmly established corporate structure. Some of the famous songwriters who came out the Brill Building publishing establishment include Carole King and Gerry Goffin, Neil Diamond, Paul Simon, Jeff Barry and Ellie Greenwich, Barry Mann and Cynthia Weil, Jerry Leiber and Mike Stoller, and Neil Sedaka. The publishers and record companies for which these individual songwriters and songwriting teams worked had a variety of artists under contract, including soloists, vocal groups, black R&B acts, and white pop acts. The musicians associated with the Brill Building songwriters who most profoundly influenced the British Invasion bands, though, were the so-called girl groups—black female vocal groups, generally with three members. Of all the Brill Building songwriting teams, the most commercially successful was the husband and wife team of lyricist Gerry Goffin and composer Carole King. Generally, the songs that Goffin and King wrote for girl groups such as the Cookies and the Shirelles—as well as the songs they wrote for black solo singers such as Little Eva—were arranged by Goffin and King so that the texture featured a solo singer supported by backing vocals.

As writers, arrangers, and producers, Gerry Goffin and Carole King made an impact on several male British bands in the crucial period leading up to the British Invasion, but perhaps most forcefully on the Beatles. In a full-page 1963 profile of the Beatles in *New Musical Express,* Paul McCartney lists Goffin and King as his favorite songwriters.[11] McCartney and John Lennon also have been widely quoted as saying that all they wanted to do when they starting writing songs together was to be as good as Goffin and King.[12] As performers, the Beatles included the Goffin-King song "Chains" (originally recorded by the Cookies) on their first album, and the band recorded another Goffin-King composition, "Keep Your Hands off My Baby" (a 1962 hit for Little Eva, with backing vocals by the Cookies), for a January 1963 BBC broadcast. In addition to these two songs, the Beatles covered girl group songs written by other Brill Building songwriters. In addition, the early compositions of Lennon and McCartney reflect structural, arrangement, and lyrical features of the material Brill Building songwriters produced for girl groups.

As with material from Motown, the R&B material from the Brill Building songwriters tended to appeal to a wider range of British bands than the purely blues-based music of singer-songwriters such as Muddy Waters. While many of the Brill Building writers had their songs covered, let us just consider as an example the Goffin and King songs that British bands recorded. In addition to the Beatles' recordings of "Chains" and "Keep Your Hands off My Baby," the Hollies recorded "Honey and Wine," the Animals recorded "Don't Bring Me Down," the Rockin' Berries recorded "He's in Town," Manfred Mann covered "Oh No, Not My Baby," and Herman's Hermits scored the biggest Goffin-King hit of all the British Invasion bands with their cover of "I'm into Something Good."

There also seems to be some evidence of a possible tie between the sound of Gerry Goffin and Carole King's arrangements and record production at the development of British Invasion rock and roll. It is difficult to imagine that Goffin and King's songwriting, arranging, and production did not make some impact on the changes in the sound of the Dave Clark Five's recordings that occurred in 1963. The increased emphasis on the drums in the recording mix, the use of short bursts of sixteenth-notes or triplets (depending on the metrical feel of the song), and the style of Denis Payton's saxophone playing when he is accompanying all seem to be anticipated on Goffin and King's arrangement of the Little Eva hit "The Loco-Motion." Songwriter Ron Ryan, who worked with the Dave Clark Five at that time, claims that the first "crash, bang, wallop" (his term) recording of the Dave Clark Five was of his composition "The Mulberry Bush." According to Ryan, though, Goffin's production was not a direct influence. Rather, he claims that Doug Sheldon's cover of "Your Ma Said You Cried in Your Sleep Last Night" directly influenced the band's new style.[13] Certainly, the full sound of "The Loco-Motion" and the emphasis on the drums was something that was in the air at the time, especially in the work of British record producer Joe Meek, who was noted for, among other things, close miking the drums. Still, it is curious that Ryan's lyrics in "The Mulberry Bush" make reference to the Loco-Motion as one of the dances that one might do at the fictional dance club of the song's title.

One of the more noteworthy points of contrast between British covers of Motown songs and British covers of Brill Building songs is that the Motown material by and large tended to be songs that originally were associated with male singers (e.g., Smoky Robinson's "You Really Got a Hold on Me," the Isley Brothers' "Twist and Shout," and Barrett Strong's "Money"), while the Brill Building material largely was that originally associated with female singers. To an extent previously not heard in American popular music, Brill Building songwriters who crafted material for female vocalists avoided traditional, stereotypical gender roles and attitudes in their lyrics. Therefore, a song such as "Keep Your Hands off My Baby," in which the lead singer's character exhibits what we in the twenty-first century might call a lot of "attitude," contains nothing of the submissiveness found in pop music sung by women in the 1950s. Likewise, "I'm into Something Good," in which the lead singer directly acknowledges premarital sex (and implies sex possibly on the first date), might be even more closely associated with the stereotypical gender roles of men than of women. Ultimately, what this meant for the male British bands was that this

R&B, with its engaging vocal melodies and harmonies, crossed gender boundaries easily. All the tweaking that was necessary was the occasional change of pronoun.

That is not to say that all the Brill Building songs that British rock bands covered in the early to mid-1960s emanated from the girl group genre. The Searchers' first hit single in Britain, for example, was a cover of "Sweets for My Sweet," a song originally recorded by the American male vocal group the Drifters. The natural affinity between Brill Building songwriters and the new beat groups that became part of the British Invasion is confirmed by the fact that after they had written hits such as "Save the Last Dance for Me" and "A Teenager in Love" for American singers, the New York–born and raised team responsible for "Sweets for My Sweet"—Doc Pomus and Mort Shuman—moved to London for a time in the 1960s to write for British performers.

Certainly, there are melodic, harmonic, and formal cues from other Brill Building teams that can also be found in the work of British rock bands in the years leading up to the British Invasion. One song in particular that deserves mention is Jerry Leiber and Mike Stoller's "Poison Ivy," a 1959 hit for the Coasters. This song made it into the repertoire of a number of British rock groups in the early 1960s and was recorded by the Rolling Stones, the Dave Clark Five, the Hollies, Manfred Mann, the Paramounts, and others. While each of these bands had its own take on the song—the Paramounts give an R&B-oriented performance, the Dave Clark Five, a high-energy, fast-paced performance with a healthy dose of flashy drum technique, while the Joe Meek–produced recording by the Puppets is thinner in texture and includes surf guitar tone color—there is not as much variation from band to band as with some other songs that were covered by British artists. One important feature of Leiber and Stoller's writing on "Poison Ivy" is the heavy use of the bVII chord, as well as extensive use of the diatonic minor chords (ii, iii, and vi). The use of the subtonic chord (bVII) became one of the defining features of British Invasion rock, as did the modal ambiguity between a major and its relative minor key, which very much is part of the sound of "Poison Ivy."

TRANSITIONAL ARTISTS

The first several years of the 1960s found new British rock and roll singers and bands making it onto the record charts in Britain; however, a fair number of these artists remain footnotes in many Americans' knowledge of British rock because these artists made minimal impact in the United States. Although there were some fundamental differences between these artists and performers such as Marty Wilde and Tommy Steele, they do not necessarily represent the entire package of what Americans labeled British Invasion rock and roll style in the 1964–1966 period. Let us examine some of these transitional artists.

One group that emerged at the start of the 1960s, the Shadows, tends to defy categorization. For one thing, the Shadows grew out of Cliff Richard's original backing band, the Drifters; however, by the time the group was recording on its own, none of the original members of the Drifters were in the Shadows. The Shadows continued to serve for a number of years as Richard's backing band; however, they also enjoyed a fruitful career, as a standalone group, mostly known for their instrumentals.

In order to document the story of the Shadows fully, one needs to go back to the Vipers Skiffle Group. This 1950s group was by all accounts second in importance and popularity among skiffle bands only to Lonnie Donegan's group. The Vipers Skiffle Group—later the Vipers—had something of a revolving door of membership, such that although they were not originally members of the Vipers, future Shadows Hank Marvin, Tony Meehan, and Jet Harris all performed with the group near the end of the skiffle craze. Originally, the Shadows, Marvin (guitar), Meehan (drums), Harris (bass guitar), and Bruce Welch (guitar) operated as Cliff Richard's backing group; however, in the late 1950s and early 1960s instrumental rock music was a viable genre—note, for example, the success of such American acts such as Dick Dale, the Ventures, and others that came out of the surf tradition, not to mention the enduring popularity of the Champs' "Tequila" and the cult-like status of Link Wray's "Rumble."

The Shadows continued to back Cliff Richard, but became independent stars with the success of their 1960 single "Apache," a recording that topped Britain's *New Musical Express* polls. In fact, *NME* readers selected "Apache" as 1960 Record of the Year and selected the Shadows as 1960 Britain's Top Small Group in a popularity poll. EMI released the group's debut album, *The Shadows,* in 1961, and their second album, *Out of the Shadows,* in 1962. By the time of the release of the second album, bassist Brian Locking had replaced Jet Harris and drummer Brian Bennett had replaced Tony Meehan. The Shadows continued to enjoy hit singles and albums in Great Britain, even as groups such the Beatles, the Searchers, and others began making their impact in 1963.

A listen to the Shadows' first two albums quickly shows the stylistic diversity of the group, as the tracks include everything from rock and roll, to middle-of-the-road, jazz-influenced ballads, and so on. Most of the songs are, however, on the light side, especially when compared with the R&B, rock, and blues music that the British Invasion bands brought to the record charts at the time. The Shadows influenced a host of imitators, instrumental bands that aped the style of the Shadows' hits. Some of the artists who were just emerging, however, later spoke disparagingly about the choreographed moves of the Shadows' guitarists and the staid rhythms of some of their material. *The Beatles Anthology* documentary film, for example, includes a segment in which the very tone of George Harrison's description of Shadows and the imitators they spawned—set against a clip of a very rhythmically sterile television appearance of the Shadows—shows his distaste for that aspect of the Shadows' work. The rhythmic sterility in the Shadows work—again, compared with the recordings of other bands—generally comes from a lack of and/or de-emphasis on syncopation. There is also a tendency in some of the pieces they recorded to employ what musicians sometimes call a hard swing rhythm, in which the unevenness of the rhythmic units of a swing feel are somewhat exaggerated. To put it into concrete musical terms, some of the swing feel moves in the direction of dotted-eighth/sixteenth-note (3:1) relationships instead of the quarter-note/eighth-note triplet (2:1) relationship in a smoother swing. The Shadows did, however, prove that a largely instrumental guitar-based band could be a popular commercial success.

The first self-penned composition by the Beatles (credited to George Harrison and John Lennon) committed to tape in a professional recording session, ironically, is "Cry for a Shadow," an instrumental piece the Beatles recorded in Hamburg, Germany, in 1961. Very few of the early compositions of the Beatles, however, were instrumentals, as were few of their covers. Among the groups that took the United States by storm as part of the 1964 and 1965 British Invasion, about the only one that recorded at least a fair number of instrumentals was the Dave Clark Five, which included instrumentals from time to time as album cuts, recorded several instrumentals as incidental music for their film *Catch Us If You Can* (released in the United States as *Having a Wild Weekend*), and released one instrumental single, "Chaquita," in both the United Kingdom and the United States. Although "Chaquita" is an obvious reworking of the Champs' "Tequila," it should be noted that Dave Clark Five guitarist Lenny Davidson uses a tremolo setting in his solo on "Chaquita" that suggests the influence of both surf guitar and the work of the Shadows. Likewise, the tremolo in the lead guitar part in several early Johnny Kidd and the Pirates singles suggests the influence of the Shadows.

One of the possible reasons for the increased diversification of rock styles and for the development of a uniquely British-sounding rock music is that many of these bands spent enough time gigging that they had to learn a wide repertoire and be conversant in a wide variety of styles in order to thrive. Compare this with the teen idols discovered and/or managed by Larry Parnes, most of whom emerged as teenagers and were suddenly thrust into the national spotlight before they had gained a great deal of professional experience.

Bands such as the Dave Clark Five, the Searchers, the Beatles, and others that either played for extended residencies at domestic clubs, played extended residencies in Hamburg, or did a regular tour of the military bases around London had to play every style of music, as well as specific songs, demanded by a diverse audience. This was especially true for bands such as the Dave Clark Five, playing for American service personnel at bases in London, and the Searchers, Beatles, Rory Storm and the Hurricanes, King Size Taylor and the Dominoes, Cliff Bennett, Tony Sheridan, and all the other British musicians who played Hamburg. An officer's dance at an American military base in Britain, for example, might include an audience with nearly all the members being older, and probably considerably older, than the musicians. This meant that a band might have to be equally conversant in 1940s and 1950s dance band music as with the latest Top 40 music. While a group such as the Shadows clearly exhibits a wide stylistic range on their first two albums, it should be noted that many of the songs lack the drive of the "true" British rock bands of the early 1960s. To put it another way, to the extent that "true" rock and roll is youth counterculture music, the Shadows are more of a rock-style band, and not really a group of rock and rollers.

Another of the important aspects of diversity that I believe helped bands to create a uniquely British approach to rock music was that of the exploration of personal taste in a band setting. For example, it seems that part of the dynamic that drove the Beatles and the Rolling Stones to develop perhaps the most lasting music of the British Invasion was the balance they achieved between band identity and individual identity. The Rolling Stones, after all, included two confirmed jazz musicians, drummer Charlie Watts and bass guitarist Bill Wyman, as well as confirmed blues musicians. Part of the unique sound of the Beatles came from the merger of the R&B-leaning John Lennon, the country and Chuck Berry–style guitar of George Harrison, and the almost bipolar combination of pop balladry and Little Richard–inspired rock screaming of Paul McCartney. But, before we delve too much into the specifics of what drove the Beatles, the Rolling Stones, the Who, the Kinks, the Yardbirds, the Searchers, Gerry and the Pacemakers, and the other bands that dominated the U.K. and the U.S. charts, let us examine some of the changes that were taking place before the British Invasion.

One of the more interesting, if not largely under-appreciated, British bands of the period just prior to the British Invasion, and one that illustrates the changes taking place in the transitional period between the rockabilly and Elvis Presley–inspired pop of the British teen idols, is Johnny Kidd and the Pirates. Born Frederick Albert Heath in Willesdon, London, in 1935, the singer-songwriter professionally known as Johnny Kidd was older than the British teen idols, as well as older than all of the members of the bands that became part of the British Invasion. Between 1959 and 1962, however, Johnny Kidd was one of the more progressive and influential rock musicians in Britain.

In 1956, Fred Heath began playing guitar in a skiffle band. Heath's band, known variously as the Frantic Four and as the Nutters, performed skiffle, rockabilly, and pop songs. Heath was also active as a songwriter, penning 30 songs in a three-month period.[14] The Bachelors recorded Heath's 31st composition, "Please Don't Touch," but the record failed to sell in significant numbers. Heath and his band were given a recording test and a contract with HMV. In April 1959, Freddie Heath and the Nutters recorded their own version of "Please Don't Touch," and were told at the session that their new professional name would be Johnny Kidd and the Pirates. Kidd donned an eye patch and the band dressed in pirate outfits for much of the rest of their career.

While the song "Please Don't Touch" is not Johnny Kidd's best-known work, it is an important piece in what it symbolizes in the development of British rock. For one thing, Kidd uses the bVII chord in the verses. "Please Don't Touch," is a hard-driving, fast-paced rock song, and the parallel harmonic motion—in which all the notes of the I chord move downward a whole-step to the notes of the bVII chord—flows more smoothly than in the contemporary works by other British singer-songwriters. In comparison, Billy Fury's use of modal mixture is more sporadic, and Marty Wilde's tends to draw attention because of how "different" it sounds. Although it is not quantifiable, Kidd's use of polymodality sounds more natural.

The overall texture of "Please Don't Touch" resembles the work of Cliff Richard and the Shadows. "Please Don't Touch" does stand out from other British rock recordings of 1959 in several important ways, however. For one thing, unlike the work of Wilde and Fury, Kidd and the Pirates do not make overt references to rockabilly in the song's rhythmic feel, harmonic feel, or texture; this is more of a rock and roll record than a rockabilly record. Also, Kidd clearly does not imitate Elvis Presley or Buddy Holly when he sings. There are no affected, Americanized pronunciations or stylized vocal hiccups.

"Please Don't Touch" reached as high as No. 20 in the *Melody Maker* polls. Apparently, sales of the single were helped by the song being played on Radio Luxembourg, which was trying to develop a youth market in the late 1950s and early 1960s, and therefore was a stronger outlet for new rock records than the BBC. Labor strife and a printing strike in the United Kingdom at the time, however, made it difficult for HMV to publicize this new band. It seems conceivable that "Please Don't Touch" could have topped out higher on the record charts had its release not coincided with the 1959 strikes.

Another important early single release was the 1960 cover of Marv Johnson's "You Got What It Takes," both for what it symbolizes and for how it sounds. This 1959 song, credited to Tyran Carlo, Roquel Davis, Gwen Fuqua, Berry Gordy, Jr., and Marv Johnson, was originally recorded by Johnson for United Artists Records. Despite this, it can be heard as an early example of the Motown sound: Berry Gordy, Jr. produced the track, Gordy was Johnson's manager, and the two had worked together just as Gordy was starting his first record label, Tamla. So here we find a British band covering what essentially is a Motown record. As we have seen, many of the British acts at the close of the 1950s were still primarily drawn to American rockabilly and pop. Johnny Kidd and the Pirates, then, take a step toward the mix that would define the British Invasion sound, and a Mod step, too, by turning to Motown-style R&B.

The other thing about "You Got What It Takes" that is important is the minimalist instrumental setting. Most obviously, the electric bass and the rhythm guitar play the same single-line backing figures throughout the song. This doubling strips the entire texture down to Kidd on lead vocals (with a few "yeah, yeahs" sung by the rest of the group), drums, and the single bass/rhythm guitar line. This thin texture defined the new sound of Johnny Kidd and the Pirates. In part, the texture of "You Got What It Takes" was retained because of lineup changes in the Pirates. For a period of time, Kidd's backing group consisted of Alan Caddy on guitar, Brian Gregg on bass, and Clem Cattini on drums. Kidd has been quoted as saying that the intent was to bring in a rhythm guitarist— Frank Rouledge, from Kidd's old skiffle band—but the Pirates' sound was so fully realized that Kidd decided to leave the instrumental trio sound in place.[15] Incidentally, a young band called the Detours (later known as the Who) toured with Johnny Kidd and the Pirates (a different Pirates lineup, but still with the lead singer-instrumental trio texture) in 1962–1963. After this experience, the Detours underwent some personnel changes and decided to adopt the Johnny Kidd and the Pirates model. The Detours' lead guitarist, Roger Daltrey, became the singer, and the band, when they changed their name to the Who, became instantly associated with the "power trio" instrumental texture.

Johnny Kidd and the Pirates perhaps will always be best remembered for the 1960 recording "Shakin' All Over." The history of the recording industry of the twentieth century contains several famous tales of spur-of-the-moment songs, written in haste but nevertheless becoming popular hits. These include Bessie Smith's "Lost Your Head Blues," the Beatles' "She's a Woman," and Ian Samwell's "Move It." Informed that they could include a self-penned B-side for a single release of a rockabilly version of the old Tin Pan Alley song "Yes Sir, That's My Baby," Kidd and the band quickly wrote "Shakin' All Over" in the basement of the Freight Train coffee bar the day before the recording session. Ultimately, the not-particularly-interesting cover of Rick Nelson's rockabilly version of "Yes Sir, That's My Baby" was relegated to the B-side, and "Shakin' All Over" became the A-side and a hit. "Shakin' All Over" made it into the top 10 in all the British pop record polls of the day, and hit No. 1 in *Record Retailer.*

In addition to Kidd and Pirates' Brian Gregg (bass), Alan Caddy (guitar), and Clem Cattini (drums), session guitarist Joe Moretti contributed to "Shakin' All Over." In fact, it is Moretti who plays the opening lead guitar figure, as well as the solo. Caddy and Gregg double the minimalist bass line. Cattini's drums seem to be placed more forward in the mix than one tends to hear in many British rock recordings of the time. Cattini includes some of the signifiers of British rock that would continue to be heard in British Invasion rock, including the "2-and, 4" pattern in the snare drum. All of this combines to give "Shakin' All Over" a feeling of power and a clear tie to the British rock that emerged over the next several years. Melodically, the song balances a short, simple descending figure in the opening phrases with a largely ascending figure that enters when the harmony shifts from the tonic (E minor) to the subdominant (A minor). The lyrics themselves concern the effect that Kidd's character experiences when his lover gets close to him: "the shakes come over me." The recording is one of the first famous original British songs that sounds as though it owes more to black American R&B than to any of the more tradition-ally white American forms.

Significantly, "Shakin' All Over" was the first British rock song to be covered by bands from around the world, and for a fairly long period of time. There were American, Canadian, British, and Australian cover recordings of the song. One of the earliest of these was by Vince Taylor, the British singer probably best known for the black leather clothing and Elvis Presley–styled long sideburns he continued to wear even as the Rocker era was waning. Taylor's version is notable for numerous rockabilly style vocal falters, which are very much in evidence in his 1961 televised performances.[16]

A cover version by the Swinging Blue Jeans on the 1964 EP *Shake,* makes for interest-ing study. This version of the song begins with the steady eighth-note bass line ostinato (two iterations of low E, two iterations of the E an octave higher, two iterations of the D a whole-step lower, two iterations of the B a minor third lower), rather than with the de-scending pentatonic line with which Joe Moretti opened the original. The Swinging Blue Jeans perform the song a half-step higher than the original version, in the key of F minor, instead of E minor, and use a slightly faster tempo than most of the other cover versions. Despite the brisker tempo, it perhaps exceeds the rock-solid heaviness of the original version, largely as a result of Norman Kuhlke's powerful drumming. It is also interesting to note that, like Pete Best (the Beatles), Ringo Starr (the Beatles), Roy Dyke (the Remo Four), and other Liverpool drummers of the 1961–1964 period, Kuhlke uses the "2-and, 4" snare drum pattern of the Pirates version, but accents the "and" of 2, more than beat 2 itself. Therefore, "Shakin' All Over" is transformed into a thoroughly workable piece of Merseybeat. Curiously, the guitar solo begins as an imitation of Moretti's solo with Johnny Kidd and the Pirates but degenerates into near chaos by its close.

In 1965, the Canadian group Chad Allan and the Expressions—soon known as the Guess Who—recorded a cover version that went to No. 1 in Canada and No. 22 on the *Billboard* pop charts in the United States. The Chad Allan/Guess Who version mimics Johnny Kidd and the Pirates' tempo and vocal style, and stays fairly close to the original arrangement. The Canadian band, though, adds steady repeated eighth-notes in a bare-bones piano part that helps to fill in some of the gaps in Kidd's original arrangement, and includes a heavier drum style, both of which are more typical of the mid-1960s than the sparse feel of the original.

Perhaps the best-known cover of "Shakin' All Over," however, is the Who's recording from their famous 1970 *Live at Leeds* album, still touted as one of the greatest live rock albums of all time. The Who's arrangement differs even more from Johnny Kidd and the Pirates' original than the 1965 Guess Who arrangement. Most notably, the Who stretch out the line "shakin' all over," and include three-part vocal harmony on the line. As might be expected from the Who, too, their version includes a more extensive electric guitar solo section than that found in any of the earlier versions. Other notable rocks acts that covered "Shakin' All Over" include the Yardbirds, the Damned, Humble Pie, Iggy Pop, and the MC5.

The fact that "Shakin' All Over" was a hit recording that is still effective nearly 50 years after it was made speaks to the importance of Johnny Kidd and the Pirates. It is an even greater testimony to Kidd (who is listed as sole composer) that the song itself and the arrangement could be given only minor adjustment and work as a Rocker-type "greaser" number (Vince Taylor), Merseybeat recording (the Swinging Blue Jeans), hard rock piece (the Yardbirds), and punk rock number (the MC5 and the Damned), continuing to be relevant material for bands years after it was written.

Unfortunately, "Shakin' All Over" represented a peak that Johnny Kidd and the Pirates never reached again. Subsequent material recorded in 1960 and 1961 failed to make the same impact. The most successful, "Restless," was an original by Kidd, Teddy Wadmore, and Stanley Dale, and essentially recreated the sound of "Shakin' All Over," largely as a result of another guest appearance by guitarist Joe Moretti and lyrical references to shaking (something that is also found in Kidd's other two most notable compositions: "Please Don't Touch" and "Feelin'"). The recording is also notable, however, for the hypnotic rhythmic groove created by the bass and drums. The groove and the minor mode character of the piece anticipate in a small way the raga rock of the 1966–1968 period.

One track from 1961 that was left unreleased for over two decades was Kidd's recording of the Willie Dixon composition "I Just Want to Make Love to You." The most famous version of the song came from Muddy Waters, who had toured Britain in 1958. Johnny Kidd and the Pirates turn the song into a stroll-style piece, and Kidd sings with exaggerated vocal falters on the high notes that, while perhaps designed to convey a sense of urgency, sound somewhat contrived. The recording, however, illustrates the kinds of changes that were taking place in the first couple years of the 1960s in British rock, changes that ultimately would be crucial to the British Invasion of 1964. Kidd and the Pirates do not copy the Muddy Waters recording, or even imitate it, as much as they try to put their own stamp on the song.

In August 1961, Brian Gregg, Alan Caddy, and Clem Cattini left the Pirates to back Tommy Steele's brother—Colin Hicks—on a concert tour to Italy. Ultimately, Cattini and Caddy formed the nucleus of the Tornados, and backed Billy Fury before their breakthrough instrumental recording of "Telstar" became the first British rock record to top the record charts in the United States. In 1963, Brian Gregg also joined the Tornados.

Johnny Kidd assembled a new version of the Pirates, which included guitarist Johnny Patto (soon replaced by Mick Green), bassist Johnny Spence, and drummer Frank Farley. Kidd, Green, Spence, and Farley performed an extended series of gigs in Liverpool at the Cavern Club, and in Hamburg, at the Star-Club in 1962. This put them in close contact with the Beatles, the Searchers, King Size Taylor, and all the other Liverpool musicians who were developing the Merseybeat sound at that time. It appears that Kidd's choice of material for some of his 1962 recording sessions might have been influenced by the Merseyside bands: he cut a cover of Richard Barrett's "Some Other Guy" (written by Barrett, Mike Stoller, and Jerry Leiber) and a cover of Arthur Alexander's "A Shot of Rhythm and Blues" (written by Terry Thompson). These two songs were favorites of the Liverpool bands, including the Beatles, who included both songs as part of their regular stage act in 1962 and 1963,[17] and who recorded both songs for 1963 BBC broadcasts. Again, it is important to note that these songs originally were associated with black American R&B singers, suggesting that British bands were turning away from rockabilly to a more direct adaptation of African American popular music.

In considering Johnny Kidd and the Pirates' residency at the Cavern and at the Star-Club, as well as the apparent influence of Liverpool bands on the group's repertoire, it is interesting to consider some of the similarities and differences between the Pirates' covers and those of groups from the north. Johnny Kidd and the Pirates treat the first stanza of "A Shot of Rhythm and Blues" differently than all the subsequent stanzas by inserting spaces between the lines. By contrast, the Beatles' version of the song from their 1963 BBC sessions is completely squared off. Pirates drummer Frank Farley plays more improvisationally than Ringo Starr, who by contrast uses a straight ahead Merseybeat style (the accentuation on the "and" of beat 2) throughout the song (aside from a few fills). Farley includes this accentuation only in the bridge. This gives the Pirates' version more stylistic variety, or less consistency, depending on the extent to which the listener values one over the other. Another major difference is that the Pirates include a guitar solo approximately halfway through their recording, while George Harrison is limited to being a second rhythm guitar except for a few brief fills in the latter stages of the Beatles' recording. Another important difference is the way in which the groups treat the female vocal harmony parts from the original Arthur Alexander recording. On the Pirates recording, it sounds as though Kidd is overdubbed singing the backing lines in unison. The Beatles, however, preserve the harmony, with Harrison and Paul McCartney answering John Lennon's lead vocal.

The biggest stylistic differences between the London-based Johnny Kidd and the Pirates and northern rock bands that managed to score hits as part of the British Invasion, though, can be found in their treatments of "Some Other Guy." For their part, Kidd and the Pirates capture some of the spirit of the blues bands from the south of England, such as the Rolling Stones. In fact, their 1962 take on "Some Other Guy" seems to anticipate the Stones' January 1964 recording of "Route 66." The Beatles' 1963 BBC performance incorporates Merseybeat-style drumming (with especially firm accentuation of the "and" of beat 2), and Ray Charles "What'd I Say"–style guitar figures. The rhythmic feel of the two versions are completely different. Incidentally, the Manchester band Freddie and the Dreamers turn the implied swing of the Merseybeat style into an actual swing feel in their recording. Another Manchester band, Wayne Fontana and the Mindbenders, however, recorded "Some Other Guy" with the "Route 66" feel. Unfortunately, the January 1963 recording of "Some Other Guy" by Johnny Kidd and the Pirates was not released until the 1980s.

When the British Invasion hit with full force in 1964 and 1965, Johnny Kidd and the Pirates were left behind. By that point, Kidd had formed a new backing group, the New Pirates, and recorded a new version of "Shakin' All Over." His recording could not compete commercially, though, with the cover version by Chad Allan and the Expressions (the Guess Who). Kidd's recordings of the 1964–1966 period included covers of R&B songs, pop songs, and even a cover of Hank Williams's "Your Cheatin' Heart." The Williams song makes for especially interesting listening. By that point—1964—Kidd's backing group included a keyboard player. The Hammond organ on the track gives the song a surprising R&B feel. There is a rhythmic break during the organ solo that sounds like an overt reference to early Jamaican ska music. Curiously, Kidd changes the original line, "You'll walk the floor, the way I do," to "You'll walk the floor, the way you do," which completely distorts the rhetorical scheme of the song. Johnny Kidd was just beginning a reemergence in 1966 when he was killed in an automobile accident.

One aspect of Johnny Kidd and the Pirates' work that easily can be overlooked is the band's visual image. The stylized pirate stage and photo shoot outfits—as well as Kidd's eye patch—made the band distinctive from all the other groups in British rock. And, playing on the pirate image, the band's stage shows featured Kidd dancing around wildly with a sword. When two of the early members of the Pirates, Mike West and Tony Doherty, left Kidd in 1960, they formed a group called Robby Hood and His Merry Men, and wore highly stylized Robin Hood outfits. Probably the most visually recognizable rock band of the mid-1960s for their stage costumes, Paul Revere and the Raiders, playing on the real name of their keyboard player and founder (Paul Revere), donned stylized Revolutionary War costumes and presented a wild stage show. Although many writers focus on the influence of Spike Jones and Billy Haley on the visual image and stage show of Paul Revere and the Raiders,[18] Johnny Kidd and the Pirates would seem to be the closest logical predecessors, especially in the rock genre.

Musically, Johnny Kidd and the Pirates was a transitional band. The growing importance of electric blues and R&B can be heard in Kidd's compositions, as well as in the covers the group recorded, especially those recorded up to 1962. Certainly, too, the unreleased 1963 recording of "Some Other Guy" captured the feel of what was to come approximately a year later on the Rolling Stones' first album. However, the band also incorporated a bit of the influence of the Liverpool bands. So, the question arises, why did this group not become part of the British Invasion? It appears that several things were going against Johnny Kidd and the Pirates. For one thing, aside from the early recordings of the Rolling Stones, the most successful and longest-lasting British Invasion bands either wrote their own material or had writers supplying them with material—they were not cover bands. By the time of the British Invasion, Johnny Kidd and the Pirates largely were releasing covers. As a transitional group, too, they seemed to become increasingly less well defined musically. The sonic texture and style that had defined the group on their first hits became too diffuse. In part, this may have been related to the wholesale personnel changes in the Pirates that plagued Kidd throughout his career. The constant personnel changes also made it difficult for fans to identify with the musicians as individuals, aside from Kidd himself. For the most part, the British bands that emerged in 1963 and 1964 were—or at least appeared to be—cooperative units. Perhaps Johnny Kidd and the Pirates just appeared too much to be a solo singer with a hired backing band. The rock and roll covers and some of Kidd's original compositions, too, use just a little too much hep cat, 1950s jive lingo such that the lyrics of these songs seem dated in comparison to new British Invasion rock songs. Kidd's best-known compositions—"Please Don't Touch," "Shakin' All Over," "Feelin'," and "Restless" also contain enough common lyrical threads that they paint Kidd as a somewhat mono-dimensional writer.

Tony Sheridan was another interesting, if relatively little appreciated, transitional artist of the pre–British Invasion 1960s. Born Anthony Esmond O'Sheridan McGinnity in Norwich, Norfolk, England in 1940, Sheridan learned to play violin as a child. He played in the school orchestra and sang in the school choir. Eventually, he dropped out in order to attend art school. He also switched from violin to guitar. Sheridan formed his first skiffle band in 1956, and by 1957 he was playing rock and roll. In 1958, Sheridan had the distinction of becoming the first performer to be shown on British television playing the electric guitar live. At the time of this writing (May 2008), at least one of Sheridan's 1959 appearances on the British television program *Oh Boy!* is available on YouTube.com. This high-energy performance of Roy Orbison's "I Like Love" by Tony Sheridan and His Wreckers makes for interesting study. Sheridan's band, himself on vocals and lead guitar, supported by rhythm guitar, acoustic bass, and drums, generally appears and sounds like Gene Vincent's group did at the time. Sheridan sings with a bit of the Elvis Presley and Gene Vincent sneer and mumble, which is in keeping with the prevailing style of British rock in 1959. However, the high-energy rock and roll reflects the contemporary work of Vincent much more than four- or five-year-old Presley-style rockabilly. Sheridan takes two guitar solos in the performance. The second solo, especially, betrays the influence of Chuck Berry, and both solos clearly are rock and roll—as opposed to rockabilly—in style.

Sheridan played lead guitar for Vince Taylor's Playboys in 1958–1959 and played as a backing musician for various American performers that toured Britain. In fact, he was one of the supporting guitarists for the infamous 1960 Gene Vincent/Eddie Cochran tour in which Cochran perished.

Tony Sheridan traveled to Hamburg, Germany, in June 1960 with his new band, the Jets, and became one of the first British acts to appear there. Over the course of the next three years, numerous British bands (especially bands from Liverpool) traveled to Hamburg for bookings at the Kaiserkeller, the Indra, the Star-Club, and the Top Ten, the most important beat music clubs in Hamburg's St. Pauli district. Sheridan's own backing band had a flexible membership throughout this period, and included such later prominent musicians as Roy Young and Ringo Starr. In addition, the British musical contingent in Hamburg visited each other's gigs—to study the competition, if nothing else—and sat in with each other's bands. Therefore, a performer like Tony Sheridan had the opportunity not only to hear the changes that were taking place in the work of the Liverpool bands but also to work with the members of those bands.

By far the most famous example of Sheridan's work with Liverpool musicians was the onstage and recording work he did in 1961 and 1962 with the Beatles, which at that time consisted of John Lennon, Paul McCartney, George Harrison, and Pete Best. Sheridan reports that he became acquainted professionally and personally with the Beatles in 1960 when they first played Hamburg. When the Beatles returned in 1961, Sheridan says, "I was without a band at that time, and so we got together. They backed me in my solo numbers, and I played guitar with them when they did their spots."[19] Sheridan came to the attention of the German bandleader and record producer Bert Kaempfert in June 1961. Attempting to capture the new sound of the British bands that was sweeping through Hamburg's St. Pauli district, Kaempfert arranged for Sheridan and the Beatles to record several sides for Polydor Records. On June 22–24, 1961, Kaempfert recorded Sheridan and the Beatles performing "Cry for a Shadow," "My Bonnie," "When the Saints Go Marching In," "Why," "Nobody's Child," "Ain't She Sweet," and "Take out Some Insurance on Me, Baby" in three sessions. On a subsequent trip to Hamburg in May 1962, Kaempfert recorded Sheridan, the Beatles, and guest pianist Roy Young performing "Sweet Georgia Brown."

Easily the most famous track from the sessions, "My Bonnie" became a hit single in Germany. Although it was not a major hit in the United Kingdom, a request for this record that Brian Epstein received at his store in Liverpool caused Epstein to seek out the Beatles, who at the time were playing not far from the store. Epstein soon became the Beatles' manager.

"My Bonnie" is a rock version of the traditional Scottish folksong "My Bonnie Lies over the Ocean," widely known to schoolchildren. The choice of a song most closely associated with children might seem like an odd choice for a pop record; however, interviews with Sheridan and others for the 2004 Universal Music film *The Beatles with Tony Sheridan—The Beginnings in Hamburg: A Documentary,* suggest that the song had appeal for the Germans, because it was one British song they knew. It also appealed to Brits, Americans, and other English-speaking people in Germany regardless of their age, because they also all knew the song. The practice of taking nursery rhymes or folk and other musical material that children learn in school and creating a rock setting continued into the British Invasion years of 1964 and 1965. Although the practice sometimes led to uneven results, Sheridan's arrangement of "My Bonnie" is a success.

The Beatles' backing role on "My Bonnie" is interesting. Paul McCartney's shouts and harmony vocals are not up to the high standards he would achieve within a couple of years when the group became famous. Pete Best maintains a unwavering "2-and, 4" beat throughout the fast part of the song (there is a slow introduction). Best's drumming is supported by hand claps, but the drums themselves are placed so far back in the recording's mix that the track lacks the percussive drive of the Beatles' later recordings. Also of note are George Harrison's brief guitar fills in the song's bridge. His playing does not sound as self-assured and the fills do not have the same sense of organic wholeness as Sheridan's playing on the track. Of course, Sheridan at this point was a 21-year-old who had been a professional musician for several years; Harrison was 18 and had far less professional experience than Sheridan.

For his part, Sheridan sings the slow introduction to "My Bonnie" in what sounds like an overt impersonation of Elvis Presley, including a quick vibrato and near mumble of some of the words. Unlike the work of some British singers of the era, notably Marty Wilde and Billy Fury, however, Sheridan sounds British: he does not affect an American accent. Still, in the fast part of the performance—the bulk of the song—Sheridan's singing betrays the stylistic influence of Presley. In the two-chorus guitar solo, however, Sheridan's work sounds nothing like rockabilly, carefully avoiding references to Scotty Moore's work of the mid-1950s or the later work of Buddy Holly, Gene Vincent, Carl Perkins, and other late 1950s figures. The melodic figures, string bends, use of sustain, and distorted tone reflect a new rock-specific approach to electric guitar, with its roots more in American R&B than in American country music. Sheridan's tone color and use of a more legato (smooth) feel stand in sharp contrast even to his performance on *Oh Boy!* of just a couple years earlier. In stark contrast to Sheridan's guitar solo on "My Bonnie," George Harrison reflects more the rockabilly/country side of rock and roll, as personified by Carl Perkins, as he plays his lead guitar fills with a clean tone and with most notes picked.

Tony Sheridan and the Beatles' cover of bluesman Jimmy Reed's recording of "Take Out Some Insurance on Me" is also worth noting. Sheridan and the Beatles incorporate the loping swing rhythmic style of Reed's version; however, the smooth, almost jazz-oriented phrasing with which Reed sings is replaced by Sheridan's Elvis Presley–influenced style. While there is nothing about the performance that hints at the growing blues scene that was developing in the early 1960s in London, it is notable that Sheridan and the Beatles turned to a song associated with the blues singer Jimmy Reed. Reed's recorded performances continued to influence white rock performers throughout the 1960s.

A very different source yielded the song "Nobody's Child." This Cy Coben/Mel Foree composition perhaps is still most closely associated with the so-called Singing Ranger, the Canadian country performer Hank Snow, for his early 1950s version. However, skiffle king Lonnie Donegan recorded the song in 1953 and 1956, and Billy Fury included "Nobody's Child" on one of his EPs. Once again, the Beatles and Tony Sheridan turn the song into a sort of hybrid between the old and the new. Sheridan's vocals incorporate the mumbling of Elvis Presley and the leaps into falsetto of Donegan. His lead guitar playing, however, uses melodic and chordal figures that come straight out of slow rural blues.

Although Beatles John Lennon and Paul McCartney already were writing solo songs and as a team at the time of the first recordings with Tony Sheridan, Sheridan and the Beatles recorded no Lennon/McCartney songs at any of their 1961 or 1962 sessions. The only original *song*—an instrumental credited to George Harrison and John Lennon was also recorded—is credited to Sheridan and Bill Compton. "Why," while certainly not the best-known British rock composition of the year 1961, is another example of how Tony Sheridan's work with the pre-fame Beatles reflects clear ties to 1950s rock and roll while simultaneously providing glimpses of new developments in British pop music.

The song is built in stylistically distinctive sections, with an introduction that is followed by the standard, Tin Pan Alley, AABA-form song proper. The introduction begins with a repeated oscillation between an A major triad and a G major triad. At first, this oscillation leaves the song's key center in doubt. However, after several repetitions of the pattern, the last G major chord moves to an E major triad, which sets up A major as the song's tonality. In retrospect, this means that the listener was in fact hearing an oscillation between I (A) and bVII (G), followed by V (E). Because the E major triad contains the major seventh scale-step (G-sharp), while the bVII chord contains G-natural, writers Sheridan and Compton provide the listener with the major-Mixolydian modal ambiguity that became one of the important calling cards of 1960s rock. Another interesting harmonic touch is Sheridan and Compton's use of the bVI chord (F major) on the "bah, da, bah, da, bah" vocal fill that follows the line "If you only knew how much I love you" near the end of each verse. Here, the bVI functions as a dominant preparation chord as the final harmonic cadence of the verse approaches. The chord moves through a brief tonic chord to the dominant (V) before coming to a rest on tonic at the close of the verse.

If the introduction and A sections of "Why" represent progressive harmonic tendencies, then the bridge section (B) reflects backwards to old-school rock and roll. For one thing, the song moves from an almost calypso, straight eighth-note feel to a hard-driving swing feel, with Beatles' drummer Pete Best pounding out accents on beats 2 and 4. Sheridan's vocal melody (D, F-sharp, A, B, C) is based on a major-minor seventh chord built on the fourth scale-degree. The melodic shape is not entirely unlike the main melody of Hank Williams' "Move It on Over" (1947), which itself is clearly imitated in "(We're Gonna) Rock around the Clock." The melodic figure is also found as a bass line in countless earlier boogie-woogie piano pieces. So the melodic figuration and the swing rhythmic feel reflect backwards musically. Curiously, the exact melodic figure with which Sheridan begins the bridge of "Why" finds its way into the beginning of the bridge in the Beatles' 1968 song "Back in the U.S.S.R." on the line, "The Ukraine girls really knock me out."

I have already commented on the use of modal mixture, and particularly the bVI chord, in songs by Marty Wilde and Billy Fury—and now on its use in Tony Sheridan's "Why." This chord, as well as the bVII, continued to find its way into the music of British Invasion bands in 1962–1964, especially in love ballads. Two well-known examples are the Beatles' "P.S. I Love You," which was first released as the B-side of the "Love Me Do" single in October 1962, and the Dave Clark Five's "Because," which first appeared in the United Kingdom in May 1964 as a B-side. Incidentally, when "Because" was issued in the United States in July 1964 it was the A-side and proved to be one of the Dave Clark Five's most enduring hits. In "P.S. I Love You," the bVI chord occurs on the first "You" in the title line as a deceptive cadence (a harmonic stopping point in which the dominant chord [V] moves to a chord built on the sixth scale-step, instead of to a chord built on the expected first scale-step). On the repeated "you, you, you" at the very end of each stanza the bVI moves up by whole-step to the bVII chord, and up another whole-step to the tonic (I). This upward whole-step motion of major triads at the cadence (bVI—bVII—I) is rare in popular music; however, it was a cadential formula used by some late nineteenth-century symphonic composers, as well as by some twentieth-century film composers.

In "Because," the bVI chord occurs as part of the turnaround at the end of each verse, as well as at the end of Mike Smith's organ solo. In this case, the bVI functions as a substitute for the dominant of the dominant (V/V). Although a thorough explanation would be too lengthy for our needs here, suffice it to say that the use of the bVI in "Because" is related to the jazz harmonic concept of tritone substitution. The bVI of "Because" falls down a half-step to the dominant (V) chord, which then proceeds to tonic at the start of the next verse.

Tony Sheridan recorded several more sides for Kaempfert between August 28, 1962 and January 31, 1963.[20] One of the August 28, 1962 recordings, a cover of the Chris Montez hit "Let's Dance," makes for especially interesting study. First, it should be noted that the Sheridan recording session took place less than a month after the Montez recording first appeared in the Top 40. So, here we have a British (albeit recorded in Germany) cover of a contemporary American rock song, as opposed to a British cover that was recorded months or years after the well-known American version. One of the first things the listener might notice about the recording by guitarist/singer Sheridan, drummer Johnny Watson, bassist Colin Melander, and organist Roy Young is that the British group performs the song at a faster tempo. Also notable is Johnny Watson's use of the famous early 1960s British rock and roll, "2-and, 4" snare drum pattern, something that is not part of the original Chris Montez version of the song. Sheridan's guitar solo, while not as rhythmically driving, or as intuitive sounding as his work with the Beatles on "My Bonnie," is also interesting, especially for an upward arpeggio figure he uses that comes right out of the melodic vocabulary of American be-bop jazz. What really captures the most attention about the performance, however, is Roy Young's technically virtuosic and rhythmically driving organ solo. In this 1962 recording, Young—who is widely known as "Britain's Little Richard"—anticipates the intricate organ work of Rod Argent of the Zombies and Alan Price of the Animals.

Because of Tony Sheridan's close ties to the members of the Beatles during their Hamburg period, I posed a question to him about the possible validity of the line that Ringo Starr delivers in *A Hard Day's Night*—about being a "Mocker," as opposed to a Mod or a Rocker. Sheridan responded, "My 'old drummer'—Ringo—was, at his own admittance, a Teddy boy (at least outwardly). He missed the rocker stage; Pete Best still being the drummer with the Beatles when we were wearing leather gear, *etc.* A mod he wasn't—can one imagine Ringo on a Vespa? Perhaps it follows that Teddy boys were the mockers of their time."[21] In his response, Sheridan raises important points about the changes the were taking place in the early 1960s in British youth sociology and music, and something important about the appeal of the Beatles: (1) the pre-Starr Beatles, with their leathers, were aligned with the Rocker aesthetic; (2) the Beatles had changed direction somewhat by the time Best was fired and Starr joined them in August 1962; and (3) the Beatles, and especially Ringo Starr, bridged the gap between the Mods and the Rockers. Incidentally, and possibly unintentionally, Sheridan's observation also aligns with the view of some sociologists that the Teddy Boys shared some traits with both the Rockers and the Mods, while being most closely tied with the Rockers.[22]

The extent of Tony Sheridan's influence on the development of British Invasion music is difficult to judge. Sheridan never enjoyed fame during the 1960s. In fact, during the mid-1960s he was virtually invisible commercially as he undertook an extended tour of

Vietnam, performing rock and roll for American troops, apparently turning his back on fame. Today, he lives in Germany, and is viewed as something of a cult figure in the development of British rock.

Keyboardist-singer Roy Young, however, recalls that John Lennon and George Harrison spent considerable time observing Sheridan's performances in Hamburg. Young claims that Lennon's famous guitar-playing stance was fashioned from that of Sheridan.[23] Sheridan himself discussed his use of a playing position with the guitar held relatively high—at chest level—as well as a wide stance in an interview for Genesis Publications. He acknowledges Lennon's use of a similar position and speculates that Lennon held the guitar in the same manner for playing comfort and stability.[24] While Sheridan does not claim to have directly influenced Lennon in his famous stance, he does claim that the Beatles called him "the teacher." For their part, members of the Beatles acknowledged studying Sheridan: Ringo Starr referred to Sheridan as "a really good player" and George Harrison called him "a pretty good singer and guitar player" who possessed considerably more professional experience than the Beatles.[25] Lending even more credence to the view of Tony Sheridan as an influence on the Liverpool beat groups that performed in Hamburg are the recollections of Gerry Marsden of Gerry and the Pacemakers. Marsden calls Sheridan "a terrific singer and guitar player with a strong sense of showmanship," and adds, "we all learned a lot of guitar licks from Tony. I watched him carefully and learned a lot about singing and presentation."[26] Marsden also asserts that the Beatles thought so much of Sheridan that they considered asking him to join their group.[27] Even if Tony Sheridan had not possibly been a direct influence on the Beatles at a crucial period in their development as a band (the extended stays in Hamburg in 1960, 1961, and 1962), he would still be a viable example of how British rock music was changing from the Billy Fury/Marty Wilde model to what mature British Invasion rock was by 1963 and 1964.

Brian Poole and the Tremeloes is another important transitional band that is not particularly well known in the United States. This band came together in approximately 1959 in Dagenham, Essex, England, and consisted of Brian Poole (vocals), Ricky West (lead guitar), Alan Blakeley (rhythm guitar), Alan Howard (bass guitar), and Dave Munden (drums). Their initial inspiration came from Buddy Holly and the Crickets, a band that they heard in concert in 1958. By 1961, the group had progressed to the point that they appeared on the BBC radio program *Saturday Club.* On January 1, 1962, Dick Rowe, an Artists and Repertoire (A&R) representative at Decca Records, recorded two bands that his assistant, Mike Smith,[28] had scouted: the Beatles and Brian Poole and the Tremeloes. Rowe selected only one of the groups for a recording contract: Brian Poole and the Tremeloes. While it would appear that part of the attraction for Decca was that they were based closer to London, a listen to some of the selections the Beatles taped that day (widely available in 2008 on CD and as a download from several legitimate online sources) also suggests that the Beatles performance was far from one of their best. The Beatles' audition tapes find Paul McCartney's voice breaking on high notes, George Harrison playing notes in his solos that do not fit into the tonality of the song, and tempos that fluctuate more than they should.

While Brian Poole and the Tremeloes had a Decca contract at the start of 1962, it was not until 1963 when their records enjoyed major success. In 1963–1964 the band had four singles that made the U.K. Top 10: "Twist and Shout," "Do You Love Me," "Candy Man," and "Someone Someone." Brian Poole left the group in 1966 for a solo career, and bassist Alan Howard was replaced by Chip Hawkes. The Tremeloes enjoyed seven more Top 10 British singles between 1967 and 1970. The post–Brian Poole version of the band made it into the U.S. Top 40 only three times, for the 1967 singles "Here Comes My Baby," "Silence Is Golden," and "Even the Bad Times Are Good."

In comparing Brian Poole and the Tremeloes with bands such as the Beatles, the Dave Clark Five, the Rolling Stones, Gerry and the Pacemakers, the Animals, Herman's Hermits, the Searchers, and others that were part of the British Invasion in 1964–1965, several factors emerge as possible reasons that their U.K. success was not parlayed into U.S. success. First, Brian Poole and the Tremeloes was a covers band. In fact, the 20 tracks included on the 1996 CD *The Very Best of Brian Poole and the Tremeloes* (Spectrum Music 551 321-2) include such songs as "Do You Love Me" (originally recorded by the Contours), "Candy Man" (Roy Orbison), "Twist and Shout" (the Isley Brothers), "Time Is on My Side" (best known through the Rolling Stones hit recording of 1964, but recorded in 1963 by both Kai Winding and Irma Thomas), a medley that includes "The Loco-Motion" and "Don't Ever Change" (Little Eva and the Crickets, respectively), and so on. The "Best of" disc also includes covers of hits originally recorded by the Four Seasons, Buddy Holly, Elvis Presley, Freddie Scott, and a variety of others. Only a couple of the songs on the disc were written specifically for Brian Poole and the Tremeloes, and those were B-sides and album cuts. By contrast, the majority of the singles by the Rolling Stones and the Beatles that made the U.S. Top 40 in the British Invasion years were self-penned. Even the British Invasion successes that primarily recorded songs written by outside songwriters enjoyed U.K. and U.S. success from songs that were unique to that band (the Searchers' "Needles and Pins," written by Americans Sonny Bono and Jack Nitzsche) or so different from earlier versions of somewhat obscure songs (e.g., the Animals' "House of Rising Sun" and "Don't Let Me Be Misunderstood" and Herman's Hermits' "I'm Henry the VIII, I Am" and "Mrs. Brown You've Got a Lovely Daughter") that their "covers" either stood completely apart from the earlier versions or were of songs not widely known in the United States, and thus were not perceived as covers. Incidentally, another highly successful band on the U.K. record charts, the Hollies, also failed to make a great deal of impact in the United States until 1966, despite all their U.K. and European success. Like Brian Poole and the Tremeloes, a fair number of the singles the Hollies' record company released in the United States were covers of well-known American hits.

Another possible disadvantage that Brian Poole and the Tremeloes had when it came to making a commercial impact in the United States was that the group in retrospect appears to have been too closely tied to the star-plus-backing-group paradigm of the British singers that emerged between 1956 and 1960 (e.g., Richard, Steele, and Fury). It is true that some of the bands that did enjoy success in the United States were configured as a lead singer (who perhaps played the occasional percussion instrument or harmonica) with three to four instrumentalists. Examples of groups of this type include the Rolling Stones, the Yardbirds, the Hollies, the Who, and the Animals. Unlike Brian Poole and the Tremeloes, however, these groups had strong hooks that distributed the audience's attention more equally around the band. When it came to television appearances, the Rolling Stones are especially notable in this regard. In their 1964–1966 appearances on *The Ed Sullivan Show, Hullabaloo,* and *Shindig!,* each of the Rolling Stones exhibits a clear identity—Mick Jagger, the R&B singer with the fancy footwork; Brian Jones, the blond playing the curious lute-shaped guitar; Charlie Watts, the drummer who seems not to show any expression or even be working at playing the drums; Bill Wyman, with his bass guitar held at an unusual, acoustic-bass-derived upward angle, and so on. The Who, too, with Pete Townshend's windmill guitar strokes and Keith Moon's let's-see-how-different-from-Charlie Watts-I-can-be approach to pounding the drums and bashing the cymbals, come across as four important individuals, and not Roger Daltrey plus three backing instrumentalists. The Hollies, with their extensive use of vocal harmony and tossed-around lead vocals on songs such as "Too Much Monkey Business," again, have the sound and appearance of a group, and not lead singer Allan Clarke plus backing musicians. Of the groups listed above, the Animals sound and appear to be the closest to the star plus backing group model, and they only lasted in their most famous form until 1966, when personnel changes turned the group into Eric Burdon and the Animals in name as well as in reality. The prototypical British Invasion ensemble exhibited a strong group identity while allowing the individual personal and/or musical identities of its members to shine.

Another disadvantage that Brian Poole and the Tremeloes had when it came to making a chart impact in the United States was sonic, and included the production on the group's records and the rhythmic approach that the group took. Compared directly against covers of the same American R&B songs by other bands that were part of the British Invasion, the Tremeloes' recordings seem rhythmically square, with clean, almost sterile-sounding production. For example, Poole's lead vocal on "Time Is on My Side" contains noticeably less syncopation than does Mick Jagger's vocal on the Rolling Stones' cover of the song. Although stylistically certainly not identical to Jagger's singing, Denny Laine's lead vocal on the early Moody Blues' cover of the same song is also more rhythmically syncopated and soulful sounding than Brian Poole's vocal. The relative rhythmic lightness of Brian Poole and the Tremeloes can also be heard in a side-by-side comparison of their hit version of "Do You Love Me" with the Dave Clark Five's contemporary cover of the song. The Tremeloes' tempo is slightly faster, but the recording is not as energetic, mostly because of the power of the Dave Clark Five's lead singer, Mike Smith, and the high impact, in-your-face record production of Clark. Likewise, Poole and the Tremeloes' cover of the Isley Brothers' hit "Twist and Shout," although recorded after the Beatles' cover and largely based on the Beatles' version, moves away from the heavy, passionate R&B feel of the Beatles and more toward a light, almost generic British beat group style.

Despite the light feel of the group's recordings, the old-fashioned leader/backing group structure, and the fact that so much of their energy was devoted to covers, in 1963 Brian Poole and the Tremeloes enjoyed some real advantages over their contemporaries at home, including their musicianship. The precision and technique of the band, however, does in retrospect give them less personality than their contemporaries. And, personality—musical and otherwise—was important for the bands that made lasting impressions beyond the United Kingdom and Europe. In 1963, however, the band seems to have been received as very professional and technically accomplished.

Another advantage that Brian Poole and the Tremeloes had in 1962 and 1963 over rival bands was timing. For one thing, it seems apparent that their audition for Decca Records on January 1, 1962 caught the Liverpool band that auditioned that day at far from their best. Poole and company, however, seemed to have arrived ready to play. Decca executives also found their proximity to London a plus over the Beatles, who would have had a more difficult time making it to recording sessions. Also, Brian Poole and the Tremeloes and their producers at Decca recognized and exploited the commercial potential of covering particular American songs more fully than other groups and record companies. For example, Decca recorded Poole and the Tremeloes performing "Twist and Shout" after the Beatles' cover of the song had already been issued on the album *Please Please Me*. The Beatles' label, Parlophone, had not issued "Twist and Shout" as a single, despite the commercial potential of the recording. By the time Parlophone released "Twist and Shout" outside the context of the *Please Please Me* album—over four months after the album appeared—on an EP, the Beatles' recording was in direct competition with a single of the song by Brian Poole and the Tremeloes, an arrangement that incorporates many aspects of the Beatles' version. Despite the fact that the Beatles' version has endured, in part because of the power of John Lennon's lead vocal and the power of George Martin's production, and even in 1963 might well have been appreciated as the better of the two recordings, the recording by Brian Poole and the Tremeloes sold nearly as well. Again, this was a direct result of timing by Decca Records.

EMI's Parlophone label was not alone in missing the commercial potential of "Twist and Shout." According to Ron Ryan, he brought the song to the attention of Dave Clark well before the Beatles' EP and Brian Poole and the Tremeloes' single version appeared. He says that Clark was not convinced of the potential of the song and therefore procrastinated on recording it. By the time the Dave Clark Five got around to finishing their recording, the other two recordings were on the charts. Because the instrumental tracks were finished, Ryan was commissioned to write new lyrics to fit the backing tracks.[29] The resulting song, "No Time to Lose," was finally issued by the Dave Clark Five on an EP in November 1963, two months after the Beatles and the Tremeloes were battling it out on the British charts with "Twist and Shout." In retrospect, Brian Poole and the Tremeloes' "Twist and Shout" pales in comparison with the Beatles' "Twist and Shout" and the Dave Clark Five's "No Time to Lose." It came out at the right time, and the musicianship is precise; however, the Poole recording does not have the intensity of the Beatles and Dave Clark Five recordings. The tempo, too, is just quick enough that some of the heaviness that marks the other recordings is missing. Another aspect of the recording of Brian Poole and the Tremeloes that tends to give it less of a feeling of personality than the others is the thinness of the record production. Unlike the production work of Dave Clark (the Dave Clark Five), George Martin (the Beatles), and Andrew Loog Oldham (the Rolling Stones), the work of Poole's producer, Mike Smith, seems thin—very clear and precise, but thin compared with what was becoming the standard of the time.

Another example of the importance of timing in the music industry, and specifically how good timing played to the commercial benefit of Decca Records and Brian Poole and the Tremeloes, comes in the form of competing cover versions of Berry Gordy's composition "Do You Love Me." The original version, recorded by the American group the Contours, hit No. 3 on the *Billboard* Top 40 and No. 1 on the *Billboard* R&B charts in the United States in late 1962. Once again, Brian Poole and the Tremeloes scooped the Dave Clark Five in covering the song. The story (unverified) goes that the Dave Clark Five actually recorded the song first, but that some musicians who were visiting the studio recognized the commercial potential of the song and rush recorded and released the version by Brian Poole and the Tremeloes. It should be noted that on his official Web site, studio drummer Bobby Graham claims to have played on both sessions.[30] Perhaps Graham was the link, or perhaps others associated with Poole's band were in the studio when the Dave Clark Five recorded "Do You Love Me." Ultimately, the song was a No. 1 hit in the United Kingdom for the Tremeloes, while the Dave Clark Five's slightly later version only made it to No. 30 on the British charts. It has been suggested that one of the reasons that Clark later closed recording sessions to visitors was because of losing the hit version of "Do You Love Me" to Poole and the Tremeloes. Again, the Dave Clark Five's recording of the song is slightly slower and heavier feeling. As a producer, Clark emphasizes the lower part of the audio frequency spectrum. And, again, while timing and precise musicianship may have driven Brian Poole and the Tremeloes to the top in Britain, their version of "Do You Love Me" never charted in the United States, while the Dave Clark Five's version made it to No. 11 on the U.S. pop charts.

Because the period framed by the years 1960 and 1963 was so fertile in Great Britain, and because there were so many bands that could legitimately lay claim to being part of the musical transitions that were taking place, it is impossible to include all of them in this chapter. Let us conclude this focus on some of the stylistic changes that were taking British rock by storm by looking at the first British rock group to have a No. 1 single in the United States: the Tornados.

In order fully to appreciate the history of the Tornados and to see some of the complexities involved in the family trees of the early 1960s rock bands in the United Kingdom, we need to revisit the careers of Billy Fury and Johnny Kidd. Because of the fact that studio musicians accompanied Billy Fury on his first recordings—Fury was signed as a solo singer-songwriter and not as part of a band—it was necessary for Fury's manager, Larry Parnes, to assemble backing bands for Fury's concert tours. In 1960, just after Fury's earliest recordings, the Beatles, which at that time consisted of John Lennon, Paul McCartney, George Harrison, Stuart Sutcliffe, and revolving drummers, auditioned to back Fury on a tour. The Beatles did not get the job, because they refused to leave Sutcliffe, a friend of John Lennon who at the time had minimal ability on the bass guitar, behind. The Beatles were signed on by the Parnes organization, though, to back Johnny Gentle on a tour to Scotland. By 1961 and 1962, it was decided that Fury should have a permanent backing band, so Georgie Fame and the Blue Flames were signed. The band had the advantage of music stands that were already painted "B.F.," which could stand for Blue Flames or Billy Fury. The group backed Fury for only a matter of months before being fired, allegedly for sounding too jazzy.[31] Producer Joe Meek's in-house studio band was christened the Tornados and began backing Fury in early 1962. This group consisted of George Bellamy (rhythm guitar), Alan Caddy (lead guitar), Heinz Burt (bass guitar), and Clem Cattini (drums). Eventually organist Roger LaVern was added. Caddy and Cattini had been members of Johnny Kidd and the Pirates until 1961, when they left Kidd's band to back up Tommy Steele's brother, Colin Hicks. Curiously, when bassist Burt left the Tornados for a solo career, one of his eventual replacements was Brian Gregg, the other original member of the Pirates. So, for a period of time in 1963, all of the members of Johnny Kidd's original backing group (Cattini, Gregg, and Caddy) were Tornados.

However, let us backtrack for just a moment. It was in 1962 when the Tornados were first backing Fury that manager Parnes and producer Joe Meek tried to establish the Tornados as a dual-purpose independent and backing group. The obvious model was that of the Shadows, which continued to serve as Cliff Richard's backing group even as they also recorded on their own. Meek's composition "Love and Fury" was issued as the A-side of the Tornados first single; however, the record was not a success. Their second single, Meek's "Telstar," however, became one of the most successful instrumental records of the rock era. Not only did "Telstar" top the singles charts in the United Kingdom—hitting No. 1 on October 4, 1962—it also topped the *Billboard* pop charts in the United States—reaching No. 1 on December 22, 1962—a first for a British rock band. "Telstar" held the top spot on the *Billboard* charts for three consecutive weeks, and when it finally was knocked out of the No. 1 spot by Steve Lawrence's recording of "Go Away Little Girl," it remained at No. 2.

Despite the commercial success of "Telstar" in both the United Kingdom and the United States, the record does not so much signal the start of the British Invasion as the success of a novelty number. For one thing, "Telstar" is an instrumental, and is a fairly impersonal instrumental. In other words, there is no way of knowing that the record is by a British rock band, or even an established band at all—it sounds fully like a studio production. In part, this is because of the larger-than-life nature of Meek's arrangement and production, which includes the unlikely combination of electronic sound effects and harp glissandi. Part of the novelty aspect of the recording comes from the use of a deliberately distorted electronic keyboard that is manipulated in the studio so that it sounds like a synthesizer—this was back in the days before people such as Robert Moog miniaturized synthesizers and thereby made them practical for use in commercial music. The keyboard carries the melody throughout the piece, except in the bridge section, in which the lead guitar plays the melody. Even Clem Cattini's drum playing includes an aspect of novelty to it. Much of the percussion part is focused on fast, repeated sixteenth-notes on the high-hat cymbal. And, even though the tone color and sustained melody of the electric guitar in the bridge section resembles the work of the Shadows, American listeners of the day could connect the guitar sound to surf music. On "Telstar," the Tornados could be any assemblage of studio musicians. Because of its novelty status, then, "Telstar" is closer to British clarinetist Mr. Acker Bilk's recording of "Stranger on the Shore" (perhaps best remembered today because of its appearance in the film *Mr. Holland's Opus*), which hit No. 1 on the *Billboard* Pop charts May 26, 1962, than to the Beatles' "I Want to Hold Your Hand." Incidentally, another popular 1962 recording by the British singer Frank Ifield (*Billboard* Pop No. 5 in late 1962), "I Remember You," is also something of a novelty number because of the focus on Ifield's yodel on the title phrase. Interestingly, the Ifield recording also features a short refrain-like phrase that is played on the harmonica, something heard in some of the Beatles' earliest recordings from autumn 1962 (e.g., "Love Me Do" and "Please Please Me"). Like Mr. Acker Bilk's "Stranger on the Shore," "I Remember You" is middle-of-the-road pop, and decidedly not rock and roll.

Ironically, Billy Fury and the Tornados were touring the United States when "Telstar" broke as a hit record in America. The Tornados and Fury adopted the Cliff Richard and the Shadows paradigm in their concerts: the Tornados opened for Fury, and then provided accompaniment for Fury when he made his appearance on stage. Because Fury himself had made no commercial inroads in the United States, the sudden unexpected success of "Telstar" in the United States meant that the opening act had the big hit and the headliner was a near unknown. Billy Fury and the Tornados soon parted company, and while the Tornados enjoyed some further chart success in Great Britain, they never had another hit record in the United States.

In conclusion, the period 1960–1963 saw a decisive move away from direct imitation of Elvis Presley, Bill Haley, and 1954–1955 American rockabilly. In its place, British musicians turned to the influence of white rockabilly and rock and roll artists such as Carl Perkins, Gene Vincent, Eddie Cochran, and Buddy Holly, as well as black rock and roll stars such as Chuck Berry and Little Richard, contemporary Motown and Brill Building R&B, and rural and Chicago-style electric blues. In short, British musicians increasingly turned to the direct influence of African American musical forms and styles. Instead of directly imitating the American source material—regardless of from what racial or ethnic group it emanated—the British musicians of the early 1960s began to put their own stamp on the material. They had finally reached a point where their blending of American influences had taken on a life and character of its own. It was only then that it could come back to the United States and be perceived as a new style of popular music.

4

The Beatles and Merseybeat: Balancing the Sides

Why the British Invasion, and why early 1964? One of the oft-repeated theories is that the assassination of President John F. Kennedy on November 22, 1963 left a huge void in the lives of young people. This has been confirmed anecdotally by informal conversations I have had with nonmusicians who were teenagers at the time of the Kennedy assassination. When four young men from Liverpool, England, performed on *The Ed Sullivan Show* on three consecutive Sundays (February 9, 16, and 23, 1964) the void was filled.

It must be remembered that *The Ed Sullivan Show* was much more than just a popular Sunday evening television program. Sullivan, an entertainment gossip columnist, hosted the program from 1948 to 1971. During that period, nearly every major American star of music, movies, television, and sports appeared, as did many international stars. Sullivan's program featured all the latest acts, and was an especially important outlet for rock music. It has been said quite widely that *The Ed Sullivan Show* did not show popular culture; it *was* popular culture. The Beatles, the Animals, the Kinks, Gerry and the Pacemakers, the Rolling Stones, Cilla Black, the Searchers, Dusty Springfield, Herman's Hermits, Petula Clark, the Dave Clark Five, and other British musicians appeared on Sullivan's program between 1964 and 1966.

While *The Ed Sullivan Show* was *the* entertainment program in the United States at the time of the British Invasion, it was a variety show; therefore, the focus was not on rock music. For example, the Rolling Stones might be followed by a troupe of circus acrobats, a film celebrity, or a ventriloquist. Because the focus was not on rock music, this allowed the performers who appeared on the program to be seen by a wide audience demographic.

When ABC's pop music–focused program *Shindig!*—which was developed by Jack Good, the developer of the British programs *Six-Five Special* and *Oh Boy!*—began its 1964–1966 run on American television, rock music and a younger audience demographic were the focus, and British groups were well represented. At one point, *Shindig!* was so popular that it aired two times per week. Rival network NBC countered with *Hullabaloo,* which ran from 1965–1966. Like *Shindig!, Hullabaloo* brought a wide range of rock music to the American public, and like *Shindig!, Hullabaloo* gave British bands quite a lot of exposure. In fact, during the first three months of *Hullabaloo,* Beatles manager Brian Epstein taped a segment in London that focused on performances by British artists. The Beatles themselves appeared on *The Ed Sullivan Show, Shindig!,* and *Hullabaloo* at various points between 1964 and 1966. But the reasons that the Beatles became the major star group of the British Invasion do not end with the need to fill a void after the assassination of President Kennedy, or with the television exposure they received on *The Ed Sullivan Show, Shindig!,* and *Hullabaloo.* A complex set of factors contributed to the band's success, including the following: the blurring of gender boundaries; the balance of Mod and Rocker tendencies; an antiauthoritarian sense of humor; the celebration of individualism within a cohesive collective; a mix of personalities that came across well in interviews; the record production of George Martin and his engineers; and the high quality of the Beatles' music—both covers and original compositions. Let us take a look at some of the developments that took place in the Beatles between 1957 and their breakthrough in the United States in 1964, as well as some of the influences that pre-date the formation of even early incarnations of the group.

In tracing important influences on the Beatles and what they symbolize at the time of the British Invasion, we must go back to the teen and preteen years of each of the members of the group. Because the Beatles are but one of the groups with which we will deal in this book, there is not space for detailed biographical study of the individual members of the band, or even of the band's history. The reader is advised that there are numerous good biographies and autobiographies of the Beatles as a group and as individuals. Perhaps the most comprehensive of these is *The Beatles Anthology,* both the documentary film and the book.

We will begin our look at the influences on the Beatles with a BBC Home Service radio program that aired from 1951–1960: *The Goon Show.* This program featured absurdist satire, often directed at the entertainment world, the police and military, the British class structure, and literature, to name a few. Created by comedian Spike Milligan, *The Goon Show* starred principally Milligan, Harry Secombe, and Peter Sellers. In addition to the Beatles, *The Goon Show* left its imprint most clearly on British comedians Peter Cook and Dudley Moore, the British troupe Monty Python's Flying Circus, and the lesser-known American comedy troupe, the Firesign Theatre. The clearest outward signs of the influence of Milligan, Sellers, and Secombe on the Beatles can be found in the Beatles' comedy sketches on their annual Christmas radio broadcasts, and in the writings of John Lennon (*A Spaniard in the Works* and *In His Own Write*).[1] The occasional unintelligible mutterings that Lennon added to some of the Beatles recordings from 1967 onward also owe a debt of gratitude to the Goons. Add to that such let's-see-what-we-can-get-away-with touches as the "tit, tit, tit . . ." backing chorus in the song "Girl." Even a few early preprofessional recordings of the Beatles illustrate the influence of the Goons. For example, the Paul McCartney/John Lennon composition "You'll Be Mine,"[2] which the group informally recorded in 1960 in a home studio (available on vol. 1 of *The Beatles Anthology* CD set, Capitol Records CDP 7243 8 34445 2 6), finds lead singer McCartney wildly exaggerating the style of the American vocal group the Inkspots, while Lennon adds the absurdist phrase "National Health eyeball" to the spoken middle section.

Paul McCartney first met John Lennon at a church fete in 1957 at which Lennon's skiffle band, the Quarry Men, was performing. Largely as a result of his ability on guitar and for knowing all the lyrics to Eddie Cochran's "Twenty Flight Rock," McCartney soon joined the group. Although younger than Lennon by approximately three years, George Harrison—who was a friend of McCartney—also soon joined the group. Various other musicians passed in and out of the Quarry Men, and the group went through a series of name changes. By 1960, Lennon's art school friend, Stuart Sutcliffe, joined the group on bass guitar; however, his membership in the band by all accounts was based on his friendship with Lennon and not on musical ability. The name "Beatles," which was adopted after Sutcliffe joined the group, is a play on words: the insect "beetle," directly inspired by Buddy Holly's group, the Crickets, combined with "beat" for the type of rock music the band played. From 1960 until his dying day, Lennon claimed that he invented the name; however, Harrison and McCartney recalled that the Marlon Brando film *The Wild One* was one of Stu Sutcliffe's favorite movies. In one scene in the film, Lee Marvin's character tells Brando's character, "the Beetles missed you." The reference to "beetles" has been attributed variously as referring to the motorcycle gang or to the (as Paul McCartney calls them) "motorcycle chicks." Harrison and McCartney suspect that Sutcliffe played as much a role in developing the name "Beatles" as did Lennon.[3] Incidentally, it should be noted that American motorcycle gangs, such as the fictional gang in *The Wild One,* were an antecedent to the Rockers. Indeed, photographs of the Beatles in 1960 find them with Rocker-like hairstyles and clothing.

The Beatles as a band came together even more solidly when Pete Best, the son of a club owner in whose establishment the Beatles sometimes performed, joined on drums. Early bookings in Liverpool and backing the Larry Parnes–managed singer Johnny Gentle on a tour to Scotland proved that the Beatles were a functioning unit; however, they were far from the upper echelon of Liverpool groups. It was in 1960, however, that club owners in Hamburg, Germany's St. Pauli district began hiring British groups. The Beatles' manager at the time, coffeehouse owner Allan Williams, secured a contract for the group to take up a residency in Hamburg.

One of the most telling quotes from the Beatles about the experience of playing extended gigs in Hamburg came from John Lennon, who said, "I grew up in Hamburg, not Liverpool."[4] The growing up process that took place in the Beatles' 1960, 1961, and 1962 stays in Germany came in several forms: musical, personal, sexual, and so on. One thing that is easy to overlook is the fan base the Beatles attracted in Hamburg and the way in which it affected members of the band. The Hamburg clubs in which the Beatles and other British groups performed, located in the St. Pauli district (and some more specifically in the notorious Reeperbahn red-light district), had a varied clientele. Chief among the groups that were attracted to the Beatles, though, was the Bohemian art student crowd. Stu Sutcliffe, who was still the Beatles' bass player on their first trip to Hamburg, and John Lennon had attended art college, so perhaps that explains the synergism between the Beatles and German art students. As Paul McCartney says, the German students were not Mods and they were not Rockers; they were "exis: existentialists."[5] Among the traits of the existentialist art students, such as Astrid Kirchherr and Klaus Voorman, were that they dressed in black and celebrated the boredom, alienation, and absurdity of life, and nothingness associated with existentialists such as Jean-Paul Sartre, Albert Camus, and Simone de Beauvoir. It is important to note that absurdity was one of the traits associated with existentialism—a trait that is shared with the humor of the Goons. This means that the Beatles felt the influence of an emphasis on the absurd as teenagers growing up in Liverpool, and as young men "growing up" in Hamburg because of fans-turned-friends such as Kirchherr and Voorman. It is also important to note that the themes of boredom, alienation, and nothingness run through the core of what sociologists found ran through the Mods in the early to mid-1960s in Britain.[6] Supporting this view of the Mod leanings of the "exis" is the fact that, as Steven Stark writes of the German existentialists in his sociological study of the Beatles, "they embraced modern music but disliked Bill Haley's image and weren't too keen on Elvis's either because they thought he had the wrong look (what was later described as too macho)."[7]

While Paul McCartney's aforementioned statement detaches the German existentialist art students from the confines of the British Mods and Rockers, the existentialists would seem to be more closely allied to the Mods, even through their somber dress also suggests ties to groups such as the American beatniks of the 1950s. Certainly, the fact that they were intellectuals, artists, and blurred gender lines with a fairly unisex approach to clothing and hairstyles all lean heavily in the direction of the self-identification of the Mods, as described by Nuttall.[8] And it was the nonmacho, unisex approach to hairstyle that often is cited as one of Astrid Kirchherr's principal contributions to the development of the image of the Beatles. Kirchherr urged her boyfriend, Beatle Stuart Sutcliffe, to wash the Rocker-style grease out of his hair, and to comb his hair not backward—as was the Rocker fashion—but forward. Three of Sutcliffe's fellow Beatles—John Lennon, Paul McCartney, and George Harrison—followed suit; however, drummer Pete Best continued to wear his hair in the Rocker style. Lennon, McCartney, and Harrison have been quoted extensively as saying that musical and personality differences with Best eventually led to his firing in August 1962. Perhaps the personality differences emerge symbolically in the issue of hairstyle: Sutcliffe, Lennon, McCartney, and Harrison rejected part of the Teddy Boy and Rocker image when they changed their hairstyles; Pete Best did not. All of the Beatles continued to wear black leather jackets; therefore, they did not entirely reject ties to the 1950s and the Rocker aesthetic during the 1960–1962 period. Stu Sutcliffe quit the Beatles in 1961 in order to remain in Germany with Astrid Kirchherr. Unfortunately, he died of a brain hemorrhage on April 10, 1962, just as Lennon, McCartney, Harrison, and Best were on their way to Hamburg for a third and final residency. As for the outward move from Rocker to Mod, Brian Epstein, shortly after becoming their manager in winter 1961–1962, convinced the four Beatles to give up their leathers on stage for suits. This (along with their ever-lengthening hair) represented another visual move in the direction of the Mod aesthetic. By the time of the British Invasion, Epstein had the Beatles wearing highly stylized collarless suit jackets, another move away from the Rocker image and in the direction of the self-consciously Mod.

The Beatles were not, however, all about image: they were really about music. Because I have mentioned some of the band's musical influences in the previous chapter, I will not detail them here. However, let us take a look at how some of these seemingly disparate influences—as well as the addition of Ringo Starr to the Beatles—came together to create a balanced approach to pop music found in few other bands of the early 1960s.

Once the Beatles' membership was fixed at John Lennon, Paul McCartney, George Harrison, and Ringo Starr in August 1962, the group's sound stepped up a level or two on the energy scale. Not only was Starr a flashier drummer than Pete Best in the technical sense, he also emphasized bass drum rhythms and played the snare drum with a louder sound. Starr also gave the Beatles a greater sense of implied swing feel—even in the songs they performed live and recorded that featured a straight eighth-note feel—because of his greater emphasis on syncopation, particularly with accentuations of the "and" of beat 2. Comparison of the extant Pete Best recordings of the Beatles in 1961 and 1962—the Hamburg recordings produced by Bert Kaempfert, the Decca audition tapes, and the Parlophone audition tapes—with the extant Ringo Starr recordings from 1962–1963, reveals that Starr's greater virtuosity and volume as a drummer paradoxically both (1) give the rhythm section of drums and bass guitar a greater feeling of drive and cohesion and (2) give Paul McCartney greater opportunity to play more melodically inspired bass lines. The other major feature that Ringo Starr brought to the Beatles was a strong, likeable personality with a self-effacing sense of humor.

An important part of the Beatles' success was because of the balance the four achieved between individualism and ensemble cohesion. Because they had interests ranging from rockabilly to girl-group R&B, Motown, Chuck Berry, Little Richard, the Everly Brothers, Buddy Holly, musical theatre, and beyond, the Beatles presented a wide stylistic range on stage and on their recordings. Not only was this range evident in the cover material that was part of their repertoire, but it can also be heard in their compositions. And, even in the covers they performed, the range of influences gave the Beatles one of the widest possible ranges of texture of any of the British Invasion bands. The textural diversity that can be heard in live performances and recordings from 1962 and 1963 (before the band broke in the United States) includes the following: (1) solo vocals; (2) the girl-group texture of lead singer supported by two backing singers; (3) the Everly Brothers–style two-voice harmony texture in which the vocal blend is such that it is difficult to determine which voice has the "true" lead line; and (4) three-part block harmony. Multiply the textures by the fact that all four of the Beatles could and did perform as lead singers (Starr, less frequently than the others, but he generally was afforded one lead vocal per album and one featured vocal in live sets), and the fact that Lennon, McCartney, and Harrison were all effective backing vocalists, and a wide range of tone colors can be heard in the Beatles' early work.

Let us briefly consider just one of the textures associated with a particular portion of the pop song repertoire—the so-called girl-group songs—and examine some of the ways in which the style found its way not only into the cover recordings the Beatles made, but also into the compositions of John Lennon and Paul McCartney.

Musicologist Ian Inglis writes that, "The customary vocal arrangement in which members of the girl groups repeated the lead singer's words in close succession—on tracks such as 'Will You Love Me Tomorrow'—was freely employed on songs like 'Hold Me Tight,' 'You Won't See Me,' and 'You're Going to Lose That Girl.'" In his study of the craft and impact of the Brill Building songwriters in the journal *American Music*, Inglis also notes that Lennon and McCartney's songs resembled those of Brill Building songwriters—such as Goffin and King—in "standard reliance on the AABA form, a melodic contrast between the A and B sections, an unusual complexity in chord progressions, and a routine modulation to a different key in the bridges of their songs."[9] These traits, by the way, are especially true of some of the Lennon and McCartney compositions through 1964.

Despite this tendency for some of the group's songs to follow the lead of Brill Building songwriters, I feel that a big part of the Beatles' appeal rests in the diversity of the group, from the country and jazz-influenced guitar playing of Harrison, the R&B

leanings of Lennon, and the eclectic mix of everything including and in between pop balladry and Little Richard–style rock and roll in McCartney. On one of their American tours, the Beatles spent time with Elvis Presley at Presley's Graceland mansion, certainly not a particularly "Mod" move. And, when given the chance in later years to revisit old favorite songs (e.g., during the Beatles' *Let It Be* sessions, on Lennon's *Rock and Roll* album, and on McCartney's *Run Devil Run* album) they covered rockabilly songs just as often as R&B or Chuck Berry–style rock and roll. This suggests that although their outward appearances moved from Rocker to Mod between 1960 and 1962, musically the Beatles maintained a balance between the opposing aesthetics.

The qualities that enabled the Beatles to become the most commercially successful band of the British Invasion, and indeed one of the most successful popular music phenomena of the age of sound recording, were not necessarily fully evident on the band's earliest recordings for EMI's Parlophone label. The band's first single, "Love Me Do," for example, is catchy but in retrospect is also derivative. John Lennon's harmonica solo, for example, clearly is based on Delbert McClinton's solo on the Bruce Channel hit "Hey! Baby." In fact, the Beatles were one of the opening acts when Channel and his group toured Britain on the strength of "Hey! Baby," and McClinton is said to have taught Lennon the solo backstage.[10] The acoustic guitar accompaniment and the Lennon-McCartney vocal harmony style on "Love Me Do" also strongly suggest the Everly Brothers. And, lyrically, "Love Me Do" is not nearly as rich as the songs that Lennon and McCartney wrote even very soon thereafter.

The Beatles' second single, "Please Please Me" is edgier: on one level it is easy to understand Lennon's plea as a request for sexual satisfaction. The recording is altogether more energetic, and the band's new rhythm section of McCartney, Lennon, and Starr is altogether more cohesive and powerful than that on any of the Beatles' previous recordings. "Please Please Me" also illustrates the kind of fruitful relationship that the Beatles and producer George Martin established very early in their working relationship. Martin wanted the group to record Mitch Murray's composition "How Do You Do It" (later a hit for Gerry and the Pacemakers), but the Beatles held out for the self-penned "Please Please Me." They did, however, heed Martin's advice and greatly increase the tempo of the song. It hit No. 1 in the United Kingdom.

Other tracks on the Beatles' 1963 debut album, *Please Please Me,* find the group turning to McCartney/Lennon songs (as they were credited on the album cover), girl group songs, a little Motown, and pop. Of the self-penned songs, "There's a Place" is notable, like Brian Wilson's "In My Room," for dealing in a personal-feeling way with rejection, loneliness, and introspection. "Do You Want to Know a Secret" (with a lead vocal from George Harrison) still holds up pretty well, but some of the other songs, such as "Ask Me Why," do not necessarily hint that Lennon and McCartney would soon become

Part of the credit for the commercial and critical suc-
cess of the Beatles' recordings belongs to producer
George Martin. Before his 1962–1969 work with the
Beatles, Martin had been a classical oboist and a
producer of skiffle and comedy records. Courtesy of
Photofest.

the top songwriters in pop music. It is telling that easily the most powerful, and still the
best remembered track from *Please Please Me* is a cover: John Lennon's definitive interpretation of "Twist and Shout."

All of the components that made for the Beatles' success at home, in Europe, and in
North America really come together on their other 1963 album, *With the Beatles*. Even
the Robert Freeman photograph that graces the cover of the album suggests a completely
different, German existentialist approach than what had been seen on any popular music
album cover before. Lennon's interpretation of "Please Mister Postman," "You Really
Got a Hold on Me," and "Money" highlight his strong, effective approach to popular
R&B, while Harrison's singing and guitar solos on "Roll over Beethoven" make that one
of the Beatles' covers that remains popular. Paul McCartney's performance of the show
tune "Till There Was You" manages to succeed in part because of a fine jazz-inspired
guitar solo from Harrison. McCartney, though, really shines forth on his own composition "All My Loving."

While some of the other Lennon and McCartney compositions on *With the Beatles,* including "It Won't Be Long" and "Not a Second Time," hint at the complete musical package that was the Beatles (including unexpected chromatic chords, tonal ambiguity between tonic major and relative minor, rhythmic vitality, and a disparate range of influences), "All My Loving" perhaps is the most definitive illustration of these features on the album. McCartney's melody has a natural rise and fall and uses solely the notes of the tonic major scale. His harmonization, however, includes unexpected chromatic chords (including the bVII chord and an augmented triad build on the third scale step) and the subtle mixing of motion toward the major tonic chord and its relative minor, such that the listener is left wondering at first hearing whether the song is in major or minor. The genius of this tonally vague approach is that it fits squarely in with the lyrics, which both describe the love McCartney's character will send to his partner, but also makes it clear that he feels unhappy about the fact that he soon will have to leave her for a period of time. In addition, the triplet chords Lennon plays, McCartney's walking bass line, and Starr's swing-feel playing gel solidly, and Harrison's guitar solo allows him to show the influence that country and rockabilly guitarists such as Chet Atkins and Carl Perkins had on his playing.

The Beatles' first North American hit, "I Want to Hold Your Hand," was by all accounts a fully calculated attempt to break into the U.S. market. As such, it informs us of what the Beatles, Brian Epstein (their manager), and George Martin (their producer) thought young American consumers wanted to hear. It is, unlike the song "Please Please Me," thoroughly innocent and teen-oriented. "I Want to Hold Your Hand" includes strong, easily identifiable musical hooks, too, including the opening rhythmic stumble and the overdubbed handclaps. All of this, it must be remembered, was calculated. For example, the handclaps clearly had to be conceived for the recording medium: with each member of the group playing their instruments, the handclaps could not be performed live. The innocence, too, is calculated. These were, after all, men in their twenties, some married, and all of whom had spent considerable time in the notorious red-light district of Hamburg.

The song "She Loves You," which was a hit in Britain and Europe before the Beatles "invaded" North America, also become a significant hit in the United States, albeit after the fact. "She Loves You," in part because it does not appear to be so calculated as "I Want to Hold Your Hand," is in fact a far more interesting and significant song.

Insofar as the accentuation of the "and" of beat 2 was a Merseybeat signifier, "She Loves You" exploits this syncopation more fully than perhaps any other recording of the era. Unlike most Merseybeat songs in which the "2-and, 4" (with a slight accentuation on the "and") pattern is solely or primarily felt from the drums, the arrangement of "She Loves You" places a massive stress on the syncopation in all the instruments. This can be heard within the line "She loves you and you know that can't be bad" immediately after the phrase "she loves you." The rhythmic vitality of "She Loves You," a vitality against which any of the Beatles' prior recordings pale, also comes from the cross rhythms created by Ringo Starr's incorporation of triplet quarter-notes in some of his fills. The song is made instantly distinctive because of several other hooks, including the famous "yeah, yeah, yeah" and the unusual (in 1963 rock music) inclusion of the added major sixth on the final chord of the song. Much has been made over the years of the old-fashioned sound (George Martin has been quoted ad infinitum as saying that it reminded him of something out of the early 1940s Glenn Miller dance band idiom); however, I believe that, whether intentional or not, the addition of the sixth fits squarely into the tendency of Lennon and McCartney at that time to use vague harmonic motion that obscured the distinction between the major tonic key and its relative minor. For example, the tonic chord in the key of G major (the tonality of "She Loves You") consists of the notes G, B, and D; the relative minor chord (E minor) consists of the notes E, G, and B. In "She Loves You," the note E (the sixth scale degree) is added to the final tonic chord; therefore, the final chord in "She Loves You" (G, B, D, E), can be understood as the combination of tonic and its relative minor. Another way in which "She Loves You" stands out from the bulk of the songs of the period is in its rhetorical scheme. In order to see how this scheme differs from the norm, we must consider the Beatles' approach to gender role stereotypes.

One aspect of the Beatles' work that represented a break with the music of their 1950s predecessors is the degree to which they blurred gender lines and gender stereotypes, especially when they first appeared in the United States. Keep in mind that a fair number of the covers that were part of their live repertoire and that they recorded on their first several albums were taken from the girl groups. These songs tended to be fairly gender neutral to begin with—that was part of the reason that the songs worked rhetorically for female and male singers. But, in addition to including songs in their repertoire that did not rely on obvious stereotypical traditional gender roles as much as did a considerable amount of the pop music that was around at the time of the British Invasion, they also wrote a number of songs that moved toward gender neutrality. While one can find references to traditional gender roles in some of the compositions of John Lennon, Paul McCartney, and George Harrison, even early on they wrote songs that bucked stereotypical roles. The song "She Loves You," for example, finds lead singer Lennon telling a male friend that he should try to reconcile with his girlfriend. Lennon plays the role of friend of both the man and the woman as he tries to get the couple back together—in the context of the early 1960s, this was not necessarily a stereotypical male role. While one of the assumptions that one can make about the song is that it implies that he (Lennon) might very well move in on the young woman if his friend does not heed Lennon's advice, a literal reading of the text finds Lennon's character playing the role of the nurturing intermediary in a relationship between two of his friends.

By 1964 and 1965 the Beatles incorporation of modal ambiguity and modal mixture was becoming so smooth in the compositions of Lennon and McCartney that it is a natural part of the songwriters' harmonic vocabulary. It is handled more subtly, so that the occurrence of the bVII chord, for example, in songs such as "I Don't Want to Spoil the Party," and "The Night Before" do not draw attention to themselves. However, it should be noted that while this is true of the songwriting of both Lennon and McCartney, it is not necessarily true that the use of the bVII chord was smoothed into the compositions of all British Invasion songwriters in 1964 and 1965. For example, the most famous songwriters most closely associated with Mod trends, Pete Townshend (the Who) and Ray Davies (the Kinks), by contrast with Lennon and McCartney seem almost to slap the listener in the face with the whole-step root motion between tonic and the subtonic (bVII)—Davies in particular. This is part of the balancing act that one can hear in the music of the Beatles—they used new harmonic and scalar materials and used some of the new lyrical imagery that was around in 1964 and 1965, but generally in a subtle way. Some other bands, by contrast, tended to draw deliberate attention to the newness of what they were doing.

In part, the Beatles succeeded as well as they did because of what in retrospect seems to be a very real sense of tension within the band. Although early in their career the focus of the four individuals was on building audience and enjoying commercial success, there is still an underlying, if unspoken, tension. This is manifested in image: the stereotypes of John Lennon as the cynic, Paul McCartney as the lovable puppy dog, and so on. However, those stereotypes also were challenged by what appear to be polar opposites at times between public persona and artistic persona. For example, the wisecracking Lennon of press conferences was also the Beatle most closely associated in songs that he wrote and sang with vulnerability and introspection. And it was that lovable puppy dog McCartney who sang the mysterious lines, "Well she was just seventeen, if you know what I mean," that imply a wink-wink-nudge-nudge acknowledgement of desire for an underage female in "I Saw Her Standing There." The musical tension sometimes is manifested in the deliberate rhythmic conflicts between a straight eighth-note and a swing feel, such as in the Beatles' 1964 recording of Little Richard's "Long Tall Sally." The Beatles also created stylistic tension in "Long Tall Sally" with Harrison's rockabilly and country references in his guitar solo within the context of a straight-ahead R&B-based rock and roll song.

The eclecticism of their musical influences, the reasonably democratic nature of the band, their good looks, their Goons-influenced humor, and other factors all came together in Britain and Europe in 1963 to create Beatlemania. As concert promoter Sid Bernstein said, "Only Hitler ever duplicated their power over crowds."[11] While one of the major reasons Americans give for the impact of the British Invasion starting in early 1964 is that it filled a void left by the assassination of President John F. Kennedy, that certainly did not play a role in the unprecedented commercial and popular success and adulation the Beatles received in the United Kingdom and in Europe the year before they hit the United States. Ultimately, I suspect that while there may have been better looking, better singing, better playing, and quicker witted individual personalities in British pop music at the time, the ultimate answer to the question, "why the Beatles?" probably is that everything that leads to stardom aligned in this group more solidly and more thoroughly than in any other group of the time.

While none of the other numerous Liverpool bands enjoyed the commercial success of the Beatles, there were several things that they shared with Lennon, Starr, Harrison and McCartney—things that helped them to achieve stardom at least for a period of time in the United Kingdom and in the United States. First, the Liverpool bands that were a successful part of the British Invasion tended to be the groups that performed live countless times at the Casbah, the Cavern, and Jacaranda, and the other clubs and coffee bars of their hometown often over the course of several years before the actual British Invasion. These also tended to be the groups that were hired to perform in Hamburg, Germany, during the same period. In the case of groups such as the Beatles, Gerry and the Pacemakers, the Searchers, as well as lesser-known groups such as King Size Taylor and the Dominos, and Rory Storm and the Hurricanes, the long sets, as well as the diverse clientele, encouraged a wide stylistic range and an extensive repertoire of mostly American pop, rockabilly, R&B, and other material. Although few of the Liverpool bands included successful songwriters—the Beatles and Gerry and the Pacemakers being the two most notable exceptions—the wide stylistic range necessitated by the kinds of gigs these groups played provided ample opportunity for songwriters to build their repertoire of compositional styles and devices. And this is an area that was especially crucial in the success of the Beatles in particular. With Lennon and McCartney both being prolific writers on their own and helping each other complete songs, and with George Harrison doing at least a little writing even in 1963, the Beatles could pen original material that had a sound basis in then-current popular styles to an extent not evident in any other Merseybeat band.

Another thing that factored into the success of the Beatles and some of the other Brian Epstein–managed artists—such as the Fourmost, Gerry and the Pacemakers, Billy J. Kramer and the Dakotas, and Cilla Black—was the record production of George Martin. In his autobiography, *All You Need Is Ears*, Martin chronicles his pre-rock work as a recording engineer and producer, but focuses on his most famous work—that with the Beatles and other Epstein-managed acts.[12] Perhaps because Martin had a wide range of experience, including his work as a classical musician, recordings he made of the Goons, and his production work with the Vipers Skiffle Group, he found ways to capture the energy of the rock bands with which he worked, to write arrangements and devise recording strategies to deal with less-than-perfect-voices, and to provide some of the most commercially effective production of British Invasion bands. A comparison of Martin's production with the contemporary work of Ron Richards, Andrew Loog Old-ham, Dave Clark, Mike Smith (the Decca producer), Tony Hatch, and others suggests that he achieved a balance between clarity and sonic impact that allowed some of the power of artists who were really live stage musicians to emerge, while putting it in a pop chart–friendly studio format.

Even though Martin balanced clarity and impact more thoroughly than most of his contemporaries, studio recordings of the day could not duplicate the sheer power of live performances. Perhaps because live recording of rock and roll bands was not a technolog-ically feasible possibility in the early 1960s in Britain—George Martin tells of EMI not owning its first four-track tape machine until as late as 1963—or perhaps because live re-cordings would be too apt to expose musical flaws, a good deal of the live development of Merseybeat that was taking place in the Cavern and other clubs is undocumented today. A notable exception, however, and one that illustrates the extent to which a band's live sound might be quite at odds with how the band was presented in studio recordings, is the EP *Live at the Cavern* (Decca DFE 8552) by the Big Three, a band not associated with George Martin. The historical significance of this recording—there were no commercial recordings issued of the most famous Liverpool bands that appeared at the Cavern actu-ally playing there (there is even precious little film footage of groups such as the Beatles and Gerry and Pacemakers performing in what might be called their home venue)—is confirmed by the fact that it was reissued again on vinyl in the 1980s and in the twenty-first century as part of a the CD collection. The fact that this fairly short recording has been reissued several times is significant, because the Big Three was a group that enjoyed minimal commercial success as a recording unit, and really had a very short career.

Within the context of a discussion of the desire of himself, Paul McCartney, and George Harrison to replace Pete Best with Ringo Starr as the Beatles' drummer, John Lennon stated that "there were two big groups in Liverpool—the Big Three and Rory Storm and the Hurricanes" and that "the two best drummers in Liverpool" were in those bands.[13] Given the high level of music making in Liverpool in 1962, with local bands such as the Beatles, the Searchers, Gerry and the Pacemakers, the Merseybeats, the Swinging Blue Jeans, and numerous others enjoying sizeable audiences, Lennon's assessment of the Big Three suggests that this group was something truly noteworthy.

The most famous membership of the Big Three was drummer-singer Johnny Hutchinson (who, in fact occasionally sat in with the Beatles when they needed a sub-stitute drummer for gigs), bass guitarist-singer Johnny Gustafson (who later joined the Merseybeats and later was in Roxy Music), and guitarist-singer Brian Griffiths. The Beatles' manager, Brian Epstein, eventually managed the Big Three and secured a recording contract with Decca Records for the group. Decca, however, made the Big Three record lightweight pop songs, and they were never a successful recording act. The Big Three's one notable U.K. hit, a cover of the R&B song "Some Other Guy," was not a proper studio recording: unbeknownst to the band, Decca released the recording from the Big Three's audition tape.

The Big Three made its greatest impact as a live act, and in particular as perhaps the best and most powerful band to play the Cavern on a regular basis. Their rare live EP consists of four tracks: a cover of Ray Charles's "What'd I Say," the original "Don't Start Running Away," a cover of Bob B. Soxx and the Blue Jeans version of "Zip-a-dee-doo-dah," and a cover of Chuck Berry's "Reelin' and Rockin'." "What'd I Say" is packed with the kind of energy that drives the so-called cave dwellers to screams, and the kind of energy that unfortunately the Big Three's studio recordings completely failed to capture. The Hutchinson-Gustafson-Griffiths composition "Don't Start Running Away" is marred by too many lyrical clichés and by the fact that it sounds too obviously modeled on "Some Other Guy," a favorite of Cavern bands. While "Zip-a-dee-doo-dah," the hit song from the 1946 Walt Disney film *Song of the South,* at first glance might seem like unusual material for what was arguably the most powerful Liverpool rock band, the song works particularly well in the hands of the Big Three. The inspiration comes not from the original version of the song from the film, but rather from Bob B. Soxx and the Blue Jeans' recording of 1962. The soulful lead vocals and powerful instrumental work from Hutchinson, Gustafson, and Griffiths stand up well against just about any other covers by any other northern band in Britain at the time. And the Big Three's live version of "Zip-a-dee-doo-dah" blows the Dave Clark Five's later studio version out of the proverbial water as an example of powerful rock music, and this despite the fact that the Big Three was a trio.

Ultimately, the Big Three was unhappy with Epstein's management (which focused increasingly on the Beatles at the expense of other artists), and with the studio recordings they made with Decca. Griffiths and Gustafson departed shortly after the *Live at the Cavern* recording, and Hutchinson carried on only for a short time with a new bassist and guitarist before the group disbanded. In addition to possible inattention from Brian Epstein and unconvincing record production, the Big Three's commercial success outside the live context probably was also hindered by the fact that material written by members of the group (e.g., "The Cavern Stomp" and "Don't Start Running Away") lacks the originality of some of the contemporary songs written by other Liverpool songwriters, such as Gerry Marsden, John Lennon, and Paul McCartney.

Another Liverpool band, the Merseybeats, had the distinction of appearing at the Cavern on the same bill as the Beatles more than did any other group. Their studio recordings are popish, even more so than those of the Beatles. Although the singing and playing is good, the group doesn't display much rhythmic drive. They also had a tendency in their early recordings to turn to songs that predominantly had short, narrow-range melodic phrases, which tends to make them sound less diverse than a group such as the Beatles. It should be noted, however, that George Harrison's 1968 Beatles song "It's All Too Much" clearly is based on the song "Sorrow," which was recorded by former Merseybeats members Tony Crane and Billy Kinsley, billed as the Merseys. The music and the lyrics of the phrase, "with your long blond hair and your eyes of blue" is shared by the two songs. Incidentally, this resembles the way in which Harrison built his famous 1969 song "Something" from a fragment of the opening of James Taylor's 1968 song "Something in the Way She Moves." The fact that the influence of the Merseybeats, and especially of the song "Sorrow," exceeded their run of popularity in the United Kingdom from 1962–1966 is also confirmed by David Bowie's inclusion of "Sorrow" on *Pin Ups*, the 1973 album on which he covered songs that he frequently performed in his prefame days. Many of the Merseybeats' songs, such "It's Love That Really Counts" (1963) and "I Think of You" (1964), however, are ballads, so the band's canon lacked the stylistic range of the Liverpool groups that were a commercially successful part of the British Invasion.

The Swinging Blue Jeans enjoyed their brief period of fame in the United States in early 1964 when their 1963 cover of "Hippy Hippy Shake" went to No. 24 on the *Billboard* pop charts. The quartet of guitarist Ray Ennis, bassist Les Braid, drummer Norman Kuhlke, and guitarist Ralph Ellis (later replaced by Terry Sylvester, who himself replaced Graham Nash in the Hollies) enjoyed several additional hit singles in the United Kingdom, but these, as well as the band's two albums, did not generate as much interest in the United States. While "Hippy Hippy Shake" has endured, it is not the group's strongest presentation on vinyl. Other riff-based Swinging Blue Jeans covers, such as "Good Golly Miss Molly" and "Shakin' All Over," feature the same kind of instrumental virtuosity, but with more upfront (and less studio reverb-laden) production. Norman Kuhlke, in particular, may have been close to the quintessential Merseybeat-style drummer of the British Invasion era. The Swinging Blue Jeans were favorites at the Cavern Club and the other Liverpool venues at which the Merseybeats, the Beatles, Gerry and the Pacemakers, the Big Three, and all the other major local stars appeared. With reissued recordings as evidence, the Swinging Blue Jeans failed to connect with the record-buying public not because of musical deficiencies. It would seem, rather, that the fact that the group relied so heavily on nonoriginal material worked to their disadvantage in the recording environment of 1964–1965. Because the band excelled on riff-based hard-rocking pieces, too, they did not have the kind of stylistic range of some of their better-known fellow Liverpublians. Ray Ennis, one of the founding members of the Swinging Blue Jeans back in 1962, continues to front the group over 45 years later; however, he is the only original member remaining in the band.

While no British band of the 1963–1966 period enjoyed anywhere near the commercial success of the Beatles, some of the Beatles' fellow Liverpublians did enjoy some success both on the British and the U.S. charts. In particular, the Searchers recorded hit singles in the form of "Love Potion Number Nine" and "Needles and Pins." The band also charted several other singles and ultimately between early 1964 and spring 1965 placed a total of 7 records in the *Billboard* Top 40 in the United States. Although the Searchers' commercial impact in the United States lasted only for a little more than a year, the band made important contributions beyond just the commercial success of these singles. For one thing, the Searchers was one of the first bands to merge folk and rock, this in the form of "Where Have All the Flowers Gone," issued on their 1963 debut album. The jangling 12-string electric guitar sound of the band is a direct antecedent of Jim McGuinn's sound in the American folk-rock band the Byrds. Ultimately, the Searchers' success was probably stunted most by personnel changes, a generally laid-back sound, record production that stripped the band of some of their power, and a lack of original material.

Like the Searchers, Gerry and the Pacemakers placed 7 singles in the *Billboard* Top 40; however, Gerry Marsden and his band stretched their run on the U.S. charts from summer 1964 to autumn 1966. Of these seven singles, "Don't Let the Sun Catch You Crying," "How Do You Do It?," and "Ferry Cross the Mersey" made it into the Top 10. The self-penned "Don't Let the Sun Catch You Crying" and "Ferry Cross the Mersey" were two of the most significant non-Beatles singles to come out of Liverpool and are still considered British Invasion standards into the twenty-first century. Marsden's lyrics in these two songs are idealistic, and his musical settings betray a sophistication that was rare in rock music in the early 1960s. Both songs, for example, make use of major-seventh chords, emphasize nonchord tones in the melodies, and exhibit a sense of balance between repeated motives and contrasting phrases in the melodies that go beyond the work of many British Invasion bands. "Ferry Cross the Mersey" is an especially important song because of what it symbolizes in terms of the maturation and worldwide acceptance of British popular music by 1965. While a group such as the Beatles literally and figuratively left Liverpool for London in the wake of Beatlemania in 1963, Gerry Marsden reassures his hometown fans, "here I'll stay." It is sentimental, but it cuts to the heart of the sense of loss that was felt in places such as the Cavern Club when hometown heroes such as the Beatles left the city of their birth never to return. When Merseybeat became a style owned by the nation and then by the world, it metaphorically ceased to be the property of the young people of Liverpool.

5

A Different Sort of Balance:
The Dave Clark Five

It seems that Dave Clark was one of the few British Invasion musicians who was not part of a skiffle band back in the 1950s. Clark, who was born in Tottenham, North London, took up the drums and formed his band in approximately 1961 in order to raise money so that his local youth football club could travel to the Netherlands to play against a Dutch team. The other original members were Stan Saxon (lead vocals and saxophone), Rick Huxley (rhythm guitar), Mick Ryan (lead guitar), and Chris Walls (bass guitar). The band went through personnel changes, and by the time they made their recording debut in 1962, they included Clark (drums), Huxley (bass guitar), Denis Payton (saxophone, harmonica, guitar, and vocals), Mike Smith (lead vocals, keyboards), and Lenny Davidson (guitar).

The early work of the Dave Clark Five is especially interesting because it contrasted so much with that of the other famous British Invasion bands. The Dave Clark Five became part of the upper echelon of London dance bands, playing in officers' clubs in the numerous military bases in the London area, in addition to other venues. The band's early repertoire included everything that one might dance to in the late 1950s and early 1960s, even including Glenn Miller, swing-style pieces.[1] Because Stan Saxon was both the lead singer and the saxophonist, the early Dave Clark Five's repertoire included more instrumentals than most British Invasion bands. When I asked early group member Mick Ryan about the influence of jazz in his own work back in the early 1960s, he confirmed that he "loves trad jazz," but that traditional jazz, which was accepted in some venues, was at odds with the rock and roll music that was expected in other venues.[2] This suggests that in its early days the Dave Clark Five was torn between two gigging and career possibilities: (1) continue the jazz and instrumental focus and meet the needs of the officer's club dance circuit or (2) change the approach in order to move into the world of rock and roll.

Even after Mike Smith replaced Saxon as lead singer and Denis Payton took over saxophone duties, the Dave Clark Five's repertoire continued to include instrumentals. Recordings from 1962 and 1963 support this: the band's first single, "Chaquita," from mid-1962, is an obvious reworking of the famous Champs instrumental "Tequila." Likewise, other early recordings, such as the cover of Johnny Cash's "I Walk the Line," are instrumentals. These early instrumentals betray a stronger influence of jazz than is the case in many of the other commercially successful British Invasion bands. While Denis Payton's role on later Dave Clark Five recordings centers on 1950s rock-band and R&B-style honking solos and multitracked almost chorale-like backing, some of his solos on the 1962 and 1963 recordings suggest at least a familiarity with jazz and Boots Randolph-style—as opposed to rock and roll or R&B—tenor saxophone playing. Despite this, even some of the Dave Clark Five's early recordings find Payton relegated to the simple honking 1950s R&B-style tenor sax. Lenny Davidson's occasional guitar solos exhibit the influence of surf guitar, but especially of the Shadows, a band that was still quite popular on the British charts at the time. The presence of ballads, covers of instrumental pieces, and instrumental versions of songs all betray strong ties to the 1950s and the requirements of a working dance band that did not necessarily have teens as its only audience.

Despite the occasional guitar solo on the Dave Clark Five's early, prefame recordings, one of the more noticeable features of the band's overall sound once they developed their well-known, high-impact style was that the instrumental solos tended to focus on the saxophone or keyboards. In this respect, the basic sound of Dave Clark Five records stands out from just about every other group that hit the U.S. record charts as part of the British Invasion.

While the emphasis on 1950s-style saxophone clearly ties the basic Dave Clark Five sound to the Rocker aesthetic of the 1950s, Clark's production, with its in-your-face emphasis on the beat of the drums and the rhythm instruments, suggests the sonic impact of Mod bands such as the Who and the Kinks. Mike Smith's keyboard playing, too, adds significantly to the Rocker-Mod balancing act that was the Dave Clark Five's British Invasion–era sound. Smith's organ tone color and the organ figures he plays inhabit the world of modern rock keyboard. However, on tracks such as "Reelin' and Rockin'," a Chuck Berry composition, Smith plays piano in a style consistent with late 1950s pianists such as Little Richard and Jerry Lee Lewis.

The Dave Clark Five's transition from (1) a dance band that would even go so far as to program virtuoso jazz tunes such as "The Peanut Vendor" as showstoppers to (2) a Top 40 British beat group has not been particularly well documented in official biographies of the group. Incidentally, the band's original lead guitarist, Mick Ryan, recalls that, "The Peanut Vendor" "was brilliantly played by [guitarist] Jeff Rowena at the 'Royal' Tottenham [the London ballroom where the Dave Clark Five made its mark outside the dance circuit] . . . We were on a roundabout stage and as Jeff and his band were playing his signature instrumental, similar to guitar boogie, the stage revolved round and we appeared continuing playing this theme tune. The effect was tremendous, and the first time I played this it was the first time I played to so many people. I just ducked my head down and hoped for the best. I took some time learning this and everywhere I played it they loved it and ["The Peanut Vendor"] was always requested."[3] Ron Ryan, who remained associated with the band as a songwriter even after his brother Mick left the group,[4] claims that after the group tried to move in the prevailing beat group direction without much commercial success—at least as measured in record sales—he brought Doug Sheldon's cover of "Your Ma Said You Cried in Your Sleep Last Night" to Clark's attention. The Sheldon track features heavy drum playing, close miking of the drums, an emphasis on the tom-toms, and a multitracked, growling saxophone. According to Ryan, the sound of the Sheldon recording, which he defines as "crash, bang, wallop," became the basis for the Dave Clark Five's new style.[5] Ryan suggests that the style fit Clark's approach to the drums perfectly, since Clark liked to use the lower-pitched tom-toms for his fills. Indeed, the fills on the Dave Clark Five's 1963 recording of Ryan's composition "The Mulberry Bush" (issued as a single in the U.K. and apparently the first example of the new "crash, bang, wallop" style) all revolve around the lower drums. Interestingly (and perhaps not entirely accidentally), the main melodic phrases of one of the Dave Clark Five's early major "crash, bang, wallop" hits, "Bits and Pieces," closely resemble those of "Your Ma Said You Cried in Your Sleep Last Night."

The stylistic transition of the Dave Clark Five can be heard by comparing the band's earliest recordings, such as the 1962 instrumentals "First Love" and "Chaquita" and the early song "That's What I Said" (also from 1962) with "The Mulberry Bush," "Over and Over," "Bits and Pieces," "Any Way You Want It," and the band's other 1963–1964 high-impact songs. The light percussion style and the vocals-forward production on "That's What I Said" and other 1962 songs is not particularly distinctive and makes the Dave Clark Five resemble other anonymous, competent beat groups of the day. The adoption of the "crash, bang, wallop" style is what truly moved the Dave Clark Five away from being a popular dance group to being a rock and roll group that could elicit screams from fans.

One of Clark's principal contributions to his band was the record production he provided. It was exceedingly rare in the 1963–1965 period in both the United Kingdom and in the United States for artists to produce their own material—Brian Wilson of the Beach Boys being the notable exception. However, Clark worked out early business deals that allowed him to produce, that granted the Dave Clark Five a higher royalty rate than any of their contemporaries, and that gave Clark control of the master recordings. As a producer, Clark employed techniques that others—including that grand experimenter of British pop record production, Joe Meek—had used, including close miking, bringing the percussion forward in the mix, and using deliberately artificial-sounding studio echo; however, the overall sonic impact that Clark and the engineers with whom he worked achieved gave the group's 1963 and 1964 recordings a level of power that few other groups' recordings possessed.

I mentioned that "The Mulberry Bush" found Clark using a different approach to the drums than that which is heard on the band's earliest recordings. However, there are not necessarily just two (e.g., pre–"Mulberry Bush" and post–"Mulberry Bush") drum approaches on Dave Clark Five recordings. By the time of the band's biggest hits

In late 1964 and early 1965, the Beatles were challenged on the U.S. record charts more by the Dave Clark Five (pictured here at the height of their popularity) than by any other British Invasion group. The Dave Clark Five maintained an unusually strong tie to the musical aesthetics of the 1950s because of the prominence of group member Denis Payton's tenor and baritone saxophone playing. Courtesy of Photofest.

of 1964–1965, there seems to be another approach: the incorporation of military rudiments into the fills on the snare drums and the famous repeated snare drum triplets or sixteenth notes (depending on the metrical feel of the piece). Album cuts from 1963 and 1964 suggest the use of the two distinct approaches: (1) tom-tom fills largely without military rudiments versus (2) the snare drum fills that include classic rudiments. This would seem to support the persistent rumors that Clark himself did not play drums on all of the group's recordings.

Rumors about the use of studio musicians on Dave Clark Five recordings reached a peak in 2004 when famed studio drummer Bobby Graham detailed his extensive work on dozens of hits from the 1960s, including the major hits of the Dave Clark Five.[6] Graham's official Web site also includes a discography of his session work, including his purported performances on such Dave Clark Five hits as "Glad All Over," "Do You Love Me," "Bits and Pieces," "Catch Us If You Can," "Over and Over," "Can't You See That She's Mine," "Any Way You Want It," and other songs.[7] Because of the fact that Clark produced the band's recordings, it would make sense that he could not be playing the drums at the same time he would otherwise be occupied at the studio console, and eyewitness evidence to counter Graham's claim would be difficult to come by: Clark maintained closed recording sessions after being scooped by Brian Poole and the Tremeloes on covering the song "Do You Love Me." However, Graham's presence on some sessions would explain the differences in drum approaches between the hit singles and some album tracks.

What must be emphasized, however, is that the use of session musicians per se does not denigrate the importance or the musical abilities of a band or the individual musicians within a band. Studio musicians were employed far more frequently than is generally acknowledged. Bobby Graham's autobiography and Web site maintain that he performed on hit singles and albums by such well-known bands as Herman's Hermits, the Ivy League, the Animals ("Baby Let Me Take You Home" and "We Gotta Get out of this Place"), Brian Poole and the Tremeloes ("Twist and Shout," "Do You Love Me," and "Candy Man"), the Pretty Things, and the Kinks ("All Day and All of the Night," "Tired of Waiting for You," and "You Really Got Me").[8] And there is supporting evidence that Graham played on some of these sessions: Ray Davies of the Kinks confirmed that Graham played drums on all but one track on the band's first album.[9] That a group such as the Kinks could replace a band member with a studio musician for recording sessions, yet maintain strong street credibility and favor among critics suggests a double standard for the Dave Clark Five, a group that has been derided for using studio musicians.

Rumors about the use of other studio musicians on Dave Clark Five recordings probably were also exacerbated by the group's extensive use of miming for many of their "live" television appearances. Some bands and managers did not trust the audio quality of television and preferred to have their televised product sound its best (and just like the record), even if the lack of authenticity of the performance might be detected by viewers. In the case of the Dave Clark Five, lip synching is all too easy to spot because of the way in which Clark as a producer used overdubbing in the studio and because of the visual focus on Clark at the drums. For example, in appearances on programs such as *The Ed Sullivan Show* and *Shindig!* on which the group appears to perform "Over and Over," Denis Payton plays the harmonica solo at the same time as his tenor saxophone is heard. At other times, the drum pattern that Clark is seen playing does not match the audio track. Some television appearances of the group seem to have them performing live, but along with a partial backing track. In these performances, such as at an ASCAP awards ceremony hosted by Ed Sullivan that has circulated widely on the Internet, Mike Smith appears to be singing live, and the microphone that is placed next to Clark's tom-tom picks up its sound; however, there are still places in which the visuals and what is heard do not entirely jibe. Because so many of these appearances are available on the Internet and on "best of" DVDs from 1960s musical variety shows, it makes for intriguing detective work, particularly for the viewer who wants to try to match up Clark's drumming, Payton's saxophone fingerings, and other aspects of the visual performance with what is heard on the audio track. In comparison, many of the Beatles' performances on American television programs in 1964 and 1965 clearly are live: the vocals, tempos of the songs, guitar solos, and drum fills vary from the studio recordings, and the visuals match the televised audio track.

The Dave Clark Five was not alone in miming for television. For example, one can find appearances of the Rolling Stones (one of the rare British Invasion bands that actually issued live recordings back in the 1960s) in which close-ups on Mick Jagger's mouth, Charlie Watts's drums, or what Brian Jones or Keith Richards appear to be playing on guitar reveal a discrepancy between the visuals and the audio track—a discrepancy that cannot be explained by a sound delay. Likewise, some television appearances of the Searchers performing "Love Potion Number Nine" have an audio track with Tony Jackson's original lead vocal, even though he was no longer in the band and was nowhere to be seen on the television screen.

While lip synching, miming—call it what you like—caused persistent rumors about the Dave Clark Five's musical credibility, it should be noted that the rare televised segments that actually show the band performing live (such as the jams at the conclusion of each episode of *Shindig!* in which each of the week's guest stars perform a truncated spot in quick succession) make it clear that they really did play. The Dave Clark Five toured extensively, and before they achieved worldwide fame, they performed at the top clubs and at what we today would call the A-list military base venues—as well as ballrooms— around London. Clearly, they had to be a top-notch live unit to rise to the peak of what was a highly competitive circuit. Still, the miming on American television in a period in which many other major British bands performed live helped to perpetuate questions about the Dave Clark Five's musical credibility.

The group's musical credibility has also suffered as a result of questions that have arisen over the authorship of some of the Dave Clark Five's major hits. In particular, Ron Ryan claims that he played a role in writing more than the few songs for which he actually received credit on the group's record labels. According to Ryan, he agreed to ghostwrite songs for Clark so that it would appear that the group's material was self-composed. Ryan claims that only when a report appeared in the *Sunday Mirror* in 1964 that suggested he was planning to sue Clark over unpaid royalties did any compensation come his way. He claims, however, that the out-of-court agreement remunerated him far less than the amount of royalties Clark collected, especially for hits such as "Because" and "Any Way You Want It." According to Ryan, after this he was barred from any contact with the group.[10] Apparently none of Ryan and Clark's alleged agreements were ever recorded on paper, so it is difficult to establish the validity of Ryan's claims. However, there is some evidence of stylistic connections between songs for which Ryan received credit and those for which he did not. It should be noted that investigation suggests that at the very least there are some curious anomalies in some of the songwriting credits as they appear on record labels and album covers. For example, the single release of "No Time to Lose" (Epic 5–9692) and the credits on the U.S. album *Glad All Over* list Dave Clark and Mike Smith as the writers; however, the database maintained by the American Society of Composers, Authors, and Publishers (ASCAP) (under title No. 440055736) credits Clark and Ryan with the song.[11]

Let us take a brief look at some of the musical connections between songs for which Ron Ryan received credit and other material not credited to him. These connections revolve around the use of modal ambiguity (the mixing of chords and melodic intervals that create a deliberate ambiguity about whether the piece is in a major key or that key's relative natural minor key), chromatic voice leading, and chromatic harmonies. For example, Ryan's composition "Sometimes,"[12] an AABA form song that the Dave Clark Five included on their 1964 album *American Tour,* although in the key of F major, makes heavy use of the three diatonically occurring minor chords of the key (ii, G minor; iii, A minor; and vi, D minor) in the A sections, while almost studiously avoiding the tonic (F major) chord. In fact, "Sometimes" begins with an oscillation between the G minor and the A minor chords, which creates an even stronger minor mode feel to the piece. It is only after hearing the delayed move to F major (which itself moves to the D minor chord) that the tonic key is confirmed. The result is that the music has an inherently mournful quality to it. This mournful quality fits the sense of loss that is integral to the lyrics. The bridge (section B) of "Sometimes" features chromatic upper voice motion in the harmony and vocal line that results from the section's opening B-flat major chord (with the pitch D, the third of the chord, in the upper voice) moving to a B-flat minor chord (with D-flat in the upper voice). The emotional and musical tug of war between sorrow and optimism (minor and major) is not entirely unlike that heard in such songs as Lennon and McCartney's "It Won't Be Long"; however, "Sometimes" is more subtle and subdued—whereas John Lennon (as lead singer and principal writer) leans toward the optimistic, Ron Ryan (as writer) and Mike Smith (as singer) lean more toward sorrow.

The song "Because," easily the Dave Clark Five's best-known ballad, is credited to Clark alone; however, it is one of the songs for which authorship is a matter of contention.[13] Although the two songs clearly are not clones of each other, "Because" exhibits the same kind of chromatic voice leading from chord to chord as "Sometimes." "Because" contains an even stronger signifier of British pop in the form of the bVI chord that directly precedes the V chord at the end of each iteration of the A section (it also occurs just before the end of the organ solo). The B section of this AABA form piece contains a touch of the modal ambiguity of "Sometimes." It is also worth noting that there are melodic shape relationships between the opening melodic phrase of "Because" and a significant phrase in the B section of "Sometimes."

In addition to the modal ambiguity and chromatic voice leading that is shared by "Because" and "Sometimes," songs such as "Can't You See That She's Mine," "That's What I Said," and "Glad All Over" include chromatic melodic motion to a greater extent than what one hears in the music of other British Invasion groups. This can be heard in "That's What I Said" on the line "I need you like I need a hole in the head," the chromatic motion on the words "pull us apart" in "Can't You See That She's Mine," and the chromatic scale fragment on the words "And I'm feelin'" in "Glad All Over." Regardless of who wrote these five songs, the chromatic melodic and inner-voice motion sets them apart from the work of many other British Invasion bands and thereby give the Dave Clark Five a melodic style hook that pulls a chunk of their 1962–1964 repertoire together. And perhaps that is the most important thing: the musical connections themselves are so general that it is doubtful they prove that the same writer was responsible for all of the songs for which royalties have been in dispute; the alleged agreement apparently was never put on paper, and questionable label credits were commonplace in the recording industry in the 1950s and 1960s. The quality of this repertoire and its staying power—some of the Dave Clark Five's recordings are still heard on oldies radio stations and on piped-in music systems 45 years after their initial run of popularity—is really what counts.

Stylistic connections between the melodies of the songs named above, though, are not the biggest or the most important hooks that set the Dave Clark Five apart from other British Invasion bands. In fact, *All Music Guide*'s Rick Clark and Richie Unterberger point to Clark's production, the emphasis on the drums, and Mike Smith's "leathery vocals" as the band's most important hooks.[14] Smith's vocals, though, are easy to overlook, perhaps because of the emphasis on rhythm and power in the overall mix. Mike Smith sang with a wide pitch range, and despite Rick Clark and Richie Unterberger's characterization of his voice as "leathery," he covered a wide stylistic range, from the rock and roll screaming to gentle ballad style. Compared with other British Invasion successes, Smith's appeal is almost a natural. His singing was not idiosyncratic like some lead singers; it could be alternately powerful or pretty, but it was instantly recognizable.

While the Dave Clark Five balanced Mod and Rocker tendencies, they are one of the few groups of the British Invasion that managed to continue to have hits both in the United Kingdom and the United States through the psychedelic era without following current trends. The closest they ever really came to psychedelia in the 1966–1967 era was the song "Inside and Out," a recording that anticipated the emphasis on the cello and the tempo and meter changes of the Beatles' "Strawberry Fields Forever." The Dave Clark Five essentially remained a rock and roll band right up until they disbanded in 1970, carrying on the balance of the Mod and Rocker aesthetics far longer than most of their British Invasion colleagues. And, while their record sales dropped off in the late 1960s in both the United Kingdom and the United States, over the course of 1964–1967 the Dave Clark Five, with their unique blend of references to the old and the new, enjoyed 17 Top 40 singles in the United States, including 8 Top 10s. The Dave Clark Five was inducted into the Rock and Roll Hall of Fame in 2008, unfortunately a week after the death of Mike Smith.

6

The Who and the Kinks: Mod to the Core

The conventional wisdom about the importance of the various British Invasion bands is that while there were lots and lots of artists who made it onto the U.S. record charts and radio airwaves, there were "the big four," and everyone else. The so-called big four consists of the Beatles, the Rolling Stones, the Who, and the Kinks. These were not necessarily the biggest-selling artists of the British Invasion in terms of pop singles: for example, between 1964 and 1967 Herman's Hermits and the Dave Clark Five each had over twice as many U.S. Top 40 singles as the Kinks; and the Who, which had Top 40 singles in the 1960s, 1970s, and 1980s, never did garner as many as either Herman's Hermits or the Dave Clark Five. In their own ways, however, the Beatles, the Rolling Stones, the Who, and the Kinks either dominated the charts or influenced other songwriters and bands for decades, while most of the other British Invasion bands did far less to influence musical trends. One member of the big four, the Beatles, exhibited the influence of everything from R&B, to 1950s rock and roll, to Broadway, to the British music hall, to the issues of gender and identity of the Mods. Another member, the Rolling Stones, started as a blues band, but aside from a few forays into folk, country, and psychedelia, they pretty much remained a blues-based rock and roll band. The other two members of this exclusive club, the Kinks and the Who, however, represented Mod aesthetics through and through.

THE KINKS

We shall begin our look at the truly Mod bands of the British Invasion with the Kinks, because their earliest hits, "You Really Got Me" and "All Day and All of the

Night," pre-date the earliest famous Mod recordings of the Who. Even though the Kinks were not a commercial force on the same level of the Beatles, the Rolling Stones, Herman's Hermits, and several other British Invasion bands, they were among the most influential. Perhaps because this band came together closer in time to the British Invasion than groups such as the Rolling Stones, Gerry and the Pacemakers, and the Beatles, the covers that they recorded early in their career seem a bit dated, even by 1964 and 1965 standards. Early on, too, the Kinks recorded songs written by their record producer, Shel Talmy that, in the words of *All Music Guide*'s Richie Unterberger, "were simply abominable."[1] However—and it is a big however—the brilliant songs written by Ray Davies made the Kinks' first two albums much better and more influential than the work of any other competent British R&B band of the day, and this despite the inclusion of other material of dubious quality.

Before delving into this repertoire and the unique musical contributions of the Kinks to the gamut of sounds that formed the British Invasion, let us first look briefly at the development and early career of the band. Brothers Ray (born June 21, 1944) and Dave (born February 3, 1947) Davies, from the Muswell Hill section of London, began playing skiffle and rock and roll music as teens. It must be remembered, though, that because of their ages, the Davies brothers' first experience with skiffle and rock and roll came not during the skiffle craze of 1954–1957, but later, by the time the more folk-oriented aspects of earlier skiffle had given way to rockabilly.

The Davies brothers, along with Peter Quaife (guitar and bass) and Mick Willet (drums) formed the Ravens in 1963. By early 1964, a demo recording by the group found its way to the American record producer Shel Talmy, who worked at Pye Records. By the time the Ravens were signed and recorded their first single, Mick Avory had replaced Willet on drums. The band also changed its name to the Kinks sometime between the recording of their first single in late January 1964 and the record's release in February. This single, a cover of Little Richard's "Long Tall Sally," was not a hit. However, study of the recording provides some insight into what made the early Kinks different from other British Invasion bands.

The Kinks' recording of "Long Tall Sally" differs from Little Richard's original recording and most of the British covers in several respects. First of all, instead of the shuffle rhythm feel of the original, the Kinks perform the song with straight eighth notes. This instantly moves "Long Tall Sally" from 1950s R&B/rock and roll and securely into the 1960s. By comparison, the Beatles in their well-known recording from March 1, 1964 create rhythmic tension by combining the shuffle feel and implied swing of Ringo Starr's drum part with straight eighth notes in the piano, thereby balancing the 1950s and the 1960s feel. The Kinks, too, limit their arrangement to two guitars, bass, drums, and a harmonica solo. This, too, is significant. It has been well established that Ray Davies sometimes wrote at the piano, and on recordings that the Kinks made shortly after their "Long Tall Sally" single, studio musicians Arthur Greenslade, Perry Ford, and Nicky Hopkins were employed to play the occasional piano parts. Therefore, it would not have been completely out of the question for the Kinks to have included piano on "Long Tall Sally." The absence of the instrument—the instrument that Little Richard played—is another rejection of the sonic aesthetics of 1950s rock and roll and establishes the Kinks as an intentionally guitar-based 1960s-style band. The expressionless vocals also contrast with the impassioned approach taken by Little Richard and by the Beatles' Paul McCartney on their recordings of the song. The vocal approach here aligns with the sense of "boredom, listlessness, ennui, a sense of drifting aimlessness and lack of any specific plans"[2] that was part of the Mod mentality. In general, the almost technique-less vocal style of the Davies brothers contrasts with that of all the other British Invasion groups. Other singers tended to sound pretty, or passionate, or even menacing. Here, though,

The combination of the focus on alienation and life on the fringes of society and musical experimentation in the songwriting of Ray Davies, and the deliberately distorted guitar playing of Dave Davies, helped to make the Kinks (pictured here circa 1965) one of the most prominent Mod bands of the British Invasion. Along with the Beatles, the Rolling Stones, and the Who, the Kinks were among the most highly influential British Invasion bands on rock music of the 1960s and 1970s. Courtesy of Photofest.

one hears a garage-band, punk quality. While the Kinks' anticipation of the edginess of later punk rock became even more evident in the distorted electric guitar tone that Dave Davies employed at recording sessions in August and October 1964, the vocals on "Long Tall Sally" anticipate not only slightly later Mod groups, such as the Creation, but also the approach taken by the Ramones in the 1970s.

Incidentally, this almost expressionless vocal style probably is easiest to detect on covers, because the listener can compare the Kinks' version to other recordings. For example, their version of Chuck Berry's "Too Much Monkey Business" does not capture the mix of anger and resignation of the original, in large part because of the general vocal approach. Incidentally, though, the Kinks were not alone in missing some of the subtle undertones of Berry's singing. The Beatles' live recording of the song for the BBC finds John Lennon singing in such a straightforward style that he, too stresses words and tune over the recreation of Berry's mood. The Hollies come closer in their recording from the same time period, and they use tossed-around lead vocals to play on some of the humor of the lyrics.

Ray and Dave Davies are not as well known to the general public as some other rock songwriters of the British Invasion era, such as John Lennon, Paul McCartney, Keith Richards, Mick Jagger, and Pete Townshend. It can be argued, however, that Ray Davies in particular was at least as forward thinking as a composer and lyricist as were any of his perhaps better-known contemporaries. He also was at least as influential as any of his contemporaries on later generations of rock musicians. In order to see some of the forward-looking and ultimately influential traits of Davies as a writer and the Kinks as a musical unit, let us examine three of the Kinks' most popular early hits.

Although the song became best known in 1965 and, therefore, came to the attention of the record-buying public after "You Really Got Me" and "All Day and All of the Night," let us first examine the Ray Davies composition "Tired of Waiting for You." This song illuminates a great deal about Davies's musical and lyrical style—features that became essential defining ingredients of the Kinks style throughout the 1960s. The lyrics are minimalist, with a haiku-like brevity that basically just describes a state of being. The Zen-like minimalism and state-of-being focus anticipates not only some of Davies's later songs but also anticipates some of the work of David Bowie. Unlike most pop songs, which have several stanzas of poetry for each verse and perhaps a refrain or chorus section that features the same words each time it is heard, here Davies associates only one set of words with each section of music. Musically, the song clearly has three distinct sections, but none function like a verse section in conventional rock songs—in other words, there seems only to be one stanza of poetry, built in three sections. Another feature of the lyrics that is unusual for the early 1960s, but is fully consistent with the work of some later writers, is the vagueness of the exact nature of the relationship between the character who waits (the singer) and the one for whom he waits. They could be lovers, but the also could be friends, or in some other kind of relationship. Some listeners might associate lyrical impressionism and vagueness more with the psychedelic rock of 1967 than with a song from this period, but here Davies anticipates the trend. It should also be mentioned that the lyrics of "Tired of Waiting for You" contain clear Mod signifiers, particularly in the prechorus section (some of the musical attributes of this section will be discussed shortly). Here, Davies tells the person for whom his character waits, "It's you life, and you can do what you want." The expression of personal freedom runs through many Mod songs: the Who's "My Generation" may be the most famous example. Also at the heart of this song and other Mod songs from the mid-1960s is the somewhat contradictory expression of belonging, yet somehow still being an outsider. Just the fact that the song is about the process of waiting also makes it part of the Mod scene. As Stanley Cohen writes in his sociological study of the Mods and Rockers, *Folk Devils and Moral Panics,* "their aim was excitement, but for most of time nothing happened and so the dominant feelings were boredom, listlessness, ennui, a sense of drifting aimlessness and lack of any specific plans."[3] So, with its early composition date, "Tired of Waiting for You" anticipates the music of the Who, the Creation, and other Mod groups. These lyrical traits would find their way into the music of the British punk rock and postpunk music of the late 1970s, particularly in Paul Weller's compositions for his band, the Jam.

Musically, too, "Tired of Waiting for You" is quite unlike other early 1960s rock. For one thing, the melody of the chorus—easily the most memorable part of this song melodically—outlines the Mixolydian scale. In fact, the harmonic oscillation between the tonic chord (I) and a major triad whose root is a whole-step below tonic (bVII) is fully compatible with the use of the Mixolydian mode. So Davies goes one step beyond the modal mixture of songwriters from Buddy Holly (in the United States) to Marty Wilde, Billy Fury, Johnny Kidd, and some of the British Invasion songwriters toward modality. The use of the church modes was at the time exceedingly rare in popular music; however, Davies experimented with modal melodic writing over a harmonic drone very early in the history of the Kinks, anticipating the influence of Hindustani music on the Byrds, the Beatles, and other groups that used modality in 1966 and 1967. In "Tired of Waiting for You," the Mixolydian mode of the chorus confirms the Zen-like state of being nature of the lyrics: unlike the major scale, which provides the listener with a sense of goal-directedness in part because of its leading tone (the seventh scale-step), which tends to "feel" to Western listeners, the Mixolydian scale has a seventh scale-step that is a whole-step below the key note (upward-moving scalar whole-steps tend to have less of a sense of goal-directed urgency to Western ears).

The key changes and structure of "Tired of Waiting for You" also defy early 1960s conventions. Since the Tin Pan Alley era (roughly the 1880s into the 1940s), several key relationship conventions have governed a large number of popular songs. For example, in the 1930s and 1940s, the bridge section of George Gershwin's "I Got Rhythm" provided a harmonic paradigm that numerous writers used. In that particular song, Gershwin begins the bridge with a focus on the major quality mediant chord (E major, in the key of C major) and then moves around the circle of fifths (chords whose roots are the interval of a perfect fifth apart) until the dominant of the original key is reached. This gives the bridge of "I Got Rhythm" a goal-directedness back to tonic (E, A, D, G [the dominant, which resolves back to C]). A fair number of popular songs of the late 1950s and early 1960s used what some musicians call the oldies progression (I, vi, IV, V) as a repeated harmonic pattern that continued throughout the entire song. Other songs were in classic 12-bar blues form. In popular songs that changed key for the bridge, the most common motion was to the subdominant (e.g., to the key of C major in a song in the key of G major). In "Tired of Waiting for You," the verse sections begin a whole-step below the original key center (e.g., F major, when one performs the song in the key of G). Interestingly, because the chorus section (which is heard at the beginning and in the fade out of the piece) frames the song, and features an oscillation between I and bVII (G major and F major), and because the principal modulation is to the key of F, Davies gives the listener the I to bVII oscillation on a micro and on a macro level. Incidentally, just as the lyrics of "Tired of Waiting for You" contain Mod subthemes, the remote modulations and the extensive use of the subtonic chord are musical signifiers of Mod rock music.

Another unusual feature of "Tired of Waiting for You" that deserves special mention is the prechorus section. This nine-measure section[4] ("It's your life, and you can do what you want") includes vague harmonic relationships (e.g., the modal mixture of B minor, F major, D7, and G major chords). Because it begins with the B minor chord (an unusual starting point in a G major song), the section seems to leap out at the listener. It is as if the music shifts harmonic focus the way in which a person's mental focus might shift from thought to thought as they are waiting for someone who seems to be taking far too long to arrive.

Although it is described by noted rock critic and historian Dave Marsh as "Ray Davies's original 'Louie Louie' rewrite,"[5] "You Really Got Me" is really much more than the Kinks' version of the 1956 Richard Berry R&B composition made notorious by the Kingsmen's 1963 garage band recording. Certainly, the two songs share the use of an oft-repeated riff, but the electric guitar riff in the Davies composition is fundamentally different. The melodic contours of the opening phrases of the verse of "You Really Got Me" also resembles the opening melodic material of "Louie Louie"; however, the Davies composition moves in such a fundamentally different direction after the opening of the verse that, while it may bear the influence of "Louie Louie," the Davies work is much more than a rewrite.

"You Really Got Me" opens with a minimalist distorted electric guitar riff that uses power chords[6] on A-flat (I) and G-flat (bVII).[7] The guitar riff continues through the first phrase of the vocals. Then the pitch center moves up a whole step to B-flat. Ray Davies did not invent modulation by ascending whole step. That tonal relationship is unusual enough in pop music, though, that it adds to the feeling of novelty of "You Really Got Me." It should be noted that unusual and somewhat unpredictable modulations, which were written both by Davies and by Pete Townshend in some of the most overtly Mod songs of 1964–1965, were one of the signifiers of "Mod-ness."

One of the important things to note about the guitar riff on "You Really Got Me" is that it is unquestionably a *guitar* riff. Using barre chords, the guitarist keeps the same basic fingering shape and simply moves up or down on the fretboard. This riff does not as easily translate to keyboard. So, just as rural blues seems to represent a harmonic practice based on the guitar as a performing medium, the extensive use of power chords moving in completely parallel motion on "You Really Got Me" also suggests a guitar-specific approach to composition. Incidentally, credit for this probably should go to guitarist Dave Davies; the song's composer, his brother Ray, is said to have written the music at the piano. This is where "You Really Got Me" fundamentally differs from "Louie Louie" and other earlier riff pieces with which it sometimes is compared. The harmonic ostinato of "Louie Louie" is not necessarily guitar specific—it can be played on the piano just as easily as on guitar. Likewise, riff-based pieces from the boogie-woogie repertoire do not necessarily suggest a guitar-specific technique (those riffs can be played just as effectively on, say, piano)—"You Really Got Me" (as it was eventually arranged and recorded), with its sliding parallel motion, is a guitar-based piece.

The Kinks' "You Really Got Me" was an impressive hit, reaching No. 1 on the U.K. pop charts and No. 7 in the United States. One thing that is immediately apparent is an almost punk-rock-like rhythmic drive. The edgy, driving, distorted sound of the record is part of its appeal. While "You Really Got Me" was not alone in this regard—the Kingsmen's slightly earlier "Louie Louie" probably owed part of its popularity to a grimy, garage band sound—the record bucked the style usually heard on radio at the time.

Unfortunately, the Kinks were barred from touring the United States after their first tour for reasons that have never been explained. The result was that, despite the success of "You Really Got Me" and the singles that immediately followed it ("All Day and All of the Night" and "Tired of Waiting for You") it took the Kinks considerably more time to develop a widespread following in the United States than other British Invasion bands.

Over the years, discussion of the early recordings of the Kinks has been rife with speculation about the extent to which studio musicians were used. In the case of "You Really Got Me," the first time the Kinks recorded the song, they were somewhere in the process of changing drummers. Therefore, producer Shel Talmy hired session drummer

Bobby Graham to play. The Kinks were not pleased with Talmy's thin production and the fast, Merseybeat style they affected for the recording, so they held out for a second session on the song. By the time the second recording—the one that became the smash hit—was made, Mick Avory was the Kinks' drummer. In a scene reminiscent of Ringo Starr's start with the Beatles, producer Talmy did not trust the new drummer and therefore hired Graham to play. Just like Starr on the Beatles' single version of "Love Me Do," Avory was relegated to the tambourine. Arthur Greenslade played the minimal piano part on "You Really Got Me," and for other early Kinks recording sessions, studio musicians such as Nicky Hopkins (piano), Jon Lord (organ), and Jimmy Page (guitar) were hired to fill out the group's sound.[8]

The story of the Kinks struggle to recreate the essence of their live sound in the studio, and the initial reluctance of Shel Talmy to capture the power of the band, calls to mind the Rolling Stones' first recording, a cover of the Chuck Berry composition "Come On," on which the band was forced to adopt a pseudo-Merseybeat style that bore little resemblance to the band's live sound. That the Kinks were able to rerecord "You Really Got Me"—and with the deliberate use of distortion, no less—illustrates the changes that were going on in 1964 in the British recording industry. The R&B scene was showing itself to be popular enough that hard-edged bands such as the Kinks, the Rolling Stones, the Animals, and the Yardbirds at least stood a chance of having something that came close to their natural style committed to vinyl.

Ray Davies' well-known song, "All Day and All of the Night," moves even farther away from the prevailing pop music of 1964. For one thing, Davies builds the song on a short riff motive, which basically surrounds the tonic pitch with the subtonic (a whole step below) and the minor submediant (a minor third above tonic). All of these notes are harmonized with open fifths (power chords). Not only does Davies base the motive and its harmonization on a fully saturated use of modal mixture—at least as fully saturated as three open fifths can imply—he also writes unconventional modulations. The four-measure-long transition from the verse to the chorus revolves around the dominant of the dominant (an A major chord in this G major song). The chorus moves to the key of the dominant (D) and uses a transposition of the riff motive from the verse. This total reliance on a single motive gives the song an organic feel. The move to the key of the dominant is not particularly common in rock music; generally, most rock songs move to the key of the subdominant. The fact that "All Day and All of the Night" modulated up a whole-step higher than what is conventional gives the song a feeling of moving into a higher energy feel as the lyrics find the singer telling his lover, "Girl, I want to be with you all of the time."

Now, let us examine the Mod aspects of the work of the Who before comparing the two bands and examining their impact on later rock music.

THE WHO

When one considers the Who as a British Invasion band, it is always important to keep in mind that some of their best-known and most acclaimed work comes from closer to the end of the 1960s. Indeed, as unlikely as it might seem, the Who did not place a single into the U.S. Top 40 until 1967. The Who's influence and their role as one of the quintessential Mod bands, however, go well beyond mass record sales.

As ironic as it might sound based on the Who's eventual style, bass guitarist John Entwistle and guitarist Pete Townshend first performed together as teenagers in a Dixie-land band in which Entwistle played trumpet and Townshend played banjo. Entwistle, incidentally, remained a competent brass player, eventually playing the French horn part on the Who's recording of the "Overture" from *Tommy*. In 1962, Entwistle joined a rock band called the Detours, which was led by guitarist Roger Daltrey. Townshend then joined the band on rhythm guitar. By the time Keith Moon, formerly a drummer in a surf band called the Beachcombers, became the Detours' drummer, Daltrey took over lead vocals, which left Townshend to carry on as the sole guitarist. Apparently, this was in part influenced by the fact that the Detours opened for Johnny Kidd and the Pirates and were impressed with that band's texture of lead singer supported by three instrumentalists.

At the suggestion of Townshend's roommate, Richard Barnes, the Detours renamed themselves the Who.[9] They subsequently became the High Numbers (a Mod slang term) and adapted their stage dress in order to appeal to R&B fans. After changing names and working to define themselves stylistically, Entwistle, Moon, Daltrey, and Townshend returned to calling themselves the Who, and they adopted a thoroughly Mod appearance. With the encouragement of their managers, Kit Lambert and Chris Stamp, the Who wore shirts imprinted with the Mod target in a direct attempt to appeal to members of the subculture.

Mods of the day were very style and clothes conscious. The members of the Who came from the Shepherds Bush area of London, a hotbed of Mod activity, and it was in that area that the band performed most often in their early days. Ironically, considering the working-class nature of the locale and the Mods themselves, fashion was a concern. Whatever money was available for young people who were part of the scene seemed to go into stylistically appropriate clothing. Despite the cost, this was seen as a way of, symbolically at least, breaking free of the dreariness of working-class life.

The early Who's live sets were focused on covers of American blues, Motown, R&B, and soul songs. They dubbed their energetic, sometimes double-tempo approach to African American music "Maximum R&B." While the Who focused on Mods and those young people who shared the aesthetics of the Mods, it must be remembered that the actual Mods were a gang. Possibly, part of the Mod appeal of the Who was the almost manic approach that Keith Moon took to playing the drums, as well as Pete Townshend's eventual practice—which first developed because of an accident—of smashing his guitar at the conclusion of performances. The implied violence of the Who's live performance was enhanced by Townshend's deliberate use of feedback.

Pete Townshend's use of feedback, his smashing of guitars and dramatic windmill strumming patterns, combined with Moon's wild, virtuosic drumming, and Roger Daltrey's near-snarl as he sang and moved about the stage, fit squarely in with the world of gangs in general. The band's R&B-based repertoire and Townshend's early compositions—such as "I Can't Explain"—that dealt in part with issues surrounding identity, however, had specific appeal to the Mods and not to the Rockers.

After some early unsuccessful singles that were recorded before the band defined its style (or adopted its eventual name), Lambert and Stamp brought Townshend's song

From his Mod anthems "My Generation" and "The Kids Are Alright" to the rock opera *Tommy* and beyond, the Who's Pete Townshend (pictured here circa early 1970s) is one of the most important songwriters to come out of the British Invasion. Courtesy of Photofest.

"I Can't Explain" to the attention of record producer Shel Talmy. Talmy, an American working in the United Kingdom, had established solid credentials within the emerging British Mod musical community with his production of the Kinks' early hits.

Britain's Decca Records released the Who's recording of "I Can't Explain" in January 1965. After an initial lack of sales success, the single took off when the Who appeared on the television program *Ready Steady Go!*, a program that continued the tradition of bringing new rock music to the attention of British youth that had been established in the 1950s with *Six-Five Special* and *Oh Boy!* It seemed as though the group's energetic, violent performance (both Townshend and Moon destroyed their instruments on the television show), formed a synergy with Townshend's music to create a complete package—something that the music itself did not necessarily accomplish without benefit of the visual image of the band. The Who and those surrounding them at the time also credit the ship-based pirate station Radio Caroline with the single's success: while airplay on Britain's official radio service, the BBC, was minimal, Radio Caroline placed "I Can't Explain" in its rotation.[10]

This brings up an important part of the Who's work: their live performances formed the basis for their recordings to a greater extent than most of their British Invasion colleagues. In other words, of all the British bands of the 1960s, the Who probably sounded the most similar when their live recordings and studio recordings are compared. The combination of music and the visual aspects of their live performances, however, also move in the direction of performance art. The tradition of using at least implied destruction and violence can be found in avant-garde performance art back in the Dada movement of the post–World War I era, as well as in the Fluxus movement of the 1950s and 1960s. In both of these movements, various art forms were combined (e.g., music, visual arts, poetry) in new ways that broke free of the traditional and formal genre boundaries of the past. Both Dada and Fluxus had at their core an anti-art basis—hence the emphasis on breaking down traditional boundaries—as well as the use of destruction as an act of creation. While all of the members of the Who might not have had an extensive knowledge of the work of Marcel Duchamp, John Cage, Dick Higgins, Jackson Mac Low, and others, the organized near-chaos of their performances fits into a greater extent with Dada and Fluxus aesthetics than does the work of bands such as the Beatles and the Rolling Stones, not to mention more pop-oriented artists such as Herman's Hermits and a host of others. Pete Townshend states that he was aware of the auto-destructive art of Gustav Metzger from a lecture he attended at art school.[11] So, while Townshend saw the deliberate destruction of instruments as performance art, it just fit in with the over-the-top personality of Keith Moon, who took to destroying drum sets, even to the point of secretly placing explosives in his bass drum for an appearance on the *Smothers Brothers Comedy Hour*.

Even before the deliberate destruction of guitars, amplifiers, and drum sets, though, the Who was very much a band of atmosphere. In the early twenty-first century, film footage that Kit Lambert and Chris Stamp shot of the Who in 1964—when they were known as the High Numbers—surfaced. Lambert and Stamp shot the footage in and around the Railway Hotel as part of a proposed documentary on the London Mod scene. Although Lambert and Stamp never completed the documentary, the footage they shot shows much about the scene and provides a rare look at a soon-to-be-famous band in its developmental stages. Perhaps just as impressive, the visual and audio quality are quite good compared with the poor quality news documentary footage of, say, the Beatles performing "Some Other Guy" at the Cavern Club before they were a worldwide entertainment phenomenon. Lambert and Stamp's footage—as included as bonus material in the 2007 documentary *Amazing Journey: The Story of the Who*—begins by showing a group of Mods gathered around their Vespa scooters outside the performance venue. The High Numbers perform two R&B songs. Even at this early stage, Pete Townshend includes a few dramatic windmills, and Roger Daltrey (who wears dark sunglasses in the film) sings with some of the vocal sneer that he developed further within the next year. The texture of the band—with its one guitar, one bass, and drums supporting Daltrey's lead vocals—is already fundamentally different than that of contemporary bands with two guitarists and/or a keyboardist. While not as fully developed, bass guitarist John Entwistle clearly plays in a more technically advanced style than what is conventional in British R&B bands of the day. In addition to maintaining a bass line, he plays some of the fills that might more conventionally be played by a lead guitarist. But Entwistle's Who personality as the stoic, never-moving figure is not quite fully formed: he moves as he plays and sings backing vocals in a manner close to that of other rock musicians of the day. Keith Moon plays in a manner closer to that of typical British R&B drummers than the almost manic approach he would take in live performances by the next year. All of this suggests that the extremes that the Who's live performances exhibited by 1965 might have been based on the deliberate exaggeration of tendencies that each of the musicians had.

The Mod audience themselves behave quite differently than the manic, screaming audiences of Liverpool's Cavern Club, as captured in early news footage of Gerry and the Pacemakers and the Beatles, and as captured on the Big Three's EP, *Live at the Cavern*. For one thing, the crowd is less densely packed at the Railway Hotel. For another, the Mods appear to be more into their own dancing in their own disparate styles and not as fixated on the band, or as uniform in their movement as the so-called Cave dwellers. This less communal-looking atmosphere surrounding the High Numbers suggests alienation from society, emphasis on the individual, and an intentional sense of coolness.

Incidentally, it was at a performance at this venue—the Railway Hotel—that Pete Townshend first destroyed a guitar. Even though the first time was an accident, it created such a stir in the Mod community that the band's audience immediately grew: some young people came just to see if the destruction was part of the act. It became an audience expectation that Townshend was obliged to meet.

What is missing from the High Numbers' filmed performance at the Railway Hotel is the brilliance of Pete Townshend's slightly later Mod anthems. The first of these, "I Can't Explain," makes for interesting study on several levels. For one thing, because Shel Talmy produced the Who's recording, it is interesting to note that the song is based primarily on a short oft-repeated guitar riff. Although the chord progressions and the melodic riffs are not the same, the riff-based *nature* of the piece resembles songs such as "All Day and All of the Night" that Talmy earlier had produced for the Kinks. In considering "I Can't Explain," though, let us begin by examining the lyrics.

On the surface, Townshend creates a character that describes unusual physical feelings he has, because he is in love for the first time. Beneath the surface, however, Townshend's lyrics explore the broader issue of identity. This theme emerges because Townshend places the emphasis not on the character's maladies but on the title line: the fact that he cannot explain his maladies. This suggests a lack of self-identity on the part of the character. His own definition of self is called into question, as it is not too much of a stretch to hear him expressing as much concern over the fact that he "can't explain" why he feels as he does, as he expresses over the new feelings themselves. Listeners who have not heard "I Can't Explain" that way—with an emphasis on the definition of self—are encouraged to try to hear that the theme of identity, because it sets the stage for a large amount of Pete Townshend's work from that point forward in his career as a songwriter. And the concern with self-definition was at the core of the Mod experience, at least as documented by Lambert and Stamp in their 1964 film footage of the prefame Who. For the Who, the broader issue of identity—both self-defined identity and how one perceives the real or hidden identity of another—is at the core of individual songs (e.g., "My Generation") and larger works (e.g., *Tommy* and *Quadrophenia*).

Between early 1965 and early 1966, the Who released a series of important singles that succeeded in expanding the group's audience and showing the range of their performing and writing abilities. "Anyway, Anyhow, Anywhere" and "My Generation" found songwriter Pete Townshend (collaborating with Roger Daltrey on "Anyway, Anyhow, Anywhere") defiantly expressing the freedom that he and other young people have in determining their own destinies. "Substitute" continued the exploration of identity and alienation that was at the background of "I Can't Explain." In the case of "Substitute," though, Townshend (as writer) and Daltrey (as singer) portray a character whose sense of self-identity here is obscured by the way he has been treated by society, by his parents, and by individuals with whom he has been romantically involved.

The focus on identity that paints these songs as products of the Mod aesthetic is confirmed to a certain extent in each song by musical signifiers. Because of the fact that "I Can't Explain" is most closely associated with the musical style of the Kinks (e.g., "All Day and All of the Night," which features a similar emphasis on a guitar riff), this song is the richest of the four important Who songs in Mod harmonic and voice-leading touches; however, all four of the songs have at least one attribute that places them squarely within the Mod genre.

The song "I Can't Explain," which is in the key of E major, includes the bVII chord in the main guitar riff, which moves as follows: E major (I), D major (bVII), A major (IV), E major. The whole-step parallel motion from I to bVII (the parallel motion comes from playing the same barre-chord shape and moving down two frets) itself comes squarely from guitar technique, much like the parallel motion of Dave Davies's guitar playing on "All Day and All of the Night" and "You Really Got Me." Like the Kinks' songs, "I Can't Explain" also includes major-Mixolydian modal mixture: the bridge of the song is preceded by a B major (V) chord, which contains the major seventh scale step; the bVII chord contains D-natural, the lowered (Mixolydian mode) seventh scale step. In addition, "I Can't Explain" finds Townshend playing what would throughout the 1960s be almost a trademark of his rhythm guitar sound: the suspended-fourth chord (Asus4, which he uses in the bridge). It should be noted that while the use of a suspended fourth (the note D in the Asus4 chord) moving down to the third of the chord (C-sharp) is not new with the songs of Pete Townshend—it can be found occasionally in jazz standards and it is a standard practice in classical music—it becomes a guitar-specific-sounding technique in Townshend's work. Other guitarists would pick up on this, so that by the early 1970s it became almost a stereotypical figure in the work of some rhythm guitar players. Incidentally, other notable rock and pop examples that emphasize the suspended fourth chord include the 1968 Rolling Stones song "Child of the Moon," and numerous early James Taylor hits, such as "Fire and Rain."

The song "My Generation" finds Townshend writing in a more harmonically mini- malist manner. Basically, each stanza of this song is based on a single chord; however, the bass line, played by John Entwistle, for the most part oscillates between the tonic pitch (G, in the beginning of the song) and the lowered seventh scale-step (F-natural). While the bVII chord itself is not used, the whole-step motion gives "My Generation" the Mixolydian mode feel that is heard in parts of "I Can't Explain," "All Day and All of the Night," and "You Really Got Me." Like the contemporary work of the Kinks' Ray Davies, "My Generation" also features unconventional modulations. "My Generation" begins (in the studio version), in the key of G; it then moves up a whole-step to A, up a half-step to B-flat, and finally up a whole-step to C. The fact that the modulations move by both whole-steps and half-steps lends the shift of tonal reference points a somewhat unpredictable feel. While the key relationships are not exactly the same as those in contemporary songs by the Kinks, it is important to note that both Ray Davies and Pete Townshend, the two most famous Mod songwriters, incorporated unusual and unpredictable key relationships. They did so to a greater extent in their famous overtly Mod songs than did their not-as-overtly-Mod contemporaries in British rock.

Likewise, in addition to its sentiments of generational identity and freedom ("I can go anyway, way I choose; I can live anyhow, win or lose"), "Anyway, Anyhow, Anywhere" also contains the bVII and parallel motion signifiers that mark the piece as part of the Mod genre. Because of the fact that Pete Townshend's harmonic progression includes both the V (A) and the bVII (C) chords in this D major song, "Anyway, Anyhow, Anywhere" also features the mixture of the major and Mixolydian modes that, while notable for its unusual sound in a few compositions of Billy Fury and Marty Wilde back in 1959–1960, became a standard part of rock compositional vocabulary—in part thanks to its heavy exploitation by songwriters such as Pete Townshend.

As a writer, Townshend grew increasingly more interested in extended, multimovement works. Large-scale works such as *A Quick One While He's Away, Tommy*, and *Quadrophenia*, helped to establish rock opera—an extension of the unified concept album approach—as a viable art form. Even in these works and the Who's other recordings from the 1960s and early 1970s, however, Mod lyrical themes and musical signifiers continued to form the core of the Who's sound.

It should be mentioned that even without the cacophony caused by feedback and the destruction of electric guitars, amplifiers, and drum sets, the fundamental instrumental tone quality of the Who was edgier than many of the other British rock bands of the day. The Who succeeded, though, in developing a broad commercial appeal in part because the energy, drive, and edgy tone of the instruments, and Daltrey's lead vocals were balanced by the increased use of beautiful backing vocals in the 1966–1967 period.

Despite the outward differences in their music and their stage performance style, the Kinks and the Who share important things in common. For one thing, both Ray Davies and Pete Townshend explored the ambiguities of how one arrives at one's self-identity to a greater extent than their colleagues in other bands did. It is true that in 1965 and 1966 John Lennon did this in some of his songs, but in the work of Davies and Townshend it seems almost like a leitmotif for much of each songwriter's output. Both songwriters also created characters that represented the fringes of British society. Both bands made creative use of distortion and feedback—sounds that defied the traditional definitions of sonic beauty in 1964–1966—to a greater extent than other bands did. Their hard-hitting styles found a more difficult time gaining commercial acceptance in both the United Kingdom and in the United States than their more musically moderate or conservative colleagues did; however, the influence of both bands' songwriting and musical performance styles can be heard in the work of later artists perhaps even more fully than the influence of the more popular British bands of the era. For example, the Jam, a 1970s–1980s British band that came out of the punk movement, explored the lyrical themes of identity and defining British-ness that can be heard in the compositions of Davies and Townshend. The basic power trio texture of the Jam owes much to the live texture of the Who. And, like Pete Townshend's work with the Who, Paul Weller's guitar playing in the Jam left room for melodic bass guitar fills from Bruce Foxton that were not necessarily typical of other bands of the era. In fact, to a certain extent the entire package of Mod aesthetics, lyrical and musical, that the Kinks and the Who put together during the British Invasion period formed the basic framework from which the Jam expanded. Interestingly, like the Kinks and the Who, the Jam made less impact in the United States than in Britain, probably in part because Paul Weller's social commentary and observations about self-identity were too closely tied to British identity, just like the work of Davies and Townshend. In addition to the Jam, the entire punk rock scene of rave up tempos, loud distortion, feedback, and the destruction of instruments all have precedents in the mid-1960s work of the Kinks and the Who.

On a more mainstream note, David Bowie's songs of alienation and exploration of identity can be heard as an extension of the work of Davies and Townshend, despite the fact that throughout his career Bowie has adopted different musical styles than his slightly older countrymen have. Even more specifically, the explorations of sexual ambiguity, perversion, and sadism that the Kinks (e.g., "Lola") and the Who (e.g., "I'm a Boy," "Do You Think It's Alright"/"Fiddle About" and "Cousin Kevin")[12] developed through various characters were taken up by Bowie. And, like the vivid characters that the Kinks and the Who created in order to explore these themes, Bowie also created psychologically vivid characters in order to explore nontraditional lyrical themes. Bowie's debt to the Kinks and the Who is confirmed by the fact that on his 1973 album of cover recordings, *Pin Ups*, Bowie included "Anyway, Anyhow, Anywhere," (composed by Townshend and Daltrey), "I Can't Explain" (Townshend) and "Where Have All the Good Times Gone" (Ray Davies). In addition, Pete Townshend later performed as a guest guitarist on Bowie albums, and Bowie performed Ray Davies's "Waterloo Sunset" on his 2003–2004 *Reality* tour.

The Kinks and the Who, to a greater extent than most of their British Invasion colleagues, also shifted their focus to albums, including concept albums and rock operas, during the late 1960s and early 1970s. Works such as *Tommy, Quadrophenia, The Kinks Are the Village Green Preservation Society,* and others by these groups extended the concept album paradigm beyond that established by Brian Wilson's *Pet Sounds* (1966), Pink

Floyd's *The Piper at the Gates of Dawn* (1966), and the Beatles' *Sgt. Pepper's Lonely Hearts Club Band* (1967). Because the late 1960s albums of the Kinks and the Who tended not necessarily to be built around hit singles, but were more unified, cohesive works, these two bands contributed significantly to the genre of album-oriented rock.

Despite the fact that at the start of the British Invasion the Who and the Kinks did not make the degree of commercial impact of the Rolling Stones, the Beatles, and others, by the end of the 1960s both bands had attained a substantial following and had garnered the widespread approval of rock music critics. The Kinks and the Who were not the only overtly Mod bands of the 1960s. The Creation, a group that originally was formed in 1963, recorded a number of songs in the 1965–1966 period, including "Painter Man" and "Making Time," that stylistically are in the same basic league as contemporary material from the Who. Like other recordings of the Mod genre, the Creation's work included Townshend-like distortion and other electric guitar special effects (in fact, early examples of what would become common in the psychedelic music of 1966–1967), celebration of the life of the artist/art student, and exploration of self-identity. The sense of coolness, the use of distortion and feedback, the unusual modulations, and the Mod exploration of self-identity of all the Mod bands continue to influence rock music into the twenty-first century.

7

The Blues and R&B Bands

Although it was connected with the traditional and modern jazz scenes in Britain in the 1950s, an independent blues scene was separating itself from jazz at the same time. The British tour of Muddy Waters signaled a keen interest among British musicians in this distinctly African American genre, especially in London. By the time of the British Invasion, musicians had to make a choice: either (1) remain true to electric blues and/or R&B or (2) find a way to achieve the mass appeal of the emerging rock and pop bands. We will begin our look at the blues and R&B bands of the British Invasion and then turn to groups that, to varying degrees, balanced a focus on the blues and R&B with an attempt to achieve mass commercial appeal.

ALEXIS KORNER, CYRIL DAVIES, AND BLUES INCORPORATED

Born April 19, 1928 in Paris, France, Alexis Korner arrived in London in 1940. Reportedly, Korner first listened to American blues music as a teen while waiting out Nazi air raids on London. Korner learned to play guitar and piano and first experimented with electric blues as early as 1947.[1] Two years later, Korner joined Chris Barber's Jazz Band, the same ensemble that later spawned Lonnie Donegan's skiffle group. Instead of the more rurally oriented skiffle music to which Donegan was attracted, Korner favored the blues. So at the same time as Donegan was starting the skiffle craze in Britain—approximately 1954—Alexis Korner and singer/harmonica player Cyril Davies began working together as an electric blues duo in London.

Younger than Korner, but still older than most of the musicians with whom he worked, Cyril Davies was born in Denham, Buckinghamshire, England, in 1932. Davies and Korner formed the Blues and Barrelhouse Club in London's Soho and sponsored the appearance of American blues artists, in addition to continuing their own performances. This work of Korner and Davies—especially in bringing American blues musicians to the United Kingdom—is credited with starting the British blues boom, which largely was centered in London.

Korner and Davies recorded together as early as 1957, a year before Muddy Waters toured England, but their early efforts met with little commercial success. The duo expanded their blues group over the years, and in 1962 established an ensemble called Blues Incorporated, as well as regular blues nights at the Ealing Jazz Club. The list of the membership of Blues Incorporated reads like a who's who of some of the most important British blues, blues-rock, and rock musicians of the 1960s and 1970s, in part because so many famous musicians passed through Blues Incorporated and into higher-profile careers in other bands or as solo artists. Some of the musicians who performed with Blues Incorporated include: Long John Baldry (vocalist), Charlie Watts (the Rolling Stones), Jack Bruce (Cream), Graham Bond, and Ginger Baker (Cream). Drummer Charlie Watts's future Rolling Stones bandmates Brian Jones, Mick Jagger, and Keith Richards also performed with Blues Incorporated, but only from time to time. Others who were fans of the group and who sat in from time to time included Jimmy Page (the Yardbirds and Led Zeppelin), Rod Stewart, and Paul Jones (Manfred Mann).

Cyril Davies left the group around the time the *R&B from the Marquee* album was released. He wanted to continue to focus on Chicago-style blues, but Korner and some of the other members of the band wanted to move more into commercial R&B. The band that Davies formed, the Cyril Davies R&B All-Stars, continued to entice talented young musicians into the British blues scene. In fact, Davies recruited several players away from the band of David "Screaming Lord" Sutch, a British blues singer known for his performance of morbid songs supported by unearthly effects courtesy of producer Joe Meek. Unfortunately, however, Davies died in January 1964. Long John Baldry took over leadership of the group, and post-Davies sessions included such future rock luminaries as Jimmy Page, Jeff Beck, and Nicky Hopkins.

After Davies left Blues Incorporated, Korner kept the group going until 1966, at which time it was widely known as Alexis Korner's Blues Incorporated. Although Blues Incorporated lasted only until 1966, it and John Mayall's Bluesbreakers were the two most important groups in the establishment of a vibrant British blues scene.

Let us examine the band's important 1962 album *R&B from the Marquee* as a document of Blues Incorporated's musical approach. Despite the album's name, it was not recorded at the Marquee, but rather in a Decca studio in June 1962. Blues Incorporated was a new group at the time of the recording; however, its membership was already in a state of flux (most of the British blues bands of the 1960s had fluid memberships). The members on this album were Alexis Korner (guitar), Cyril Davies (harmonica and vocals), Dick Heckstall-Smith (tenor saxophone), Long John Baldry (vocals), Keith Scott (piano), Spike Heatley (string bass), and Graham Burbridge (drums). On the song "I Got My Mojo Working," they were joined by Big Jim Sullivan (vocals) and Teddy Wadmore (electric bass guitar).

The selections on *R&B from the Marquee* mostly are drawn from well-known American blues songs; however, both Korner and Davies are represented as composers of instrumentals, and Long John Baldry sings one of his compositions. The album begins, in fact, with Korner's composition "Gotta Move." This introduction to Blues Incorporated instantly makes clear the stylistic range of the instrumentalists: Korner plays single-line guitar figures that are instantly recognizable as coming out of the Memphis and Chicago blues traditions but are not necessarily identifiable as coming directly from any one particular African American guitarist. Likewise, Davies fits squarely into the traditions of Sonny Boy Williamson II and Little Walter. One of the things that makes this piece and several of the others on the album stand out, though, is the jazz feel that drummer Burbridge brings into the mix. The strongest direct ties to jazz, however, are heard in the saxophone work of Dick Heckstall-Smith. While it is more noticeable on this instrumental than on the songs, throughout the album Heckstall-Smith incorporates melodic and rhythmic figures—as well as a legato phrasing—that come more out of the American jazz tradition than the blues or R&B traditions. This creates a little stylistic tension; however, it is a desirable tension, which makes for a feeling of individualism within a collective.

The Cyril Davies composition "Spooky but Nice" is an instrumental in the form and rhythmic style of a stroll. Because of the way in which Davies's melody mixes notes of the blues scale and the major scale, and because of the melodic shape of the C phrases of this ABCC-form tune, there are strong hints of the Mixolydian mode, or even a Hindustani raga. The slow rhythmic insistence of the stroll style (e.g., Link Wray's "Rumble") and the Eastern sound of the tune perhaps are what led to the piece's title.

The blues songs on the album feature either Davies or Long John Baldry on vocals. While both sing with authentic-sounding blues phrasing, figuration, and tone quality, Davies generally is a more powerful and self-assured-sounding singer than Baldry. One thing that is noticeable in both singers—and something that is also easy to hear in Mick Jagger's blues singing—is a tendency to imitate the dialect of African American blues singers both in covers and in original compositions. This is something of a double-edged sword in British blues. On one hand, it helps the performances fit within the prevailing electric blues tradition; however, on the other hand it is artificial. It does, however, raise an intriguing question about authenticity: is blues more "authentic" if it fits into a sonic stereotype (e.g., Southern African American pronunciations) or if it comes from the soul (and the accent) of the singer?

Despite the question of authenticity that the affectation of African American vocal style by some of the British blues singers raises, this tendency still does not seem as contrived as the dancing maneuvers of Mick Jagger of the Rolling Stones and Allan Clarke of the Hollies used in their appearances on American television in 1964 and 1965. While the fancy, sliding dance steps are impressive to watch, they are gleaned directly from American R&B singers. If one lead singer of a British rock band used this during guitar solos or during "groove" sections in R&B covers it would be one thing, but when two or more do it, it exposes the derivative nature of the technique. This R&B affectation is exposed especially clearly when one watches segments of the Rolling Stones and the Hollies back to back in the context of a "best of" *The Ed Sullivan Show* or *Shindig!* context.

But back to *R&B from the Marquee* . . . One of the things that may strike the listener about most of the blues songs on the album is how densely packed some of them are with almost competing melodic fills coming from the harmonica, saxophone, guitar, and/or piano. It is very much a polyphonic approach to blues music, and stands out because it contrasts with some of the well-known work of blues performers such as Howlin' Wolf, Muddy Waters, and other American bluesmen. As might be expected, this tends to happen more on the tracks on which Baldry sings, because it allows Davies to focus on the harmonica. With nothing but circumstantial evidence, however, I suspect that part of the reason for the busier sound of Blues Incorporated might come from the association that some of the members of the group, particularly Korner and Davies, had with the traditional jazz scene in the 1950s. Both Korner and Davies had been members of Chris Barber's Jazz Band. Although Barber was a trombonist and mostly focused on Dixieland style jazz, his group also included skiffle (Lonnie Donegan was a member of the group) and blues. This makes for a truly interesting mix, because in the United States, except for recordings from the 1920s, generally blues musicians and New Orleans-style or Dixieland musicians did not work together a great deal. So, Korner and Davies, as part of a group that devoted a significant amount of its effort to a polyphonic jazz style, probably had more exposure to the possibilities of this texture than even American blues musicians might have had. Therefore, not only did Chris Barber play a significant role in the British skiffle and blues scenes by including those forms in his band's bag of tricks, he also probably influenced the polyphonic style of some of Blues Incorporated's work—a style that distinguishes it from the American roots from which it came.

JOHN MAYALL'S BLUESBREAKERS

Like Alexis Korner and Cyril Davies, the other major blues bandleader of the 1960s, John Mayall, was older than the musicians who passed through his band and onto stardom as blues-rock artists. Mayall was born November 29, 1933 in Macclesfield,

Cheshire, England. Like Korner, Mayall heard blues recordings when he was young and became enthralled with the music. He learned to play piano, guitar, and harmonica, and by 1956 was working in a dance band called the Powerhouse Four. Mayall reached a major crossroads in his part-time career in music in the 1962–1963 period, when he became a member of the Blues Syndicate and was encouraged by Alexis Korner to leave his job as an art designer and take up music full time. He heeded Korner's advice and formed a group called the Bluesbreakers.

The 1963 membership of John Mayall's Bluesbreakers included John McVie (Fleetwood Mac) on bass, Hughie Flint on drums, Roger Dean on guitar, and Nigel Stanger on saxophone. At the time of their first album—a live recording from December 1964 released as *John Mayall Plays John Mayall*—the Bluesbreakers were notable for performing original songs written by Mayall in a blues-rock, R&B-based style. This contrasts with Alexis Korner's Blues Incorporated, which maintained closer links with the Chicago-style electric blues tradition and focused on songs first popularized by Muddy Waters, Howlin' Wolf, Willie Dixon, and others. In 1965, however, Eric Clapton—who had left the Yardbirds when they moved away from their blues roots in order to achieve more commercial success (e.g., "For Your Love")—joined the Bluesbreakers on lead guitar. With the change of personnel, the Bluesbreakers moved away from R&B-based rock and back in the direction of pure electric blues. Clapton's first album with the band, *Bluesbreakers with Eric Clapton,* is still considered one of the greatest British blues recordings ever. However, because it was released in 1966, it falls on the fringes of the original British Invasion. What the album did was to establish Clapton as a star of blues guitar and in general a star in the art of blues improvisation, something the Yardbirds had not allowed. When Clapton left the Bluesbreakers to form Cream in 1968—along with bassist Jack Bruce, another former member of the Bluesbreakers—the imprint of John Mayall's band was propelled into the heavy blues-rock of the end of the sixties. In addition to Clapton, McVie, and Bruce, other luminaries of late 1960s and early 1970s rock and blues-rock who performed at one time with John Mayall's Bluesbreakers include guitarists Peter Green (Fleetwood Mac) and Mick Taylor (Brian Jones's replacement in the Rolling Stones), as well as drummers Mick Fleetwood (Fleetwood Mac) and Aynsley Dunbar (Jeff Beck Group, Frank Zappa, David Bowie, Journey, Jefferson Starship, and Whitesnake).

In order to develop the theme of how some blues musicians—such as John Mayall—attempted to merge Chicago-style blues, R&B, and blues-based rock and roll at the time of the British Invasion, let us consider some of the tracks on the album *John Mayall Plays John Mayall*. In part because Mayall blends several styles together and in part because the musicians in the Bluesbreakers exhibit different musical styles, there is some stylistic tension on the album. This, the reader might recall, was also a trait in evidence on Blues Incorporated's famous *R&B from the Marquee* album of a couple years earlier.

Mayall's live album was recorded at Klooks' Kleek, an R&B club night, in the Railway Hotel, West Hampstead, London, on December 7, 1964.[2] Incidentally, the reader might recall that the Railway Hotel was also the venue at which the Who established itself as a leading Mod band of the era. Several of Mayall's original compositions, "I Wanna Teach You Everything," for example, fall squarely into 12-bar blues form and fit in with the British blues style of Blues Incorporated. In these blues pieces, though, Mayall's organ playing leans more in the direction of R&B bands such as the Animals than what one might expect to hear in a purist group. In fact, the entire album captures almost the entire gamut of blues, R&B, and beat music that was in the air at the end of 1964. For example, while Mayall's organ playing on some of the tracks calls to mind the work of Alan Price (the Animals), his virtuosic harmonica playing successfully captures the feel of Chicago-style blues. On "When I'm Gone," drummer Peter Ward mixes jazz figures and beat group signifiers. As a singer, Mayall falls somewhere in between an R&B front man such as Manfred Mann's Paul Jones, and a more heavily jazz-influenced singer, such as Georgie Fame. This mix of stylistic references might not exhibit the focus of later Mayall recordings, but it goes far in suggesting the diversity of styles that came together to form the London side of the British Invasion.

GEORGIE FAME AND THE BLUE FLAMES

Born Clive Powell on June 26, 1943, in Leigh, Lancashire, England, the keyboardist and singer who eventually became known as Georgie Fame learned to play piano as a child. As a pianist and singer, his early influences included Fats Domino and Jerry Lee Lewis. When his family moved to London in 1959, however, Powell was discovered by songwriter Lionel Bart—a sometimes collaborator with Tommy Steele and Marty Wilde. Bart brought Powell to the attention of impresario Larry Parnes, who rechristened the teenager Georgie Fame. By 1961, Fame found himself playing in a band called the Blue Flames backing Billy Fury. Unlike the Parnes-managed teen idols of the day, however, Fame (as well as the rest of the Blue Flames) had a strong interest in jazz and R&B. In fact, it has been speculated that part of the reason the band backed Fury for such a short time was because they were too inclined toward jazz for Fury's repertoire.

After leaving Billy Fury, Fame became the lead singer and the group became known as Georgie Fame and the Blue Flames. Fame became one of the first British keyboard players to focus on the Hammond B-3 organ, and he and the Blue Flames were among the first British artists in the early 1960s to incorporate Jamaican ska into their style. But Georgie Fame and the Blue Flames were also heavily R&B based, and the group's ties to jazz are evident in their recordings from the 1964–1966 period.

Although Georgie Fame was active as a songwriter, the main elements of his style might best be found in the nonoriginals he recorded. And a significant number of Fame's best-remembered and most successful recordings from the British Invasion period are not originals. In considering Georgie Fame's work, though, it would be less than fully accurate to label these recordings "covers," as one might ordinarily do when considering the nonoriginals recorded by various rock bands of the day. Because of the jazz-based nature of many of his arrangements, his keyboard playing, and his singing, Fame can best be considered as a jazz interpreter. He may not exactly be the British equivalent of Frank Sinatra, Billie Holiday, or Ramsey Lewis, but like those famous American jazz musicians Fame's creativity is based more on the way in which he interprets the compositions of others than on writing original material.

Although few Georgie Fame recordings can truly be labeled "covers," because Fame generally went beyond copying or even extensively basing his interpretation on one earlier popular version of the piece, a notable exception is his 1964 recording of Booker T and the MGs' instrumental "Green Onions." Here, Fame seems to focus on accurately reproducing Booker T. Jones's Hammond organ sound (including the tremolo style), and arrangement. Jones's registration and some of his improvised melodic lines also find their way into Fame's recording. For the most part—especially on vocals—Georgie Fame is instantly recognizable as a song stylist.

The one British Invasion–era Georgie Fame recording with which Americans might have been familiar was "Yeh Yeh." It is an interesting performance to consider because it is so unlike the bulk of what Americans heard from British groups at the time. For one thing, the arrangement has a Latin feel—perhaps closer to the popular 1950s and early 1960s jazz of musicians such as Stan Getz than to a British pop band—and features a jazz-conceived saxophone solo and Fame's mix of jazz- and rock-inflected vocals. In a sense, these are the attributes that mark the work of Georgie Fame and the Blue Flames as the natural successor of the jazz-rock hybrid work of the John Barry Seven back in the late 1950s and nearly 1960s.

The lyrics of "Yeh Yeh," a jazz piece written by Rodgers Grant, Jon Hendricks, and Pat Patrick, too, suggest a maturity beyond the typical teen situations that some purely rock and pop songs of the era describe. The domestic situations in which Fame's character and his girlfriend's character live that suggest that they are independent, urban, perhaps middle-class people in their 20s, as opposed to the teens to which many of the British Invasion songs were aimed: the characters of "Yeh Yeh" have jobs and flats, and their idea of excitement is to spend the evening listening to records on the "hi-fi" in her flat and then making love.

At the time of the British Invasion, Georgie Fame by and large did not enjoy a sizeable following in the United States. For one thing, the jazz and jazz-based R&B that he recorded fell outside the popular British beat group style; it also fell outside the British blues and blues-rock styles, too. Because the jazz focus was so strong, Fame's music would seem to have appealed to more of a niche audience. It is too mature and sophisticated, for example, to have found mass appeal among American teen, fashion-conscious consumers. In a sense, Georgie Fame and the Blue Flames took the jazz leanings of a group such as Manfred Mann and seemed to refuse to lean in any other direction. While Fame might not have been a huge Top 40 success in the United States, he has enjoyed a long career as a jazz interpreter in Britain. To the extent that the merger of jazz, R&B, and rock is considered an important development in the popular music of the 1966–1969 period—including Paul McCartney's "Got to Get You into My Life," the obscure Monkees track "Goin' Down," and the early innovative recordings of American groups such as Chicago and Blood, Sweat and Tears—then Georgie Fame can be viewed as a visionary.

CLIFF BENNETT AND THE REBEL ROUSERS

Cliff Bennett, who was born in 1940 near London, was one of the many British teenagers who was affected by American rock and roll music in the mid-1950s. Bennett took up the guitar and performed in a skiffle band, but he proved to be a much better singer than instrumentalist. He gravitated toward R&B more fully than many young British singers of the time. In fact, Bennett generally is regarded as one of the best British singers of the 1960s in his ability to create an authentic-sounding R&B style. This is confirmed by the fact that Cliff Bennett and the Rebel Rousers eventually became the first British band signed by Motown Records.

Cliff Bennett and the Rebel Rousers, originally a seven-man unit (Bennett on lead vocals, plus guitar, bass, keyboards, drums, and two saxophones), was another group that did not enjoy much commercial success in the United States at the time of the British Invasion. Most of the band's early recordings were covers of American R&B songs. The extensive use of tenor saxophone calls to mind an extension of the arrangements of American R&B bands—more so than some other groups (e.g., the Dave Clark Five) that incorporated the saxophone.

Despite the lack of commercial success of the early recordings the band made under producer Joe Meek, their work with Meek provided them with enough recognition that they secured a residency in Hamburg, Germany, where they appeared in venues such as the Star-Club, one of the Beatles' performance venues in their residencies in Hamburg. In fact, the Beatles urged their manager, Brian Epstein, to sign Bennett and his group. They became the first London band that Epstein signed.

Vocally and instrumentally, this was one of the strongest British R&B bands of the 1960s; however, even in Britain their record sales paled in comparison to other groups with whom they shared an R&B and blues-based repertoire. The visual image they presented in publicity and album cover shots (they did not look like the "mop tops" of the day), the fact that individual personalities were more difficult to define in a large band, the maturity of their musical approach (Bennett and the Rebel Rousers clearly are a professional R&B band with no discernable garage band–like ties), the lack of original compositions, and the soloist-plus-backing-group structure all combined to keep this talented band from making the commercial impact they deserved.

In a real sense Cliff Bennett and the Rebel Rousers were musicians' musicians. And although they were not a successful part of the British Invasion—and even failed to generate sales at home befitting their excellence—listeners who want to hear just how thoroughly British musicians in the 1963–1965 period had absorbed African American R&B are encouraged to listen to Cliff Bennett and the Rebel Rousers' debut album (which includes tracks cut in 1963, 1964, and 1965). Bennett gives especially strong performances on the soulful Motown standard "You Really Got a Hold on Me."

Cliff Bennett and the Rebel Rousers achieved their greatest success at home in 1966 with their U.K. No. 3 single "Got to Get You into My Life," a Paul McCartney composition from the Beatles' *Revolver* album. McCartney himself produced Bennett's recording of the song. The jazzy R&B work of Bennett and his band anticipated—although perhaps not as fully as the work of Georgie Fame—the jazz-rock genre that gained popularity later in the 1960s.

While Alexis Korner and Cyril Davies' Blues Incorporated, John Mayall's Bluesbreakers, Georgie Fame and the Blue Flames, and Cliff Bennett and the Rebel Rousers perhaps are the most representative examples of the British blues and R&B-jazz scene up to the time of the British Invasion, especially in terms of how it formed an extension of American electric blues and R&B, there were numerous other blues-based bands in the United Kingdom at the time of the British Invasion. Neither Blues Incorporated, Bluesbreakers, Georgie Fame and the Blue Flames, or Cliff Bennett and the Rebel Rousers enjoyed a great deal of commercial success in the United States in the 1964–1965 period; however some of the blues-based rock bands did. Let us take a look at some of these groups and see how they managed to reconcile a niche musical style (blues) with a desire for popular and commercial acceptance.

THE ANIMALS

The history of the Animals goes back to a group known as the Kansas City Five, an early 1960s R&B/blues group from the industrial city of Newcastle-upon-Tyne. Three members of this group—singer Eric Burdon, organist Alan Price, and drummer John Steel—eventually became part of the Animals in 1964. The Kansas City Five broke up, however, when Price left in 1962 to join the Kontours and Burdon moved south to London. Chas Chandler played bass guitar in the Kontours, and he too eventually became a member of the Animals. The Kontours underwent some personnel changes, as well as a name change to the Alan Price R&B Combo. By 1963, Burdon had returned to Newcastle and became the singer with Price's group. John Steel, too, was part of the Prince Combo. Finally, guitarist Hilton Valentine joined the group just as the Alan Price R&B Combo took on the more vivid and less cumbersome name, the Animals.

Like other R&B and blues-based bands of the era, the Animals benefited from the attention of impresario Giorgio Gomelsky, who booked the group at the Crawdaddy Club, the stepping-off point of bands such as the Rolling Stones and the Yardbirds. Around the end of 1963, the band was signed by record producer Mickie Most and EMI's Columbia label. Most (1938–2003), who was born Michael Hayes, helped the Animals by getting them signed to the British Columbia label (their records were issued on MGM in the United States); however, he was not necessarily the best producer for a band that wanted to stick to the blues and R&B genres.

Between the time of their debut single, "Baby Let Me Take You Home," in early 1964, and their May 1965 single "We Gotta Get out of This Place," Burdon, Price, Valentine, Chandler, and Steel enjoyed substantial chart success with singles both in the United Kingdom and the United States. Their 1964 recording of "The House of the Rising Sun," which they learned from a recording by the American folk-blues artist Josh White, became an iconic piece of British Invasion history, and hit No. 1 in both countries. While there had been some activity in merging folk, blues, and rock before "The House of the Rising Sun"—the Searchers, for example, had recorded Pete Seeger's "Where Have All the Flowers Gone" on their 1963 debut album—the Animals' recording proved that folk material could be placed into a thoroughly convincing, thoroughly rock-oriented context.

The Animals' adaptation of "The House of the Rising Sun" is notable in several respects. First, because the old nineteenth-century American folk song originally came from the perspective of a female prostitute who plied her trade at a brothel called the House of the Rising Sun, Eric Burdon uses the lyrics of Josh White's male-perspective version. Burdon's contribution, though, is his full-throated, aggressive delivery. His singing exudes a degree of passion that ranks with the best of the British Invasion. The track begins with Hilton Valentine's arpeggio pattern on electric guitar, a pattern that continues throughout the recording. Also notable is Alan Price's similar accompanying pattern on the electronic organ and his powerful solo. Interestingly, Price alone of the five Animals received label credit for the arrangement of "The House of the Rising Sun," despite the appearance that the entire group contributed to what was arguably the first great folk-rock classic. When Price left the band in mid-1965, the official explanation was that a fear of flying made it impossible for him to tour; however, it has long been suspected that internal strife in the group over the credit Price received for the group's biggest hit at least in part caused his unexpected departure. The iconic status of "The House of the Rising Sun" is confirmed by its continued presence on oldies radio stations. *Rolling Stone* magazine ranked the Animals' recording at No. 122 on their list of the 500 best songs of all time,[3] and rock critic Dave Marsh ranked the recording No. 91 on his list of the 1,001 greatest singles ever made.[4]

The other iconic British Invasion single from the Animals was "We Gotta Get out of This Place," a composition written by Brill Building stalwarts Barry Mann and Cynthia Weil. With Eric Burdon interpreting the song, it becomes a cry of escape from the British working class, with its poverty and widespread industry-caused illness. The song was one of the favorites of U.S. troops in Vietnam, who identified with the title line about escape from what sounds like a hell on earth in Burdon's interpretation. Although not as highly regarded by critics as "The House of the Rising Sun," "We Gotta Get out of This Place" is also widely included in lists of the most important recordings of the rock era. *Rolling Stone,* for example, includes it as No. 233 on their list of the 500 greatest songs of all time,[5] and Dave Marsh ranks it No. 798 in his list of the 1,001 greatest singles ever made.[6] Incidentally, this recording is reputed to be one on which session drummer Bobby Graham performs in place of John Steel.[7]

The other well-known Animals singles that charted in the United States in the 1964–1966 period include "Don't Bring Me Down," a composition of Gerry Goffin and Carole King, "Don't Let Me Be Misunderstood," a composition of Bennie Benjamin, Gloria Caldwell, and Sol Marcus that Nina Simone first recorded in 1964, and "It's My Life," written by Roger Atkins and Carl D'Errico. Of these, "Don't Let Me Be Misunderstood" is the most significant; *Rolling Stone* includes it as No. 315 on the magazine's list of the 500 best songs of all time.[8]

Despite the fact that even most of the band's big hit singles featured a bluesy edginess beyond that of many of the other commercially successful British Invasion bands, the Animals were not enthralled with the material producer Mickie Most selected for them for singles. Three of their hit singles ("Don't Bring Me Down," "It's My Life," and "We Gotta Get out of This Place") came from the pens of Brill Building songwriters. Unlike the Brill Building material recorded by groups such as the Beatles, however, these were not covers. The three songs were written especially for the Animals, at Most's request. Rhetorically, all three of the songs match with a band from a British industrial city in which escape from poverty and self-definition are important concerns. Still, the songs are not the authentic blues and R&B that the Animals preferred. One of the problems of the Animals was that the band did not include writers who were strong enough or prolific enough to compete with the likes of John Lennon, Paul McCartney, Mick Jagger, Keith

Richards, and others. While the Animals were allowed to record R&B and blues songs as album cuts, they were primarily known for their singles, songs that members of the band felt were outside the realm of their primary musical interest. For his part, aside from the Animals, Mickie Most's greatest commercial success probably came from the much lighter-weight hits he produced for Herman's Hermits and Donovan.

The Animals left Mickie Most in 1966 but disbanded shortly thereafter. Burdon formed an entirely new group, known variously as Eric Burdon and the Animals or Eric Burdon and the New Animals. With his new backing musicians, Burdon enjoyed Top 10 hits in the United States in 1966 and 1967 ("See See Rider" and "San Franciscan Nights"). The new band also released the significant two-sided antiwar single "Sky Pilot" in 1968. By the end of the 1960s, Burdon was recording with the band War. The original Animals reunited for touring and recording projects at various points in the 1970s and 1980s.

THE MOODY BLUES

Beginning in 1967, the Moody Blues became one of the better-known British bands by specializing in a melodic blend of psychedelic progressive rock, with a focus on songs written by guitarist Justin Hayward. In fact, the Moody Blues became so firmly etched on public consciousness through Hayward's romantic-yet-progressive songs and his instantly identifiable solo guitar style, as well as Mike Pinder's atmospheric mellotron and Ray Thomas's flute playing, that it is easy to lose sight of the fact that this group started as an R&B band fronted by singer-guitarist Denny Laine.

The Birmingham-based Moody Blues had their roots in the early 1960s band El Riot and the Rebels, which included future Moody Blues Ray Thomas (vocals, harmonica, woodwinds) and Mike Pinder (keyboards and vocals). Incidentally, another member of El Riot and the Rebels, bass guitarist John Lodge, joined the Moody Blues in 1966 when the band went through personnel changes. By 1963, Thomas and Pinder found themselves in the Krew Cats. The two decided to recruit new members so that the band could become a full-time, professional unit, so Denny Laine (guitar and lead vocals), Clint Warwick (bass and vocals), and Graeme Edge (drums) were added. Laine (born Brian Hines) had previously been the leader of Denny and the Diplomats, which also counted Bev Bevan, the future drummer of the Electric Light Orchestra, among its members. By the time Laine, Edge, Warwick, Pinder, and Thomas made their debut together in May 1964, they were known as the Moody Blues. The group specialized in R&B and secured a series of performances at London's famed Marquee Club.

On the strength of the Moody Blues' work at the Marquee, Decca signed the band to a recording contract. Although their first single did not make the charts, their second—a cover of the contemporary Bessie Banks song "Go Now"—was a hit. The single reached

No. 1 in Britain and No. 10 in the United States. On the strength of the record, the Moody Blues opened for the Beatles on one of their North American tours. The problem for the Moody Blues was that "Go Now" was the band's only major hit until the late 1960s. In 1966, both Denny Laine and Clint Warwick left the group. Their replacements, Justin Hayward and John Lodge, brought an entirely new style to the Moody Blues, one that overshadowed the R&B of the band's early days.

Despite the lack of commercial success relative to other R&B groups in the 1964–1966 period, the first lineup of the Moody Blues produced some truly interesting recordings, including not only "Go Now," but also several lesser-known songs. In particular, the originality of the compositions of Laine and Pinder, both independently and as a writing team, is noteworthy. This especially is noteworthy in light of the occasional references to the songs and styles of other, more commercially successful British Invasion bands. For example, "Every Day,"[9] with its piano and rhythm guitar accompaniment and Graeme Edge's heavy steady sixteenth-note fills all are reminiscent of the contemporary work of the Dave Clark Five. Laine and Pinder's harmonies, which include a mix of diatonic major and minor chords, as well as an expected chromatic shift at the end of the refrain, also fit within the basic stylistic framework of the Dave Clark Five's moderate-tempo ballads. The melody has a natural rise and fall; however, the story of two young people falling in love certainly is not new, nor is it as interesting as the music.

One of the things that add to the appeal of "Every Day" is the Moody Blues' use of harmony vocals. This is also notable in the bluesier R&B cover "Go Now." In this regard, the Moody Blues resemble a band such as the Hollies; however, even the early Moody Blues' vocal harmony work is more expansive than in most of the British Invasion bands. And the Moody Blues' vocal work did not necessarily rely on studio overdubs. For example, film footage of the Laine/Warwick edition of the Moody Blues performing James Brown's "I'll Go Crazy" live features a vocal arrangement that is similar to the band's studio recording of the song, with Laine on lead and with Pinder, Thomas, and Warwick all on backing vocals. A four-voice texture such as this was exceedingly rare in British Invasion bands; in a live setting, for example, one would not hear it from the Rolling Stones, the Beatles, the Dave Clark Five, or the Hollies.

Another feature of "Go Now" that can really draw the listener in, but is easier to overlook than the harmony vocals or Laine's lead vocals, is Mike Pinder's piano solo, which begins approximately two-thirds of the way through this 3:11 song. Although it is based primarily on repetitions and reworkings of one bluesy figure, the figure itself, as well as Pinder's articulation and phrasing of it, creates a fascinating metrical conflict with the triple meter of the song. The figure stresses the downbeats of the measures of music (the even-numbered measures) that are unaccented by the rest of the band. Like some of the psychedelic music for which the next edition of the Moody Blues would be famous—in particular, Ray Thomas's "Legend of a Mind"—Pinder's deliberately repetitive solo figure has a certain Zen-like feeling of a state of being. It is forward looking without necessarily seeming to be so.

Even as Edge, Laine, Pinder, Warwick, and Thomas tried unsuccessfully to duplicate the commercial success of "Go Now," the first edition of the Moody Blues progressed stylistically. While Mike Pinder's piano solo in "Go Now" might have unknowingly anticipated the state-of-being nature of psychedelic music, a style that was notable in part for its use of drones and minimalist repetitive figures, other Moody Blues songs are more consciously experimental and anticipate the more complex sounds that became more commonplace in the Justin Hayward–John Lodge edition of the band. The last great single of the Laine-Warwick years, "From the Bottom of My Heart (I Love You)," is an especially rich example of how the band was breaking free of R&B even before Laine and Warwick left the group. Laine and Pinder, the writers of this song, move back and forth between relative minor and major keys so smoothly that it is difficult to tell if the piece is really supposed to sound minor or major. This creates something of a sense of foreboding—is the love affair going to work out, or not? There is much contrast in melodic shape from phrase to phrase, which adds to the background uncertainty against which Laine sings with absolute certainty the song's title line. The Moody Blues includes some background subtleties, such as the sitar that can heard answering some of Laine's phrases in the verse sections of the piece, and Ray Thomas's flute, which enters during the song's extended fade out. The backing vocals use the Moody Blues' customary wide spacing (including high falsetto). The most dramatic aspect of the piece, though, is Denny Laine's passionate falsetto vocalization that builds up over approximately the final 40 seconds of the recording.

Likewise, Laine and Pinder's "Boulevard de la Madeleine" steps far outside the sound of a conventional British R&B band. This song sounds as though it was inspired by Denny Laine's love of the work of the jazz/gypsy guitarist Django Reinhardt, one of Laine's earliest influences on the instrument. The piece finds the Moody Blues moving between a minor mode section with faux-Parisian café instrumentation and a major mode section that is more of a beat group ballad style.

Another early Moody Blues recording that is interesting to consider, especially in comparing the band with their contemporaries (and possibly trying to explain why the Moody Blues were not as commercially successful as an R&B band as they were during their psychedelic/progressive rock heyday) is their cover of "Time Is on My Side." The Moody Blues' version certainly features a bluesier feel than the version Brian Poole and the Tremeloes recorded. While Denny Laine sings with passion and with a workable R&B rhythmic feel, and while his guitar solo finds him using sharp attacks and string bends that give the playing a bluesy rawness, the overall performance of the song just does not have the feeling of R&B authenticity of the Rolling Stones' famous version.

To a large extent, this is because of the block structure of the backing harmony vocals. The wide spacing of the chords sounds typical of the Moody Blues; however, it does not sound quite like the voicings that one would hear in American R&B music. Likewise, while Denny Laine's lead vocal has a rhythmic feel that approximates black rhythm and blues music, the backing vocals are tied to the beat enough that the listener can be left with a feeling of disconnection. "Time Is on My Side" sounds like the work of a band that was not content to conform to the conventions of R&B, even when covering R&B repertoire. Of course, the vocal harmony style and the other experimental touches (including instrumentation and song forms) that one hears on the 1964–1966 recordings of the band found a home—and a highly commercially successful home—in the work of the next edition of the Moody Blues.

When Clint Warwick and Denny Laine left the band in 1966, there was some shuffling around, but eventually John Lodge and Justin Hayward, respectively, replaced them. As mentioned earlier, John Lodge had worked with Ray Thomas and Mike Pinder in their pre–Moody Blues group. Guitarist, singer, and songwriter Justin Hayward, who in many respects came to symbolize the new sound of the Moody Blues, had, ironically enough (given his impressionistic songs and instantly identifiable sustained guitar solo style), served in rockabilly singer Marty Wilde's backing band before joining the Moody Blues. The legacy of the Moody Blues includes not only the successful work the group itself did into the 1970s, and then for long-lasting reunions into the twenty-first century, but also includes Denny Laine's work as a member of Paul McCartney's post-Beatles band, Wings, for a full decade.

In the final analysis, the first edition of the Moody Blues started out as an R&B-based band, and continued to perform and record R&B and soul covers, even as their internal writing moved in the directions of that of beat groups and early anticipations of the complex structures of psychedelic and progressive rock. In terms of the aspects that make the early Moody Blues stand out from other R&B and blues-based bands of the British Invasion, it is easy to pinpoint two particularly important distinctions: First, their use of elaborate, full vocal harmonies on R&B covers and on R&B-style songs composed by band members Denny Laine and Mike Pinder was unusual among their contemporaries. Second, because the Moody Blues primarily focused on the electric guitar, the piano, and the electric bass as rhythm instruments, each with its own rhythmically distinctive line or riff, part of the appeal of their sound comes from the cross rhythms that are created by the deliberate conflicts between the individual instruments' riffs.

THE YARDBIRDS

In the early 1960s, singer and harmonica player Keith Relf, rhythm guitarist Chris Dreja, drummer Jim McCarty, lead guitarist Anthony Topham, and bass guitarist Paul

Samwell-Smith formed the Metropolis Blues Quartet, one of many R&B and electric blues–based bands in London. When Topham left the group—which by then was known as the Yardbirds—in 1963, he was replaced by Eric Clapton. The group's name was created by Relf, and was based on a reference from the writings of the American beat author Jack Kerouac. In beatnik lingo, "a 'yardbird' was a bum who hung around railroad yards in search of a free train ride."[10] It should be noted that like a number of other British Invasion bands, including the Rolling Stones and the Beatles, the Yardbirds had art school connections. In this case, Keith Relf and Eric Clapton were art school students, and it was this connection that helped to bring Clapton into the group.

The Yardbirds received a much-needed boost when club owner/impresario Giorgio Gomelsky booked the group as the resident band at his Crawdaddy Club after the Rolling Stones finished their lengthy residency. In autumn 1963, Gomelsky promoted the American Negro Blues Festival in Croydon, which featured Muddy Waters, Otis Span, and the singer/harmonica player known as Sonny Boy Williamson II.[11] Gomelsky arranged for the Animals and the Crawdaddy Club's resident band—the Yardbirds—to back Williamson; he also recorded both groups backing the bluesman.

The December 8 and 9, 1963 Sonny Boy Williamson and the Yardbirds sets that Gomelsky recorded at his Crawdaddy Club have been widely reissued on vinyl and on compact disc. The tracks give very little indication of the direction the Yardbirds would take even within a year; however, they make for interesting study because of what they illustrate about the aesthetic roots of the band. Because of the fact that the Yardbirds play a largely supporting role to Williamson, they are tied to his style of blues and, with one exception, songs that Williamson wrote. Another caveat to consider when studying the recordings is that Yardbird's rhythm guitarist Chris Dreja's account of the rehearsals and performances suggest that the blues singer's penchant for carrying a bottle of whiskey in his traveling case led to members of the Yardbirds over-imbibing between the afternoon rehearsal and evening performance.[12] The audio document suggests that this in turn led to some sloppiness, including false endings to some of the songs and incorrectly placed drum lead ins to choruses in others. Even with those important caveats, however, the recordings Giorgio Gomelsky made of the Yardbirds and Sonny Boy Williamson show some fundamental differences in instrumental approach between this group and others of the British Invasion.

The clearest distinctions between the Yardbirds' early work and the work of other British Invasion bands can be heard in the guitar playing of Eric Clapton. On several of the faster pieces, but particularly on "Mister Downchild," Clapton's improvised solos feature highly technical blues licks that come right out of American electric blues vocabulary. The most distinguishing features of these solos are the highly technical nature of the triplet melodies, the effortless quality they have, and the legato (smooth) articulation.

Clapton's technique and articulation suggest a knowledge of the work of the more technically proficient American blues guitarists, but also suggest familiarity with American jazz guitar. Clapton's comping (accompanying) includes ninth chords, harmonies that one perhaps would expect more to hear from a jazz guitarist than from a typical British blues guitarist of 1963.

While Clapton and singer-harmonica player Keith Relf may have learned some things about blues phrasing and improvisation from Sonny Boy Williamson, within a year the Yardbirds moved into new territory. As can be heard on the group's first official album (the band's manager and producer Giorgio Gomelsky did not issue the sessions with Sonny Boy Williamson until later), *Five Live Yardbirds,* in 1964 the band was featuring lengthy, loud improvisations—essentially blues harp (harmonica) and electric guitar jams—in their blues covers. The Yardbirds called these sections "raveups." In the raveup sections on the 1964 live album, which was recorded at the famous Marquee, the Yardbirds build up and relax the intensity and volume much like was common in the work of American R&B front men such as James Brown. More than anything that any other British blues band was performing and/or recording in 1964, these raveups anticipate the later blues-based hard rock of the late 1960s. Despite the historical significance of the Yardbirds' work marrying blues and rock, performances such as those on *Five Live Yardbirds* did not translate into massive popularity or record sales for the group.

The Yardbirds' first serious foray into the record charts came with their recording of Graham Gouldman's composition "For Your Love." The fact that the work of Gouldman was in a different stylistic world than the covers of Muddy Waters, Howlin' Wolf, and Sonny Boy Williamson, which had made up the bulk of the Yardbird's repertoire previously, is evidenced by the fact that his most commercially successful songs were made into hits not only by the Yardbirds but by decidedly more pop-oriented beat groups such as Herman's Hermits. Herman's Hermits, in fact, recorded "For Your Love" at approximately the same time as the Yardbirds.

The Yardbirds' version of "For Your Love" is built in two distinctive sections, the first of which features highly technical bongo drum figures, block chords on the harpsichord, and very little instrumental contribution from the Yardbirds themselves. After the song seems to come to an intermediate stopping point, a harder, rock-oriented section follows. The song alternates between these two disparate styles. The snarl of Keith Relf's singing, the novelty of the stopping and starting, tempo changes, unusual harmonies, and unusual instrumentation broke the Yardbirds free of the blues. "For Your Love" was also a commercial success on the U.K. and the U.S. record charts. For blues purist Eric Clapton, however, it felt like a sell out to commercialism. He left the group to join John Mayall's Bluesbreakers.

To the extent that the 1960s were one of the most important periods of the rock era for guitar heroes, then the Yardbirds were one of the most important bands of the decade. Although pictured here during the period in which Jeff Beck was their lead guitarist, the band also featured Eric Clapton (Beck's predecessor) and Jimmy Page (Beck's successor). Courtesy of Photofest.

When young but well-seasoned studio guitarist Jimmy Page turned down an offer to replace Clapton, Jeff Beck joined the Yardbirds on lead guitar. Page eventually joined the band, but not for another year-and-a-half. It was during Beck's time with the group that they experienced their greatest commercial success, with singles such as "Heart Full of Soul" (another Graham Gouldman composition) and the 1966 song "Shapes of Things," a performance that generally is considered one of, if not *the* first psychedelic record. In addition to "Shapes of Things," other Yardbirds tracks of the 1965–1967 period include drones, unconventional song forms, Hindustani ragas (scalar and melodic patterns used in the music of India), impressionistic imagery, and unusual and distorted tone colors. Because of the band's extension use of these structures and tone colors during Jeff Beck's tenure in the Yardbirds, they are considered one of the most important bands in the psychedelic style.

The Yardbirds were less commercially successful once Jimmy Page replaced Beck; however, their work anticipated some of the music that Page created with Led Zeppelin after the Yardbirds' 1968 breakup. So, while the Yardbirds never returned to the pure electric blues of their early career, their work during the Eric Clapton period paved the way for the blues-based hard rock of the late 1960s, a style that ironically would be taken up by, among others, Jimmy Page's band Led Zeppelin. The Yardbirds also did much to establish the use of drones, modality, static harmony, and Hindustani ragas in psychedelic music. Despite their relative lack of commercial success compared with a number of other British Invasion bands, these contributions mark the Yardbirds as one of the most important British Invasion bands.

MANFRED MANN

While the Yardbirds essentially gave up electric blues in order to find success on the record charts and radio airwaves, Manfred Mann found a very different way in which to achieve sales success while remaining at least partially true to their roots. Keyboardist Manfred Lubowitz was born in Johannesburg, South Africa, in 1940. He studied classical piano but was most influenced by modern jazz musicians of the late 1950s, including Miles Davis, Cannonball Adderley, Dave Brubeck, and Bill Evans. Lubowitz moved to the United Kingdom in 1961 and made a living as a jazz pianist and writer. His pen name, Manfred Manne, was based on his own given name and jazz drummer Shelley Manne's family name. Lubowitz dropped the final "e," and his stage name, Manfred Mann, was established. Eventually, Mann, multi-instrumentalist Mike Vickers, keyboardist/saxophonist Graham Bond, and drummer Mike Hugg were playing a jazz-influenced brand of R&B in London clubs, including the famed Marquee. By 1963, the band, which was called the Mann Hugg Blues Brothers, included Mann, Hugg, Vickers, singer-harmonica player Paul Jones, and bassist Dave Richmond. An audition with EMI in spring 1963 resulted in a recording contract. John Burgess, who became the band's producer, suggested that they needed a shorter, catchier name; therefore, over the objections of their keyboardist/leader, the group was renamed Manfred Mann.

Although their first recordings did not establish them as stars, the late 1963 single, "5-4-3-2-1," certainly did. In addition to becoming the theme song for the popular British rock music television program *Ready Steady Go!*, "5-4-3-2-1" reached No. 5 on the U.K charts. By the time of Manfred Mann's next two singles, "Do Wah Diddy Diddy" and "Sha La La," Tom McGuinness had replaced Dave Richmond on bass and the British Invasion was in full swing. While both singles did well in Britain and in the United States, the cover of the Exciters' "Do Wah Diddy Diddy" was No. 1 on the *Billboard* pop charts for two weeks, and the recording became an iconic part of American popular culture, finding its way into numerous movies and television programs.

Bands that came out of the British blues and R&B scenes had several choices they could make: (1) maintain an absolute allegiance to blues music, (2) change to more commercial pop and British beat group style, or (3) do what the group Manfred Mann did and achieve a delicate balance between the two. Manfred Mann recorded pop songs and R&B covers for their single A-sides, but they focused on blues and jazz-oriented R&B for B-sides and album cuts. Courtesy of Photofest.

Although the commercially successful girl group covers "Do Wah Diddy Diddy" and "Sha La La" do not really reflect it, there are two important features of Manfred Mann's work that set the band apart from other R&B-based British Invasion bands. First, because of the range of instruments the members of the group played, including not only the standard rock assemblage of electric guitars, keyboards, bass, blues harp (harmonica), and drums, album cuts include such sounds as alto saxophone, flute, timpani (which are also used to a limited extent in "Do Wah Diddy Diddy"), and vibraphone. The playing style of Mann and Mike Vickers, in particular, comes more firmly out of the jazz tradition than does that of just about any other British Invasion keyboard and saxophone player. As is frequently noted, Vickers's playing on saxophone is more melodic with a more polished jazz phrasing and technique than the contemporary work of other oft-heard British Invasion saxophonists, such as the Dave Clark Five's Denis Payton.

In a sense, Manfred Mann's popular girl group covers were an anomaly in the band's repertoire: their album cuts included blues, jazz instrumentals, and R&B covers, as well as original compositions that fit squarely into these styles. Therefore, Manfred Mann maintained a balance between commerciality and focus on what the members of the band wanted to perform by recording A-sides of singles that would appeal to the masses, while focusing on album cuts that appealed to more hard-core R&B, blues-rock, and jazz fans. This nearly bipolar approach also can be seen in their television appearances. For example, on the U.S. television program *Shindig!*, Manfred Mann performed "5-4-3-2-1," a fast-paced beat song, and a vocal version of Herbie Hancock's 1962 jazz standard "Watermelon Man," which included a decidedly jazzy saxophone solo from Mike Vickers.

The members of Manfred Mann, especially keyboardist Mann himself, also did not look like other British Invasion rock stars. With Mann's closely trimmed beard and his head-swinging approach to playing, he looked more like a beatnik jazz musician than a Mod or a Rocker. So, musically and visually, Manfred Mann fit somewhere between, on one side, John Mayall's Bluesbreakers and Georgie Fame and the Blues, and, on the other side, blues-based rock bands such as the Yardbirds and the Rolling Stones. Despite personnel changes Manfred Mann (the band) continued into the early 1970s, when the group's namesake formed Manfred Mann's Earth Band. Keyboardist Mann continued to explore an eclectic mix of styles but is probably best remembered for "Do Wah Diddy Diddy," a 1968 hit version of Bob Dylan's "Mighty Quinn (Quinn the Eskimo)," and a hit 1976 recording (under the Earth Band moniker) of Bruce Springsteen's "Blinded by the Light."

In the final analysis, the initial British Invasion time period found British blues and R&B in a state of flux. The more-or-less purist electric blues and R&B bands did not achieve the broad commercial appeal of the bands that either moved away from the blues genre (e.g., the Yardbirds) or those that recorded an almost bipolar mix of R&B and pop songs (e.g., Manfred Mann and the Animals). The purist groups, however, produced numerous musicians that led the emergence of blues-rock in the late 1960s.

8

The Rolling Stones:
It All Starts with the Blues

As is the case of the Beatles, the Rolling Stones—as a group and as individuals—have generated a large number of biographies and autobiographies. Because biographical material in and of itself is not the primary purpose of this book, and because the lives of Mick Jagger, Keith Richards, Brian Jones, Charlie Watts, Bill Wyman, and others that have passed through the ranks of the Rolling Stones are so thoroughly documented elsewhere, we will focus here on the music of the self-proclaimed "greatest rock and roll band in the world."[1]

The first thing that must be remembered when one considers the development of the Rolling Stones is that in its earliest days the band was closely tied to blues and R&B. The reason that I mention this is that by 1965 and 1966 the Rolling Stones were incorporating touches of Elizabethan-era British lute song, straight-ahead rock and roll, and the Anglo and Anglo-American folk traditions in their recordings. For example, a listener familiar with the song "Lady Jane" would find it very difficult, if not impossible, to hear a connection to the early 1960s British blues scene.

As discussed in chapter 7, Alexis Korner's Blues Incorporated was one of the most important bands in the development of British blues, particularly as a breeding ground of talent. In addition to being fans of the group, Brian Jones, Keith Richards, and Mick Jagger performed from time to time with Blues Incorporated. Certainly, they were not as active in the group as was Charlie Watts—who was a regular member of Blues Incorporated before he joined the Rolling Stones—but the connection with Blues Incorporated for Jones, Jagger, and Richards was stronger than *just* that of fans. And, just as Alexis

The self-proclaimed "greatest rock and roll band in the world," the Rolling Stones, developed out of the early 1960s British electric blues scene; however, each of the members of the band brought a unique musical contribution. Drummer Charlie Watts, for example, brought to the Stones a jazz feel that made his work stand out from the work of most British Invasion drummers. Courtesy of Photofest.

Korner's first performing experience with blues came through a connection with jazz. Charlie Watts and Brian Jones were jazz fans and knowledgeable about different jazz styles. In addition to Jones, Jagger, and Richards, the other original members of the Rolling Stones (before they had officially adopted that moniker) were pianist Ian Stewart, drummer Tony Chapman, and bassist Dick Taylor. Before the formation of the Rolling Stones, Stewart, Chapman, and Taylor also had been active in the London R&B and blues scenes. Although Stewart officially left the band in 1963, he continued to perform with the Rolling Stones on tour and in the recording studio into the 1980s. Bill Wyman and Charlie Watts replaced Taylor and Chapman by January 1963.

Another facet of the development of the Rolling Stones that one must keep in mind is the Bohemian lifestyle that Jones, Jagger, and Richards lived once they had gotten together as a group but before they were joined by Charlie Watts and Bill Wyman. In his autobiography, Wyman mentions how surprised he was at the deplorable conditions in which he (someone who was a half-decade older than his eventual band mates) found Jones, Jagger, and Richards living when he first made their acquaintance in 1962. He states that he had this reaction primarily for two reasons: (1) it contrasted so highly with his own way of living (Wyman was older, had a job, and was a snappier dresser than his new bandmates) and (2) it made no sense to him because of what he knew about Jones's, Jagger's, and Richards's economically comfortable upbringings. According to Wyman, it was a lifestyle born out of choice and not out of necessity, and was connected with the influence of modern jazz and the Bohemian, beatnik lifestyle that was associated with that musical genre in the late 1950s and early 1960s.[2] Without working-class backgrounds, they turned to a counterculture lifestyle as a conscious reaction against the conventional norms of society.

In discussing the Rolling Stones, it is necessary to mention Giorgio Gomelsky, the club owner, manager, and record producer who gave the Rolling Stones their first important break. Gomelsky was born in Soviet Georgia; however, his family escaped Stalin and lived variously in France, Italy, and Switzerland. Gomelsky arrived in the United Kingdom and co-owned a coffee bar there from 1955. He played an important role in the development of the British blues scene with his Crawdaddy Club, which beginning in 1962 featured R&B and blues bands. Gomelsky's club was located in the Richmond suburb of London. In 1963, Brian Jones convinced Gomelsky to listen to his new band, then called the Rollin' Stones. Gomelsky booked the group for what turned out to be an eight-month residency at the Crawdaddy Club. It was this residency that firmly established the Rolling Stones as an important blues-rock band.

Given the strong ties that the members of the Rolling Stones had to jazz and blues, as well as the sense of rebellion that was exhibited by the Bohemian lifestyle of Jones, Jagger, and Richards, it is ironic that the band's first single was a cover of Chuck Berry's "Come On," which is performed in a fairly sterile beat group style. This debut recording, which was released in June 1963, reached No. 21 on the British charts. Despite the fact that it was not a commercial failure, the Rolling Stones themselves were displeased with the single. Even the B-side of the record, a cover of the Willie Dixon composition "I Want to Be Loved," a blues song most closely associated with Muddy Waters, features a beat group swing-feel rhythmic approach and record production that fails to capture the kind of gritty blues approach the band preferred. The group's manager and producer, Andrew Loog Oldham, continued to take the approach of trying to market the Rolling Stones as a popish rock group for several more recorded sides, but by the time of the Rolling Stones' debut album the following year, Oldham allowed the band to play and sing with the harder-edged sound that better reflected the live sound of the Rolling Stones.

Despite Oldham's early attempts to present the Rolling Stones as a beat group not entirely unlike others that had already enjoyed some U.K. chart success by the time of the Stones' recording debut, a few harder-edged gems did slip out. For example, the Rolling Stones' second single, "I Wanna Be Your Man," a song supplied by John Lennon and Paul McCartney at Oldham's request, contains a blistering slide guitar solo from Brian Jones that shows off his electric blues leanings. Incidentally, "I Wanna Be Your Man" outdid "Come On" on the charts, reaching No. 12, perhaps supporting the Rolling Stones' contention that there was a market for harder-edged material.

Already by 1963 it was clear that a new paradigm for rock bands was becoming established: in the wake of the Beatles, no longer would it be fashionable to turn exclusively to covers of American songs, nor would it be fashionable to turn to outside professional songwriters for material. The factors that helped a band establish musical credibility now included having songwriters in the group. Oldham insisted that Mick Jagger and Keith Richards learn to write their own material.

Before Jagger and Richards wrote songs that became icons of the British Invasion, such as "Satisfaction," the Rolling Stones recorded their first album, *England's Newest Hitmakers*. This 1964 collection presents a very different sound than sides such as "Come On," "The Fortune Teller," and other pseudo–beat group recordings of the band. Significantly, the album's cover photo places Mick Jagger and Brian Jones, perhaps the two most heavily blues-influenced members of the group, in the foreground, with Richards, Watts, and Wyman in the background. And, it is true that Jagger was the front man of the Rolling Stones, but Jones was the early leader of the group. The implications of the photo are played out musically on the album: this was the most blues- and R&B-focused recording the early Rolling Stones ever made.

From the blues-inspired remake of Buddy Holly's "Not Fade Away" to Willie Dixon's composition "I Just Want to Make Love to You," the album finds the Rolling Stones returning to a style that is closer to that of Blues Incorporated and other British blues bands. Even the covers of "Route 66" and the Chuck Berry composition "Carol" have an earthier, bluesier feel than the band's early singles. In contrast to every later Rolling Stones album, *England's Newest Hitmakers* features just about as many, and just about as prominent, blues harp (harmonica) solos from Brian Jones and Mick Jagger as electric guitar solos. Where this album contrasts most significantly with the contemporary work of groups such as Blues Incorporated and Mayall's Bluesbreakers is that even on this debut album, the Rolling Stones more fully integrate rock and roll with blues. One of the clearest audible differences is that the polyphony that the purist blues groups created when several instrumentalists improvised simultaneously is absent.

England's Newest Hitmakers contains some of the earliest self-composed pieces by the group. The instrumental piece "Now I've Got a Witness" is credited to Nanker

Phelge, a pseudonym used for group-composed pieces early in the band's career. It is not one of the most noteworthy pieces on the album, though, because it is essentially an instrumental jam based on the Motown song "Can I Get a Witness." The Rolling Stones (again credited as Phelge) collaborated with American producer and songwriter Phil Spector for the song "Little By Little." This piece fits easily within the blues/R&B feel of most of the songs on the album. Mick Jagger and Keith Richards's composition "Tell Me," which became the Rolling Stones' first Top 40 single in the United States in August 1964, is another R&B-style song. Although the song contains a few hints of the brilliance of Jagger and Richards's songwriting that would be heard within a year, it tends to sound an awful lot like a cover of a 1950s American R&B song, in large part because it makes such heavy use of the so-called oldies chord progression (I-vi-IV-V) in the refrain. In fact, all three of the group-composed pieces ("Now I've Got a Witness," "Little By Little," and "Tell Me") stand apart from the self-composed songs that groups such as the Dave Clark Five and the Beatles sent up the charts at the time. The Rolling Stones stick more solidly with diatonic harmonies within the tonic key, thereby avoiding the chromatic chords that mark the compositions credited to John Lennon, Paul McCartney, Ron Ryan, Mike Smith, and Dave Clark. These early Rolling Stones compositions, too, avoid the heavy use of the bVII (subtonic) chord and unpredictable modulations of the blatantly Mod groups, such as the Who and the Kinks. As Jagger and Richards developed as writers, they continued to avoid the chromaticism and upward modulations of their contemporaries. By maintaining stronger ties to the fundamental harmonies of the key, the Rolling Stones continued to tie themselves to the traditions of black R&B, blues, and rock and roll of the 1950s, even as some of the materials that they incorporated into their music sounded quite different from 1950s American music on the surface.

Despite the fact that the harmonic practice found in the three self-penned songs that grace *England's Newest Hitmakers* differs from that of Ray Davies and Pete Townshend, the Rolling Stones were embraced by Mods. The Mods favored modern jazz and black American R&B and blues. While the Rolling Stones avoid the references to jazz style of some R&B groups and blues purist groups of the day, their work on this album squarely fits within the milieu of R&B and blues. In fact, because of the early importance of blues harp answer figures and more extended solos—as well as the fact that as a singer Mick Jagger tended to phrase, pronounce, and express more like black American blues singers than many British rock singers did—it is easy to hear the Rolling Stones' debut album as one of the more authentic British R&B products of the day.

The next step in the solidification of the Rolling Stones' image and status in the world of British Invasion rock came in the form of a deliberate attempt to portray and market the group as a polar opposition to the Beatles in a sort of yin-yang relationship. A headline in the March 14, 1964 issue of Britain's *Melody Maker* magazine posed the rhetorical question "Would You Let Your Sister Go with a Rolling Stone?" This signaled the start of a campaign by the band's producer, Andrew Loog Oldham, to capitalize on the band's image as raw and dangerous. Later headlines read "Would You Let Your Daughter Marry a Rolling Stone?" With this two-pronged publicity campaign Oldham placed his charges in direct opposition to the norms held by the parents of teenagers (the "Daughter" head-line), but also reinforced the notion that it was not just parents who might be leery of these young men. The "Sister" headline suggests that some conservative, uncool young people would recognize Jagger, Richards, Jones, Wyman, and Watts as counterculture, potentially dangerous rebels. As might be expected, this strengthened the band's appeal to rebellious youth. In a very real sense, this publicity campaign represented a dramatic shift from the ways in which previous rock stars (in Britain and in the United States) were presented. For example, while earlier stars might have been presented as "bad boys," there generally was a tempering of that portrayal. In the case of Elvis Presley, for ex-ample, the hip-swiveling hepcat who countrified somewhat risqué R&B songs was also the young man who appeared on television singing "Hound Dog" to an actual hound dog, and the nice young man who recorded traditional Christian hymns.

As Oldham built up the Rolling Stones' image as the bad boys of British rock and roll, the band's music was also progressing. The band's 1964 cover of "Time Is on My Side" took the Rolling Stones into the U.S. Top 10 for the first time. Significantly, the Rolling Stones' arrangement—which receives some help from Ian Stewart[3] on organ—has a rawness and feeling of roots-music authenticity that is missing from some other contemporary British covers of the song. For example, Brian Poole & the Tremeloes re-move much of the syncopation from the song, thereby moving it from the R&B genre to the British beat group genre. The Moody Blues' cover finds Denny Laine capturing some of the blues-inflected sound in his lead vocal and guitar solo; however, the Moody Blues' backing vocals square off the syncopations and create a feeling of disconnection. Aside from the odd church organ introduction in the Stones' arrangement (which is re-moved in some mixes of the song), their take on "Time Is on My Side" is one of the more authentic-sounding British R&B covers of the period. The Rolling Stones' recording of the song also gained notoriety when it became one of the favorites of U.S. troops early in the Vietnam War. American soldiers were drawn to the implications of the title line, that if they just made it through their tour of duty, they could return home.

Even more important to the band's stylistic development was the 1965 song "The Last Time." This piece certainly is not the band's best-remembered work from that year; however, it sets the stage for the iconic songs that followed it. One of the most notable musical features of "The Last Time" is that the song is based on an oft-repeated two-measure-long electric guitar riff. Mick Jagger and Keith Richards's next two major hit songs, "(I Can't Get No) Satisfaction" and "Get Off My Cloud" were also based on short riffs. Jagger and Richards were not alone, however, in using riffs around which to base songs—it was in the air in British Invasion rock in 1964 and 1965. For example, the Kinks' "You Really Got Me" and "All Day and All of the Night" and the Beatles' "I Feel Fine" and "Day Tripper" are all riff-based compositions. Roy Orbison's 1964 song "Oh, Pretty Woman," an early example of an American rock song that contains British Invasion signifiers, is also based on a short, easily identifiable electric guitar riff. What sets "The Last Time" and "Satisfaction" off from many of the other riff-based rock songs of the period is the minimalist brevity of the riff. This is especially true of "Satisfaction," one of the most iconic songs of the entire British Invasion.

"The Last Time" also contains a sexual edge that goes beyond the bulk of British Invasion material of the day. Jagger tells his partner that she does not try very hard to please him, but that "with what you know, it should be easy," which suggests her sexual prowess. More generally, though, "The Last Time" fits in with "Satisfaction" and "Get Off My Cloud" as songs of frustration and alienation. In "The Last Time," the lyrics speak of a relationship that Mick Jagger's character is about to end because of his frustrations. In "Satisfaction," he finds frustration with the confusing modern world of consumerism, news events over which he has no control, corporate details, as well as in his relationships with women. In "Get Off My Cloud," salespeople who knock at the door, neighbors who complain about loud parties, and consumerism all contribute to the character's desire to be left alone. Jagger's lyrics—to a great extent these songs represent Jagger's lyrics and Richards' music—are not unique in expressing youthful frustrations. For example, Pete Townshend's "My Generation," Ray Davies' "Tired of Waiting for You," Lennon and McCartney's "Please Please Me," and George Harrison's "Don't Bother Me" are all 1962–1965 songs that revolve around frustration. The references in "Satisfaction" and "Get Off My Cloud" to consumerism, owning a car, holding a job, and so on, suggest that Jagger's character is probably out of school and in his early 20s. Some of the other songs of frustration and alienation of the period do not necessarily include the social commentary or the suggestions of the lead character's age. The combination of Jagger's lyrics and Richards' riff-based music, however combine to make "Satisfaction" and "Get Off My Cloud" two of the most vivid statements ever of the frustrations of early twentysomethings. Despite the fact that outwardly the two songs are not as Mod sounding as some of the work of the Who and the Kinks, the total gestalt of the statement of frustration and alienation speaks directly to the heart of what the Mod movement was all about.

The Rolling Stones continued to explore themes of frustration, alienation, and concern with contemporary urban and suburban society throughout the rest of the initial part of the British Invasion. Musically, however, they increasingly diversified, incorporating blues, rock, Renaissance lute song, music hall, R&B, and folk styles into their singles and album cuts. Despite the fact that the Rolling Stones have enjoyed a career lasting into the twenty-first century, and despite the fact that the self-proclaimed "greatest rock and roll band in the world" has placed over 40 singles in the U.S. Top 40, their British Invasion–era hits "(I Can't Get No) Satisfaction" and "Get Off My Cloud" remain two of their quintessential tracks and foreshadow the social and political discontent that marked the 1960s counterculture.

9

And That's Not All: Other British Invasion Artists

The story of the British Invasion and what led up to it tends in the minds of many Americans to focus on Liverpool, London, the blues, the Mod and Merseybeat scenes, and the male rock groups that came out of these cities and styles. There was, however, much more to the British Invasion. In this chapter, we will turn our attention to some of the solo female pop singers, folk-oriented male duos, and non-Liverpool/non-London bands that made either brief, or, in some cases, long-lasting impacts on Americans as part of the British Invasion.

While shear numbers suggest that the focus of fans' attention was on the male groups of the British Invasion, several important female British artists made significant and enduring contributions to popular music at the time. Easily the most commercially success female artist of the British Invasion was Petula Clark. Clark was born in 1932, and was a child star on radio in the United Kingdom. By the time she was 21, she had starred in her own television series in the United Kingdom and had an album released in the United States. By the time she was in her mid-twenties, Petula Clark had starred in over 20 movies. Her string of hit recordings in the United States, however, did not begin until the No. 1 pop hit "Downtown" in early 1965. In a very real sense, the invasion that British rock bands in 1964 opened the U.S. market to a wide array of British acts, including pop singers such as Clark. By 1968, Petula Clark had recorded 15 *Billboard* Top 40 singles, including "I Know a Place," "My Love," "Don't Sleep in the Subway," and "I Couldn't Live without Your Love." While Petula Clark was not a prolific songwriter, her major hits had the air of originals because Clark's producer and arranger, Tony Hatch, wrote

While one perhaps is most likely to think of bands such as the Beatles, the Rolling Stones, the Kinks, the Zombies, Gerry and the Pacemakers, and others when one thinks of the British Invasion, the 1964–1966 period also found solo British artists such as Petula Clark dominating U.S. Top 40 radio play lists and record charts. Courtesy of Photofest.

them specifically for her. Clark's recordings of "Don't Sleep in the Subway," "My Love," and "Downtown," in particular, are iconic and are among the most instantly recognizable British hits that dominated American pop radio between 1965 and 1967. And, while the single only reached No. 21 on the *Billboard* charts, Clark's 1966 recording of Tony Hatch's "Who Am I" inspired Canadian concert pianist, recording artist, and CBC radio documentary maker Glenn Gould, who used Hatch's focus on identity in the song as the basis for the 1967 radio documentary *The Idea of North*.

One female star whose story sounds like something out of a Hollywood movie script is Cilla Black. Born in Liverpool in 1943, Priscilla White worked by day as a typist and moonlighted as a hatcheck girl in the famous Cavern Club. White was called up on stage from time to time to sing a few numbers with the bands that performed there, whether they be King Size Taylor and the Dominoes, the Big Three, the Beatles, Rory Storm and the Hurricanes, or a jazz group. It was after hearing one of her amateur performances that the Beatles' manager, Brian Epstein, asked White if she would like to turn professional and be managed by him. Rechristened Cilla Black, Epstein rightly referred to her as "my little Cilla" in his autobiography *A Cellarful of Noise*.[1] Epstein took the singer and crafted her musical and public style and image based on his own sense of taste and glamour. Working with record producer George Martin, Black enjoyed numerous hit singles in Britain throughout the 1960s and early 1970s. Since the late 1960s, Cilla Black has acted in situation comedies and has hosted several television programs in Great Britain. Her only U.S. hit, however, was "You're My World," which made it as high as No. 26 on the *Billboard* Pop charts in summer 1964.

Dusty Springfield, who had been a member of the Lana Sisters and the Springfields before becoming a solo artist in 1963, did not enjoy the level of commercial success that Petula Clark achieved in the United States; however, she outperformed Cilla Black by taking 10 singles into the *Billboard* Top 40 between 1964 and the end of the decade. Of these, perhaps the most iconic is her hit "Son of a Preacher Man," a record that remained on the charts from late 1968 through early 1969. While she may not have enjoyed as much commercial success as a few other British solo pop singing stars of the 1960s (e.g., Petula Clark and Tom Jones), Dusty Springfield's 1969 album *Dusty in Memphis* remains perhaps one of the most intriguing and artistically successful British hybrids of pop and American R&B music.

Like Cilla Black, Petula Clark, and Dusty Springfield, the Welsh singer Tom Jones was not so much a part of the rock side of the British Invasion as the middle-of-the-road pop side. However, Jones—who was born Thomas Jones Woodward in 1940—did land 17 songs in the U.S. Top 40 between 1965 and 1971. He also hosted a variety show on U.S. television from 1969–1971 and made countless television appearances as a singer on other programs. The sight of women throwing their undergarments on stage at Jones's electrifying televised performances became almost a cliché by the end of the 1960s.

Another non-English male solo singer, Scottish folksinger-songwriter Donovan Leitch (professionally, he uses only his first name), was born in Glasgow in 1946. Donovan moved to England with his family in 1956. There, he took up the guitar and eventually dropped out of school in order to live the life of a beatnik folk musician. Donovan studied folk guitar technique with a number of British musicians, in addition to studying the compositions and recordings of other British and American musicians. By 1964, Donovan was a street performer; however, on the strength of a demo tape, he secured a management and publishing contract. The still-unknown Donovan appeared on the influential British pop music program *Ready Steady Go!* in early 1965 and sang his composition "Catch the Wind." It should be noted that Donovan performed the song live, in contrast to major stars (such as the Beatles) that, while they sometimes performed live on

U.S. television, mimed performances on this program. Donovan's performance resulted in a recording contract. His subsequent recordings of "Catch the Wind," "The War Drags On," and Buffy Sainte-Marie's "The Universal Soldier" find him using the texture—solo singer, acoustic guitar, and harmonica—associated with American folk and folk revival singers such as Woody Guthrie, Ramblin' Jack Elliott, and Bob Dylan. Despite the fact that he used this texture, the fact that he dressed similarly to Dylan, and the fact that he incorporated some of the pitch slides that characterized Dylan, Donovan's early folk work was not merely that of a Dylan imitator.

Donovan's originality became clear by late 1965 when he was working with producer Mickie Most. Donovan's interest in the folk-rock that was coming from the United States in 1965 recordings by the Byrds and Bob Dylan convinced the singer and the producer that Donovan's music could move in a new direction. By using the leading studio musicians of the day, including guitarists Big Jim Sullivan and Jimmy Page, and bass guitarist and arranger John Paul Jones, Donovan and Most recast the acoustic folk singer into a hippie, psychedelic figure that in late 1965 and throughout 1966 anticipated an image that became commonplace during the 1967 so-called Summer of Love. Donovan's 1966–1969 recordings, such as "Sunshine Superman," "Mellow Yellow," "There Is a Mountain," "Hurdy Gurdy Man," and "Atlantis," not only placed high in the U.S. Top 40, but they became iconic symbols of the psychedelic hippie era, songs that still symbolize that era over 40 years later.

Donovan Leitch was not, however, the only acoustic folk-influenced musician who contributed to the British Invasion. The prominent folk duo Chad and Jeremy placed seven singles in the *Billboard* Top 40 in the 1964–1966 period. In fact, Chad Stuart (born David Stuart Chadwick in 1941) and Jeremy Clyde (born Michael Thomas Jeremy Clyde in 1941) were more commercially successful in the United States than they were at home. In part, this may have resulted from widespread knowledge of their upper-class roots. It must be remembered that for the most part British Invasion rock and pop developed out of the working class, and the class system in the 1960s remained strong in the United Kingdom.

Chad Stuart and Jeremy Clyde (grandson of the Duke of Wellington) met in 1960 while they were acting students at the Central School of Speech and Drama in London. The two played London coffeehouses, and it was one of their gigs that composer, producer, and bandleader John Barry heard Chad and Jeremy and offered them a recording contract. Under Barry's leadership, Chad and Jeremy developed their unique sound, which moved from gently sung unison lead vocals to harmony and back again. Barry produced their first single, Stuart's composition and arrangement, "Yesterday's Gone." This 1963 recording was moving up the British charts when a tabloid disclosed Jeremy Clyde's connection to the Duke of Wellington. Suddenly, British working-class teens stopped buying their recordings, because they suspected that Chad and Jeremy were performing simply on a lark. In reality, the two were still working the club and coffeehouse circuit just like working-class and middle-class musicians.

Significantly, Chad and Jeremy wrote or cowrote a fair number of their singles and album cuts. In fact, the acoustic guitar–playing and singing duo's best-remembered songs in the United States are their originals "Yesterday's Gone" and the No. 7 hit "A Summer Song"—this, despite the fact that their covers of the old jazz standard "Willow Weep for Me" and of Van McCoy's "Before and After" actually performed better on the U.S. pop charts than "Yesterday's Gone." With orchestral strings, heavy use of acoustic guitar, and their relaxed vocal style, Chad and Jeremy bridged the gap between folk and middle-of-the-road pop. So many of their 1965 and 1966 recordings—even those produced by Shel Talmy, who worked with the Kinks—veer toward the middle of the road that by 1966, Chad and Jeremy's style was far removed from the direction in which rock was moving. In 1967 and 1968, however, the duo moved toward a merger of folk, pop, and psychedelic styles that, while it never caught on commercially, holds up better than some psychedelic music of the time. The folkish, somewhat lightweight nature of Chad and Jeremy's singles led to one particularly interesting phenomenon: their best-known songs, "Yesterday's Gone" and "A Summer Song," enjoyed significantly higher chart standing in *Cash Box* magazine than in *Billboard*. In the case of "Yesterday's Gone," *Billboard* ranked the single at a high of No. 21, while *Cash Box* listed it at No. 5. The single release of "A Summer Song" went as high as No. 7 in *Billboard;* it was No. 1 in *Cash Box*. While the weighting formulae used by the two trade magazines is too complicated to detail here, suffice it to say that generally *Billboard* measured unit sales, while *Cash Box* measured jukebox plays. This suggests that Chad and Jeremy's laid-back style was quite popular with American audiences, but considerably more popular when one could spend a small amount of money on jukebox play, instead of purchasing the record. Another way to look at this phenomenon is that Chad and Jeremy's singles probably appealed to a wider age demographic than the singles of rock bands. Therefore, the duo's fans included those who might be likely to buy inexpensive 45-rpm plastic records (youth), as well as those who might be less inclined to buy singles.

At the height of their popularity in the United States, Chad and Jeremy appeared both as themselves and as fictional British rock musicians on several U.S. television programs, including *Batman* and *The Dick Van Dyke Show*. Their training as actors, as well as the fact that their brand of British Invasion music was worlds apart from that of, say, the Rolling Stones in terms of acceptance by adults, made Chad and Jeremy ideal, primetime musical representatives of Britain.

Although Chad and Jeremy authored some of their own songs, they also performed jazz, folk, and R&B material in their own acoustic style. Although between 1970 and the dawn of the twenty-first century they worked together only occasionally, today they tour regularly. In their concerts, they tell the story of meeting a young American singer-songwriter who was traveling around the United Kingdom in 1964, trying to establish a career on the folk coffeehouse circuit. The young American offered Chad and Jeremy one of his new compositions, a song written in Britain about his travels and feelings of home-sickness. Although Chad and Jeremy recorded the song—Paul Simon's "Homeward Bound"—they failed to release it before Simon and Garfunkel's version appeared.[2]

Peter Asher and Gordon Waller, corporately known as Peter and Gordon, enjoyed even greater commercial success than did Chad and Jeremy. Formed in London in 1963, Peter and Gordon enjoyed the good fortune that Peter Asher's sister, Jane, happened to be Paul McCartney's girlfriend. McCartney, either writing alone or in collaboration with John Lennon (depending on the song) supplied Peter and Gordon with compositions such as "A World without Love," "Nobody I Know," "I Don't Want to See You Again," and "Woman," each of which made it well into the U.S. Top 40 between 1964 and 1966. In fact, the duo charted 10 singles in the United States before breaking up in 1968. Peter and Gordon's other successful singles include "I Go to Pieces" (written for them by Del Shannon), a cover of Buddy Holly's "True Love Ways," and "Lady Godiva." The latter, a novelty song, continued the use of British music hall influences in 1950s and 1960s pop that extended from Tommy Steele to Herman's Hermits, the Monkees' Davy Jones, and the New Vaudeville Band, and even included a few songs by the Beatles and the Rolling Stones. Although Peter and Gordon's recordings were closer to middle-of-the-road pop than the music of the Rolling Stones, the Animals, the Yardbirds, and other harder-edged British Invasion rock bands, their work tended to have more teen appeal than, say, Chad and Jeremy's recordings. The Peter and Gordon recording of "A World without Love" remains a staple of 1960s oldies compilations and oldies radio. In addition to this group's four-year run of chart hits, Peter Asher's contribution to pop music includes highly suc-cessful record production work for 10,000 Maniacs, Linda Ronstadt, James Taylor, and others.

A notable group that never garnered the amount of popularity as some of the other commercial leaders of the British Invasion was the Zombies. Most notable was Rod Argent's keyboard playing, which in 1964 and 1965 sounded almost like a prototype of the style of rock organ playing that became popular a couple of years later. Colin Blunstone's vocals were effective, and his almost cool approach contrasted with the sometimes edgy and aggressive approach adopted by some prominent British blues-based rock sing-ers of the day. The band's originals, such as Argent's compositions "She's Not There" and "Tell Her No," stood up well even against the original compositions of writers from other beat groups, such as the Beatles. Unfortunately, the band was not particularly suc-cessful in the commercial arena, except for those two singles and "Time of the Season," a 1967 recording that did not become a hit until 1969, at which time the Zombies were no more. The Zombies' block harmony vocal style and Argent's keyboard style, however, continued to be heard in the work of other rock bands through the end of the decade.

MANCHESTER, ENGLAND

The northern English city of Manchester was a particularly fertile locale for British beat groups. By and large, the groups that came out of Manchester tended to be more pop oriented than groups from the London area, which places Manchester in a similar stylistic milieu as Liverpool. Among the artists that emerged out of Manchester were Freddie and the Dreamers, David Jones, Wayne Fontana and the Mindbenders, Herman's Hermits, and the Hollies.

Although each of the Manchester artists named above made memorable contributions to pop and rock music in the 1960s and beyond, perhaps the best-known Manchester act was the Hollies. The band's incarnation extends back to a friendship that developed in primary school at age five between singer Allan Clarke and singer-guitarist Graham Nash. By the start of the 1960s, the two were working as a duo under various names. Eventually, they expanded their group and continued to explore possible names for the ensemble. The 1962 Hollies consisted of lead singer Clarke, guitarists Nash and Vic Steele, bassist Eric Haydock, and drummer Don Rathbone; however, by the start of 1964, Tony Hicks and Bobby Elliott replaced Steele and Rathbone. Before joining the Hollies, Haydock, Hicks, and Elliott had worked together in a band called the Dolphins. Bernie Calvert replaced Haydock in 1966, and Terry Sylvester (formerly of the Swinging Blue Jeans) replaced Graham Nash in 1968. Throughout the 1970s and 1980s the Hollies underwent other personnel changes, making it one of the least stable long-standing bands that came out of the British Invasion.

The Hollies' recording career goes back to 1963. From the start, the group enjoyed hit singles in their homeland. For example, their cover of "Searchin'" went to No. 12 on the U.K. charts in 1963, their cover of "Just One Look" went to No. 2 in early 1964, and their original composition "We're Through" made it to No. 7 later in 1964. The Hollies were one of the British bands that appeared on the American television program *Shindig!* at the height of the British Invasion in late 1964; however, even with the support of televised performances, they failed to garner as much interest in the United States as the Beatles, the Rolling Stones, Gerry and the Pacemakers, the Searchers, Billy J. Kramer and the Dakotas, and others.

It was not until January 1966 that a Hollies single, "Look Through Any Window," found its way into the *Billboard* Top 40, and the Hollies' first true U.S. hit, Graham Gouldman's composition "Bus Stop," reached No. 5 in autumn 1966. The self-penned

"On a Carousel" and "Carrie Anne" extended the Hollies' success in the U.S. Top 40 into mid-1967. In the early 1970s the Hollies returned to the U.S. charts with "He Ain't Heavy, He's My Brother," "Long Cool Woman (In a Black Dress)," and "The Air That I Breathe."

Despite the fact that Allan Clarke served as lead vocalist, the sound of the Hollies was unlike that of blues and R&B bands of the early 1960s with frontmen, such as the Rolling Stones, the Animals, and the Yardbirds. The Hollies' style fell in more strongly with the pop/rock sound of the Beatles and other Liverpool bands. Their 1963 residency at Liverpool's Cavern Club confirms the Hollies' stylistic ties to Merseybeat. Like the Beatles and other Liverpool groups, the Hollies frequently featured two-part and three-part harmony, covers of Chuck Berry and girl group songs, and an emphasis on pop accessibility.

The slowness with which U.S. audiences embraced the Hollies, and the fact that some lesser pop/rock acts enjoyed greater commercial success in the United Kingdom than the Hollies seem to be attributable to several factors. First, and perhaps foremost, though, was the fact that the Hollies focused their recording efforts on covers and songs written for them by outside songwriters. For example, 11 of the 22 songs on disc one of EMI's 2007, two-CD collection The Hollies Finest are covers of American songs; two of the songs came from the pen of Manchester songwriter Graham Gouldman; and of the nine originals, only three were major U.K. hits. The Hollies perhaps unwittingly also contributed to their image as a band that relied heavily on outside material. Until as late as 1966, the original songs that Nash, Clarke, and Hicks wrote were credited to several pseudonyms (e.g., L. Ransford), thereby making it appear that even their original compositions came from sources outside the group. The Hollies' drummer, Bobby Elliott writes, "The Hollies wrote all the 'B' sides of their singles, but we were bizarrely informed at the time that 'The names Clarke/Hicks/Nash, will take up too much room on the record label', so aliases . . . were born. This was not a great career move!" Elliott adds, "Sadly and frustratingly, the general public and the music press are unaware that The Hollies wrote all those great songs."[3]

The Hollies' musical style also tended to evolve a little more slowly than the most progressive bands of the British Invasion. For example, the Hollies' summer 1966 hit recording of "Bus Stop" would not have sounded out of place in late 1964 or in 1965, and the self-penned 1967 hit "On a Carousel" would not have sounded out of place at any time in 1966. That being said, and with the chart impact of the Hollies coming as late in the British Invasion of the United States as it did, it should be noted that some of the early Hollies recordings—those that are not nearly as widely known in the United States as the post-"Bus Stop" recordings are—hold up well in the twenty-first century as examples of how British bands were utilizing American influences while making them their own. Their 1964 recordings of Little Richard's "Lucille" and Chuck Berry's "Too Much Monkey Business," for example, come maybe a year or so after Liverpool bands included the songs in their stage acts; however, both show solid vocal and instrumental chops and reveal that the Hollies were working to combine American rock and roll, the Everly Brothers, and other influences as they tried to establish their own style. However, in the case of "Lucille," the influence of the Everly Brothers is a double-edged sword: the Hollies version is so thoroughly indebted to the Everly Brothers' recording of the song that some of the power of Little Richard's original is lost. The cover of "Too Much Monkey Business" includes lead vocal lines that are tossed between Allan Clarke, Graham Nash, and Tony Hicks. This is highly effective, and it was used to good effect in the Hollies' early live performances on American television. On the studio recording, however, producer Ron Richards does not fully integrate the overdubbed guitar solo in the texture, which causes it to sound artificially grafted on.

So, the answer to the question of why it took the Hollies so long to break in the United States comes down to timing (retaining songs in the repertoire that other British beat groups had used a year or two before), record production that sometimes lacks the impact and integrated sound of the more successful bands, and at least the appearance of relying too heavily on outside songwriters. To a certain extent, the Hollies' tendency not to fall heavily into the latest musical trends helped them achieve significant sales of singles and Top 40 radio airplay in 1966 and 1967—they continued to produce pop music as some bands moved to harder rock and psychedelic styles.

As *All Music Guide*'s Bruce Eder writes, "Herman's Hermits were one of those odd 1960's groups that accumulated millions of fans, but precious little respect."[4] The group first worked as the Heartbeats in 1963 and included guitarist Keith Hopwood, guitarist Derek "Lek" Leckenby, bassist Karl Green, and drummer Barry Whitwam. When the Heartbeats' regular lead vocalist did not show up for a gig one night, Peter Noone sat in. Noone became the lead singer, with Hopwood, Leckenby, and Green providing backing vocals. Several things set Herman's Hermits apart from the other successful British Invasion bands. For one thing, Noone had been a child star back in the 1950s. Therefore, despite his youth when he joined the band (he was 16), he had more show business experience than his 16–18-year-old bandmates. With all of Herman's Hermits being younger than any of the members of the Rolling Stones, the Beatles, and some of the other British Invasion musicians, they had a greater potential for teen appeal. In addition, their relative youth meant that none of the members of Herman's Hermits had experienced the development of British Invasion rock the same way as their older countrymen.

Producer Mickie Most signed the group in 1964 and capitalized on Peter Noone's good looks and accompanying appeal to young female fans. For the most part, Most selected pop and easygoing soft rock songs for the group. He also liberally employed studio musicians to play on the band's records. In part, it was the fact that band members contributed instrumentally so little—especially to their hit singles—that is behind the lack of respect that Herman's Hermits received. The band was quite popular, however, especially in the United States. Hit singles such as their cover of the Goffin-King song "I'm into Something Good," the rock version of the Edwardian-period music hall song "I'm Henry the VIII, I Am," the innocent-sounding "Mrs. Brown, You've Got a Lovely Daughter," and the ballads "The End of the World" and "There's a Kind of Hush (All over the World)" made Herman's Hermits one of the biggest-selling Top 40 bands of the 1964–1967 period.

Despite some overlooked strong album cuts, though, Herman's Hermits did not progress artistically to the extent of other British Invasion bands. Peter Noone, already a star within the band, continued to appear as a singer, actor, and television host both in the United Kingdom and in the United States. By the 1980s and 1990s, competing versions of Herman's Hermits were touring on oldies circuits, some with Noone, some without. Additional confusion about the musical identity of Herman's Hermits was created by various competing incarnations of the band rerecording their hit songs for post-1960s releases. Even in 2008, there are two versions of the band, one called Herman's Hermits Starring Peter Noone, and one simply called Herman's Hermits, which is led by drummer Barry Whitwam.

Another Manchester singer, David Jones, possessed the same sort of appeal to young female fans as Peter Noone. Born in 1945, Jones was approximately the same age as some of Herman's Hermits, although older than Noone himself. A diminutive teenager, Jones left school in 1960 to become a horse-racing jockey. Between 1960 and 1965, however, Jones pursued a career as a singer-actor and appeared on British television, radio, and on the stage. The American company Colgems signed Jones to a contract and in 1965 issued an album that failed to chart. Jones's looks, singing, and acting abilities, however, made him a natural for a new television program with which the company was affiliated: Jones was selected to star in *The Monkees*. This program about a fictional rock band ran from 1966–1968. For his part, Jones sang lead vocals on several of the group's hit singles, most notably "Daydream Believer" and "Valleri."

The British Invasion included more than one group that enjoyed a brief period of popularity in the United States and then reverted to "whatever became of" status. The Manchester group Freddie and the Dreamers is a case in point. Born in 1936,[5] Freddie Garrity was older than most of the musicians who were part of the British Invasion. Garrity worked at a variety of jobs in the late 1950s—including a stint as a milkman—but he was also active in skiffle bands. In approximately 1959 Garrity formed the Dreamers Rhythm Group; however, by the early 1960s they were known as Freddie and the Dreamers. The first incarnation of the band included Garrity on lead vocals, guitarist Roy

Crewdson, guitar and harmonica player Derek Quinn, bassist Peter Birrell, and drummer Bernie Dwyer. Eventually, EMI signed the band and released their first single, "I'm Telling You Now," in 1963. Because of the success of this single Freddie and the Dreamers holds the distinction of being the first non-Beatles, non-Brian Epstein-managed beat group to hit the top of the British charts. Interestingly, though, "I'm Telling You Now" and some of the band's other releases bear the stamp of Merseyside style. For example, like 1963 songs by John Lennon and Paul McCartney, Garrity and Mitch Murray's composition "I'm Telling You Now" includes tonally ambiguous harmonies, prominent use of the bVII chord, and touches of Liverpool-style drumming.

Like a number of British Invasion bands, Freddie and the Dreamers' recordings bore the stamp of prominent studio musicians. In the case of Freddie and the Dreamers, guitarist Big Jim Sullivan plays the solos on a number of the records. However, like Herman's Hermits, this band was a capable instrumental unit. Garrity wrote or cowrote some of the band's songs, including "I'm Telling You Now"; however, one of the apparent downfalls of Freddie and the Dreamers was that some of the material they recorded was decidedly weak. Despite the unevenness of their material, though, Freddie and the Dreamers scored several hits in the United Kingdom and, in a decidedly short run—between March and June 1965—placed four singles in the U.S. Top 40. By all accounts, the band's success was due in part to their mastery of the visual. Wearing Buddy Holly–style eyeglasses, Garrity danced around wildly on stage playing the role of the fool, while Derek Quinn lurked in the background wearing sunglasses that closely resembled those of the Yardbirds' blues-singing Keith Relf. One of the band's biggest hits, "Do the Freddie," in fact, is completely based on the slapstick humor of Garrity's dancing style.

Freddie and the Dreamers fell apart shortly after their first and only U.S. tour amid financial difficulties and because British rock music had progressed beyond their style. Garrity formed a new backing group for a time and appeared occasionally on the oldies circuit into the early twenty-first century when lung disease abruptly ended his career and his life.

Another Manchester group, the Mindbenders, placed only two singles in the *Billboard* pop charts, but they are important mid-1960s works. The band was formed in the early 1960s by singer Glynn Ellis, who used the professional name Wayne Fontana. Billed as Wayne Fontana and the Mindbenders, their 1964 recording of "Game of Love" made it to No. 1 on the *Billboard* charts in early 1965. That year, however, Fontana abruptly left the group. With guitarist Eric Stewart singing lead vocals, the Mindbenders' "A Groovy Kind of Love" made it to No. 2 on the *Billboard* pop charts in 1966.

Although not necessarily a household name like David "Davy" Jones, Peter Noone, Graham Nash, or even Freddie Garrity, for that matter, another Manchester musician, Graham Gouldman, played a significant role in the British Invasion. The early part of

Gouldman's music career was spent in Manchester, where he performed with a number of bands that failed to hit the big time. Songs that Gouldman (born 1946) wrote in the early 1960s, however, made a significant impact. His "For Your Love" was recorded almost simultaneously by Herman's Hermits and the Yardbirds. The Yardbirds' recording was their first Top 40 hit in the United States and reached No. 6 on the *Billboard* charts. Gouldman also wrote "Heart Full of Soul," the Yardbirds' first hit after Jeff Beck replaced Eric Clapton in the group. Other bands, however, also turned to Graham Gouldman for material, including the Hollies ("Bus Stop" and "Look Through Any Window") and Herman's Hermits ("No Milk Today" and "Listen People"). Gouldman's British Invasion compositions capture the spirit of the beat group style better than perhaps any other songwriter who was not known because they were part of a famous band. In other words, even though his work was original feeling, it contains stylistic signifiers of British rock, including ambiguity between tonic major and relative minor keys, major-Mixolydian mode mixture, and singable, instantly recognizable melodies. In 1968, Gouldman joined the Mindbenders; however, the group disbanded shortly thereafter. As a performer, his greatest impact came when he and fellow Mindbender Eric Stewart formed 10cc ("I'm Not in Love" and "The Things We Do for Love") in the 1970s.

10

Impact on America and Conclusions

The most self-evident aspect of the British Invasion of 1964–1965 is that it really did resemble an invasion, in the sense of a sudden, unexpected, overwhelming revolutionary change in the established order. One could quantitatively judge the commercial impact of this invasion by examining the quantity of No. 1 singles by British bands on *Billboard* magazine's pop charts for the years 1960–1966. In 1960, there were no British artists who achieved No. 1 ranking on the pop sales charts in the United States. Likewise, in 1961 no British solo act or group had a No. 1 single in the United States. In 1962, however, Mr. Acker Bilk's recording of "Stranger on the Shore" reached No. 1 for one week in May, and the Tornados' recording of "Telstar" sat at No. 1 on the charts beginning in late December. As discussed earlier, Bilk's recording was a middle-of-the-road pop instrumental that hardly had "British" stamped on it. Likewise, "Telstar" was a memorable instrumental, and while part of the appeal of the record comes from the unusual tone colors and outer-space-like electronic effects producer Joe Meek achieved using conventional electronic instruments in the studio, it could have been recorded by a group from any country that shared a somewhat similar sense of pop music aesthetics with the United States. Mr. Acker Bilk was an easily recognizable figure, in his bowler hat and goatee; however, he looked more like American Dixieland clarinetist Pete Fountain than what Americans might instantly recognize as an Englishman. Likewise, the Tornados were easily recognizable by the matching sweaters they wore; however, there was not the instant identification with British culture.

That Mr. Acker Bilk and the Tornados did not represent the real start of the British Invasion is confirmed by the fact that in 1963—aside from "Telstar," which stayed at No. 1 until January 12—no British acts reached the top spot on the *Billboard* charts. From a quantitative standpoint, though, the year 1964 stands out. The reader may recall that on February 9, 1964, the Beatles made the first of a series of appearances on *The Ed Sullivan Show*; they were followed in short order by other British rock and pop acts. The year 1964 saw nine chart-topping songs by British artists. Considering that there were 23 songs that hit No. 1 that year in *Billboard,* the fact that slightly over 39 percent of the No. 1 singles came from Britain truly represents an invasion.

Six of the nine songs by British artists that hit No. 1 in the United States belonged to the Beatles, and all six were original compositions by John Lennon and Paul McCartney. Of the other three No. 1 songs, "A World without Love," recorded by Peter and Gordon, was another Lennon/McCartney composition, the Animals' "The House of the Rising Sun" was a rock version of a nineteenth-century American folk song, and Manfred Mann's recording of "Do Wah Diddy Diddy" was a cover of the Exciters' 1963 version of the song. For all intents and purposes, then, only one of the nine chart-topping songs was a true cover of an American pop recording. This is worth noting, because it means that not only were British acts achieving commercial success in the United States, they were doing it with homegrown material. This is a far cry from state of British popular music in the late 1950s in which a performer such as Marty Wilde could enjoy considerable chart success in Britain almost entirely with cover recordings. It also suggests that for American audiences, a contemporary of the Animals, Manfred Mann, and the Beatles such as Brian Poole and the Tremeloes, a group that basically existed on cover recordings back at home, might find difficulty making a mark.

The year 1965 found a greater diversity of British acts topping the *Billboard* pop charts. Of the 25 songs that made it to the No. 1 position, 12, or 48 percent, were recorded by British acts. While the Beatles still dominated the British presence on the U.S. charts with four No. 1 singles, Petula Clark, Freddie and the Dreamers, Wayne Fontana and the Mindbenders, Herman's Hermits (two No. 1 singles), the Rolling Stones (two No. 1 singles), and the Dave Clark Five also reached No. 1.

The impact of British Invasion rock and roll is also demonstrated by the fact that two of the American singles that reached No. 1 in 1965, the Byrds' "Mr. Tambourine Man" and "Turn! Turn! Turn! (To Everything There Is a Season)," were recorded by a band that adopted a Beatles-esque spelling of their name, and based their folk-rock style on a hybrid of the instrumental, rhythmic, and vocal harmony style of British Invasion bands combined with the lyrical sensitivity and imagery of American folk revival songwriters such as Pete Seeger and Bob Dylan.

The story of British impact on the *Billboard* charts, however, goes well beyond just the records that hit No. 1. Note that some of the familiar names of the British Invasion—for example, Gerry and the Pacemakers, the Moody Blues, the Searchers, the Zombies, and the Yardbirds—did not reach the No. 1 position, although each of those groups had Top 10 singles in 1964 and/or 1965. As another gauge of the commercial impact of the British Invasion, consider that over the course of 1964–1965, the Dave Clark Five had six records that did not reach No. 1 but that did make it into the Top 10. In the same period, the Rolling Stones had a total of seven Top 40 singles (including their two No. 1 hits), and the Beatles took a full 26 songs into the U.S. Top 40 (including the No. 1 hits), including two ("My Bonnie" and "Ain't She Sweet") that had been recorded as long as three years earlier. And the list of British musicians who made dents in the U.S. Top 40 in 1964–1965 goes on to include Marianne Faithful, the Swinging Blue Jeans, the Who, and others.

By 1966 and 1967 the continuing importance of the bands of the British Invasion manifested itself in the chart appearances of the Hollies, the Justin Haywood/John Lodge version of the Moody Blues, as well as the continuing dominance of the Top 40 by the Beatles, the Rolling Stones, Herman's Hermits, and others. In addition to the Byrds, other American bands that adopted British-sounding names (the Buckinghams, perhaps most obviously) appeared on the record charts. And British solo female artists, including Dusty Springfield, Lulu, Cilla Black, and Petula Clark all enjoyed Top 40 singles.

The impact of the British Invasion was felt in the United States not just in terms of songs from Britain that dominated the radio airwaves, or by American bands that had their musical styles, names, or visual images shaped by the British Invasion: the British Invasion played a significant role in establishing a new paradigm for how rock groups operated. In the late 1950s, a number of American rock and roll musicians—as well as some of the teen idols—primarily, but certainly not entirely based in the R&B and the rockabilly styles, wrote a significant chunk of their own material. Certainly, this was the case with Eddie Cochran, Gene Vincent, Carl Perkins, Chuck Berry, Little Richard, Buddy Holly and the Crickets, Ritchie Valens, Paul Anka, and Bobby Darin. By the early 1960s, however, Holly, Valens, and Cochran were dead, Berry's career was temporarily sidelined by a 1959 sex-related conviction under the Mann Act, and Anka and Darin had moved more toward big-band music and middle-of-the-road pop. And, even when all of the musicians listed above were active as singer-songwriters, the vast majority of hit songs throughout the industry were not self written. With a few notable exceptions—surf music stars the Beach Boys and Jan and Dean chief among them—most of the solo singers and bands that enjoyed success on the charts between 1960 and 1964 did so by recording songs that came out of the Brill Building, Motown staff songwriters, or from other sources.

The prototypical British Invasion band operated differently: it was self-contained, with the instrumentalists, singers, and songwriters all being part of the group. The extent to which this had become the norm even in 1963, the year before the British Invasion, is demonstrated by Andrew Loog Oldham's willingness to obtain an original composition from John Lennon and Paul McCartney, "I Wanna Be Your Man," for the Rolling Stones' second single, apparently so that the band would not have to rely on another cover of an American song. The importance of the new paradigm is demonstrated even more forcefully by the fact that Oldham, who both managed and produced the Rolling Stones, insisted that Mick Jagger and Keith Richards write their own material. Ron Ryan, who wrote several songs for the Dave Clark Five in this same time period, states that having self-penned material on singles and albums was a major concern to Clark, both so that the group would have unique material and because of the importance to the group's image of having self-contained writers.[1] The fact that being perceived as something other than the prototypical fully self-contained band could be detrimental to a group's popular acceptance and commercial viability is also confirmed by Bobby Elliott, long-time drummer with the Hollies, who expressed frustration with the fact that the Hollies' record company forced the band's writing trio—Clarke, Hicks, and Nash—to use aliases.[2]

The impact of this paradigm was felt in the United States as well, so that newly emerging bands such as the Byrds, the Lovin' Spoonful, the Doors, and others that wrote at least some of their own material became the norm. While the songwriters of Brill Building publishing firms certainly did not go out of business—American and British bands continued to turn to teams such as Goffin and King, Barry and Greenwich, and others—reliance on professional songwriters increasingly was viewed with skepticism.

Another area of impact was in the antiauthoritarian attitudes presented by British Invasion musicians in their interviews and films of 1964 and 1965, as well as just in their general public image. While some of the American teen singing/movie stars of the pre–British Invasion 1960s might have acted in films in which intergenerational conflicts arose, the kind of open defiance that is demonstrated even in a fairly mild movie such as the Beatles' *A Hard Day's Night,* which premiered in July 1964, is rare. For example, in the film, John Lennon's character openly takes on establishment figures, and in one scene is observed making a humorous and veiled drug reference by appearing to snort a bottle of Coca-Cola (i.e., coke, or cocaine). In an era that arrived right on the heels of the commercial success of Frankie Avalon, Annette Funicello, Little Stevie Wonder, the Beach Boys, and other acts that were marketed as wholesome American music stars, a band such as the Rolling Stones represented an even more extreme break from suburban values than did the Beatles. In part, this was because of Andrew Loog Oldham's early 1964 publicity campaign for the group, and the banner headlines that ran in *Melody Maker* that read "Would You Let Your Sister Go with a Rolling Stone?" Later the rhetorical question "Would You Let Your Daughter Marry a Rolling Stone?" supported the band's counterculture image. In fact, Oldham's campaign presented the Rolling Stones as the bad-boy counterparts of the Beatles. The Rolling Stones apparently were the first British band to give up their stage uniforms and dress as they—and not the establishment—pleased. And the press and entertainment figures that commented on the group, or presented them in television programs (such as singer Dean Martin's show), picked up on the image and perpetuated it even further, sometimes going so far as to mock the Rolling Stones on their programs. The generation gap that sociologists traced to the end of World War II was stepped up a level as a direct result of the openly defiant image of some of the British acts.

Another important aspect of the British Invasion in general, and not related to any group in particular, is that it can be tied in at least an oblique way with the changes in racial relationships and attitudes that were developing in the United States at the time. It probably would be safe to say that every British Invasion rock band recorded covers of African American R&B, and/or Motown, and/or blues songs. In the case of bands that included one or more songwriters, it would also be safe to say that some of their compositions were influenced by R&B, Motown, or blues. And, in general, the best of the British rock bands tried to put the kind of intangible soul into their performances of this material that one might expect from the real deal; however, they also put their unique stamps on the material. In 1964, though, this was not necessarily commonplace in American bands.

The other important facet of the British Invasion that is important to remember is that the integration of British rock and pop music into American popular culture did not begin in 1964 and only last for a couple of years, or even just to the end of the 1960s. British bands such as King Crimson, the Moody Blues, Emerson, Lake and Palmer, and Yes led progressive rock from the 1960s into the 1970s, and bands such as Black Sabbath, Deep Purple, and Led Zeppelin established heavy metal in the early 1970s. David Bowie and Marc Bolan established glam rock in the early 1970s and brought the issue of sexual orientation and gender role stereotypes directly into the forefront of popular music in America. Similarly, British punk rock and new wave were fully integrated into American popular culture later in the 1970s, even though some of the sociological phenomena that spawned British punk were not necessary part of everyday life in the United States. These, and later infusions of British popular music into the collective unconscious of American life, suggest that one of the most important effects of the British Invasion on the United States was that it opened the United States up to more direct connections with other English-speaking cultures around the world.

CONCLUSIONS

The conventional wisdom about the British Invasion, especially as it started in February 1964, is that (1) it came about because American youth needed something to fill the gap left by the November 1963 assassination of President John F. Kennedy and (2) it was in part caused by the turn toward middle-of-the-road pop that American Top 40 music had taken after the death of Buddy Holly, Ritchie Valens, the Big Bopper, and Eddie Cochran at the close of the 1950s, the payola scandal at the end of the 1950s, as well as personal scandals that derailed the careers of Chuck Berry and Jerry Lee Lewis. Various British rock and roll performers of the 1950s and early 1960s had attempted to enter the American record charts but had not been successful. In addition to the musical void that developed at the start of the 1960s, as well as the psychological void that the assassination of President Kennedy created, the other essential component that allowed British musicians fundamentally to change America's psychic and musical landscape was that British rock musicians had finally broken free of overt imitation of American performers and had by 1964 put their personal stamps on American inventions.

Much of the discussion in chapter 4 was devoted to how British musicians moved away from an almost devotion to Elvis Presley and Bill Haley and toward a more catholic mix of American influences, especially R&B and electric blues. One of the other features of British Invasion rock and roll that undoubtedly distinguished it from what Americans were used to hearing before the British Invasion of 1964 is what we might call "the edge." Certainly, edginess of tone quality and performance style was found in some American rock and roll of the late 1950s and early 1960s. Chuck Berry employed distortion in some of his 1950s electric guitar work, as did Link Wray on his instrumental "Rumble." Even the 1951 record that some historians call the first rock and roll record, "Rocket 88," includes a deliberately distorted electric guitar riff that runs through the song. However, by the time of the British Invasion, the dominant guitar sound was the cleaner sound of Dick Dale, Carl Wilson of the Beach Boys, Tommy Tedesco, and other musicians of the surf genre. The one famous punk-ish, funky, and deliberately dirty-sounding (from the production and playing standpoint) 1960s American rock song that predates the British Invasion, the Kingsmen's recording of Richard Berry's R&B song "Louie Louie" only pre-dated the British Invasion by a little over two months. Ron Ryan, who sang and played rhythm guitar with the Walkers and the Riot Squad in the early to mid-1960s, mentions that he feels the edge of the British bands of the day directly contrasts with the 1964 sound of American groups such as the Beach Boys and that the novelty of the sound played a significant role in the appeal the British bands had to Americans. Perhaps, then, to at least some extent the same aesthetic appeal that drove "Louie Louie" up to No. 2 on the *Billboard* pop charts also helped to further the British Invasion.

Ryan maintains that in part the edginess of the sound of British Invasion bands was due to the fact that before they achieved worldwide stardom, most of the musicians had "to beg, borrow, or steal" whatever instruments they could get their hands on, even if that meant cheap "Sears and Roebuck instruments."[3] The Kinks' lead guitarist, Dave Davies, confirmed this when he told an interviewer that he used a Harmony Meteor electric guitar, "because it was the only guitar I could afford."[4] Paul McCartney and George Harrison talked about the need to buy "cheap" instruments before they became financially successful professional musicians.[5] Even proper gauge electric guitar and electric bass strings were difficult, if not at times impossible, to obtain. McCartney acknowledged cannibalizing pianos in order to get strings that would be even close to what was needed on an electric bass. His description of the gauge of these strings—"probably puts a huge strain on the guitar"—suggests that more often than not, the strings were too heavy for their intended usage.[6] Ron Ryan confirms that in London, where he lived and performed, the only available strings were so heavy that stories about players' fingers literally bleeding are not hyperbole—they literally were true.[7] Today, in 2008, guitar and bass guitar forums on the Internet are filled with discussions of the so-called inadequate equipment used by British Invasion rock bands. By all accounts, these equipment-related realities were not a general part of late 1950s and early 1960s rock and roll—they were realities in Britain where the general economic conditions were not as favorable as those in the United States. Therefore, economics—both general and related to individual musicians—played a crucial role in the development of the sound of British rock. From a technical standpoint, cheap electric guitars and bass guitars with heavy fretboard actions, inadequate electrical pickups, and overly heavy strings required that the player attack the notes more vigorously and play with more articulation and less legato flow than would be possible on better equipment. Indeed, recordings of some of the early famous lead guitarists of the British Invasion—Keith Richards, Dave Davies, Jimmy Page (back when he was a studio musician), and others—sound quite unlike recordings of their American contemporaries because of, among some other things, the articulation of the notes. It should also be noted that the work of some of these British lead guitarists was influenced by the work of African American electric blues musicians of the 1950s—musicians who, because of harsh economic conditions for them in the United States, also sometimes had to play on equipment that was less expensive and of lesser quality.

And even guitars and bass guitars that were not necessarily of the cheap variety were sometimes different than those used by American rock musicians. For example, a number of British bass guitar players used Hofner hollow-body and semi-hollow-body instruments. The most notable and iconic of these players was Paul McCartney, with the Hofner violin-shaped electric bass he bought after deciding he could no longer go on borrowing Stu Sutcliffe's Hofner right-handed, hollow-body model. However, McCartney was not alone in using the German-made basses, nor, by the way, was he alone among the British bass players in the early 1960s using the violin-shaped model. Again, though, part of the attraction of Hofner basses—violin-shaped or otherwise—was that they were less expensive than, say, the American-made Fender Precision Bass. According to McCartney, another part of the appeal of the Hofner 500/1 for him, a left-handed guitar player, was its symmetry.[8] An additional consideration for converted guitar players such as McCartney was that the Hofner model he played was a short-scale instrument, meaning that the distance between frets was closer to that of an electric guitar than what would be the case on a more normal long-scale bass. The difference between a solid-body instrument, such as the Fender Precision Bass, and an instrument such as the Hofner helped to make the tone, attack, and sustain of McCartney's playing sound different from that of American bass guitarists. So, while a bassist such as Paul McCartney might not have sounded edgier than an American bassist, he sounded fundamentally different.

It should also be noted that the amplification equipment British guitarists and bassists used differed from that of their American counterparts in the years leading up to and including the British Invasion. For example, both Vox and Marshall were British-made amplifiers, and were not as widely used or even known in the United States as were the American domestic amplifiers. The first Vox amplifiers appeared in the mid-1950s, and perhaps their greatest early widespread exposure came through the Shadows, who used the Vox AC30 amplifier on their first instrumental hit, "Apache." According to Vox's official Web site, this amplifier gave the Shadows' guitarists a unique tone.[9]

At the dawn of the 1960s, drummer and music storeowner Jim Marshall began receiving requests from young guitarists to sell amplifiers that were more appropriate for rock music than the more jazz-oriented equipment offered by stores in London's West End. Marshall, then in his late 30s, heeded young guitarists such as Pete Townshend (later of the Who) and Ritchie Blackmore (later of Deep Purple), and not only decided to sell amplifiers but also to establish an amplifier design and manufacturing business. Despite the fact that Marshall enjoys significant name recognition today in amplifiers because of the company's association with Pete Townshend, John Entwistle, Eric Clapton, and Jimi Hendrix, they were unknown in the United States as late as 1963. According to Marshall, because of the regulations of the musicians' union, on Roy Orbison's 1963 British tour "he had to use British musicians rather than his American band . . . Someone in the band backing him was using a Bluesbreaker [a Marshall model that was designed for Eric Clapton], and he decided it was the amp he had to have."[10] Marshall credits Orbison with being the first American musician to take a Marshall amplifier to the United States. Because different amplifiers produce different resonances and different overtones, which by extension produce different tone colors, the homegrown Vox and Marshall amplifiers (which were preferred by some British guitarists and bassists but were not readily available in the United States) made the players sound subtly different from their American counterparts—not necessarily better or worse, but different.

It also seems that some of the musicians tried to take notable features of their sound—even if traditional aesthetic sensibilities might dub those features "bad"—and deliberately emphasize them and thereby turn a disadvantage into an advantage. For example, the edginess that certain guitars and amplifiers might provide could be enhanced, such as in the case of the distorted Dave Davies electric guitar riff in the Kinks' "You Really Got Me." According to Davies, the distortion came from well-placed intentional razor cuts in his amplifier speaker.[11] The comparative edge of the British bands—whether because of their R&B-based style or the equipment they used—is confirmed by an observation Dennis Wilson, drummer of the Beach Boys, made to *Rave* magazine after first seeing the Rolling Stones perform live in 1964. Wilson stated, "They're tough, kinda uncompromising, no pandering to an audience. The Stones are rough, musically—sort of musical gangsters, and that's a compliment."[12] This punkish, gangster quality was fully in keeping with the need of the youth subculture to rebel against adults and against societal norms.

The high degree of influence that the British class system exerted on society during the period that includes the development of British rock and the British Invasion manifested itself in ways other than just the type of equipment that working-class young musicians used. Although white American youth of the 1950s and early 1960s did not have the same kind of identification with social and economic class, what the British musicians brought with them that related to class nevertheless resonated with American youth. In order to get at this point, let us consider subtext in three British Invasion rock films: The Beatles' *A Hard Day's Night*, Gerry and the Pacemakers' *Ferry Cross the Mersey*, and the Dave Clark Five's *Catch Us If You Can*.

One of the most famous rock and roll films of all time, *A Hard Day's Night* (1964), stars the Beatles as exaggerations of themselves. For example, the stereotypes of the four musicians, which had at least a smidgeon of basis in reality (e.g., John Lennon, the wisecracking cynic; Paul McCartney, the loveable puppy dog; etc.), were played up by the film's writers and by director Richard Lester. For one thing, this provides the audience with easily definable characters: we know (or at least we think we know) who each Beatle is. The story revolves around the fictional Beatles' trip to the big city and subsequent appearance on a television variety program. This provides the writers the opportunity, however, to poke fun at the older generation and at the upper class in the form of an encounter between the wisecracking Lennon and an older dressed-to-the-hilt veteran of World War II. This scene, which occurs fairly early in the film, incidentally, also finds Lennon's character making a veiled drug reference: he snorts a bottle of Coca-Cola (euphemistically, cocaine). All of the fictional Beatles, but Lennon's character in particular, are thorns in the side of their fictional manager and the television program's director. Because these characters (the upper-class gentleman, the manager, and the director) represent older authority figures, a subtext that encourages youthful rebellion against the older generation and particularly against authority figures runs throughout the film. The upper class and the British tabloid press are also lampooned in other scenes. Ultimately, as might be expected, the Beatles do what they have traveled to London to do, but it is clear that they have done so on their own youthful, working-class terms.

The Beatles' manager, Brian Epstein, also managed Gerry and the Pacemakers. Epstein recognized the value of the feature-film medium and secured a film, *Ferry Cross the Mersey,* for Gerry Marsden and his group. The film opens with Marsden's narration describing the tough times members of the group experienced growing up in war-torn, economically deprived Liverpool. Marsden and the Pacemakers play working-class lads, two of whom are art students and two of whom work day jobs. They have a band—naturally—in which they play in the evenings at venues such as the Cavern Club. They are, however, preparing for an important talent competition and trying to secure a management contract. Although the film mostly is filled with scenes of Gerry and Pacemakers lip-synching to their recordings in improbable locations (e.g., a warehouse and a Chinese restaurant), and romping through Buster Keaton/Keystone Cops–type escapades, there is some interesting subtext in *Ferry Cross the Mersey.* Most significant is the importance of Liverpool and the group's love of their home. The opening narration paints Liverpool as a decidedly less-than-ideal place in which to grow up in the 1940s and 1950s; however, Marsden's famous title song affirms his love for Liverpool. It is an unspoken acknowledgement that without those World War II and post–World War II hard times, the music would not have developed the way it did.

One of the less effective attempts by the film's writers, though, to project an image on Gerry and the Pacemakers comes from the insistence on having the four musicians ride around on Vespa scooters. Clearly, this and the art school experience of two of the group paint them as Mods; however, the self-penned music that fills the film exhibits strong ties to 1950s rock and roll—the Rocker side of the equation. The conflict is most apparent during the scenes of the beat group competition, in which several groups exhibit heavy R&B tendencies. This makes Gerry and the Pacemakers' ties to late 1950s pop and rock style even more apparent. Just like the Beatles' first feature film, *Ferry Cross the Mersey* also contains mild pokes at the musically conservative older generation and (albeit much more mildly than in *A Hard Day's Night*) subtle mockery of the British class structure.

The use of film to create or perpetuate an image can also be seen in John Boorman's directorial debut, the Dave Clark Five's *Catch Us If You Can.* This 1965 film, which was released in the United States as *Having a Wild Weekend,* stars the members of the Dave Clark Five as stuntmen. The principal story line revolves around Steve (Clark's character)

The bleak, working-class environment of Liverpool was the breeding ground for the Beatles (pictured here circa 1962), Gerry and the Pacemakers, the Searchers, and other Merseybeat bands. Courtesy of Photofest.

and Dinah (the star of the fictional British Meat Council's "Meat for Go" campaign) driving off the set of a television commercial in an E-type Jaguar that is owned by the production company. They set out on an adventure, aided in part by the other members of the band. Significantly, Steve and Dinah encounter a group of longhaired beatnik, nascent hippie types who are living in an abandoned building in the British military training area at Salisbury Plain. The leader of the beatniks, probably not by chance, looks very much like Brian Jones of the Rolling Stones. The beatniks are smoking marijuana and ask Steve if he has any to share, or if he has any "horse" (heroin) to share. Clark's character displays disdain for the group.

This and other scenes in the film suggest that Clark's character is just a regular urban, working-class guy. He has disdain for the counterculture and its drug scene. *Catch Us If You Can,* however, also exposes the exploitive nature of the advertising industry. Curiously, a middle-aged, upper-class couple assist Steve, Dinah, and the stuntmen. While Steve seems a bit ill at ease with this couple, they do not share the antipathy that exists between Steve and the beatniks.

So, to the extent that *Catch Us If You Can* presents a public image for the Dave Clark Five, it paints them as independent, working-class young men. They stand outside the counterculture, but also outside the world of commercialism. In short, they sound like the kinds of young men that would appeal to youth on one level, and to their parents on another level, at least in 1965. As the counterculture became more thoroughly entrenched, especially among young people, characters such as Dave Clark's Steve might be considered out of touch with the times by 1967 and 1968. Perhaps significantly, as the counterculture grew in influence groups such as the Dave Clark Five made less impact on the U.S. record charts.

In conclusion, the British music and musicians that made the greatest, longest-lasting impact in the United States tended to be at least somewhat sonically edgy, rhythmically vital, and influenced by African American R&B. This means that they were the musicians who moved away from the aesthetics of the Rockers and either (1) achieved a Rocker-Mod balance or (2) thoroughly adopted the Mod aesthetic. Image—and especially a British antiestablishment, working-class image—was important, as was the ability to write one's own songs. The artists who successfully entered the U.S. market in 1964 were those who had moved well beyond imitating American musicians of the 1950s and had started creating a vernacular music that was at once tied to American music, but also novel sounding. The impact of the musical revolution of 1964–1966 can be measured in terms of record sales, jukebox plays, and now, well over 40 years later, by the later musical styles that came out of the musical, social, and other innovations of the British Invasion, and the continued presence of British Invasion pop and rock in television shows, movies, oldies radio, and the whole of American popular culture.

Notes

CHAPTER 1

1. Stanley Cohen, *Folk Devils and Moral Panics: The Creation of the Mods and Rockers* (New York: St. Martin's Press, 1980).

2. Stanley Cohen, *Folk Devils and Moral Panics: The Creation of the Mods and Rockers* (New York: St. Martin's Press, 1980), p. 183.

3. Paul Barker and Alan Little, "The Margate Offenders: A Survey," *New Society* (July 30, 1964), pp. 6–10.

4. *The Beatles Anthology*, episode 1, VHS videocassette, Apple Corps 3392V, 1996.

5. Tom Brokaw, *The Greatest Generation* (New York: Random House, 1998).

6. William Strauss and Neil Howe, *Generations: The History of America's Future, 1584 to 2069* (New York: Quill, 1991).

7. Bill Wyman, foreword to *Bill Wyman's Blues Odyssey: A Journey to Music's Heart and Soul* (New York: DK Publishing, 2001), p. 9.

8. *Amazing Journey: The Story of the Who*, Murray Lerner, director, DVD, Universal Pictures 2003895, 2007.

9. Ron Ryan, personal e-mail to the author, February 9, 2008.

CHAPTER 2

1. Ron Ryan with Peter Dintino, telephone interview with the author, October 22, 2007.

2. Not to be confused with the well-known American vocal group of the same name.

3. *Amazing Journey: The Story of the Who,* Murray Lerner, director, DVD, Universal Pictures 2003895, 2007.

4. Paul McCartney, liner notes for *Run Devil Run,* CD, Capitol Records CDP 7243 5 22351 2 4, 1999.

5. Ron Ryan with Peter Dintino, telephone interview with the author, October 22, 2007.

6. "The Man," Billyfury.com, accessed November 6, 2007.

7. John Lennon, quoted in *The Beatles Anthology* (San Francisco: Chronicle Books, 2000), p. 11.

8. George Harrison, quoted in *The Beatles Anthology* (San Francisco: Chronicle Books, 2000), p. 27.

9. Ron Ryan with Peter Dintino, telephone interview with the author, October 22, 2007.

10. The audio fidelity on this recording, as well as on some of the other live and amateur recordings on the Viper Label's three *Unearthed Merseybeat* albums, is fairly primitive.

11. Wyman discusses this in several locations in his autobiography; Bill Wyman with Ray Coleman, *Stone Alone: The Story of a Rock 'n' Roll Band* (New York: Viking, 1990).

12. Ron Ryan with Peter Dintino, telephone interview with the author, February 6, 2008.

13. *The Official Cliff Richard Website,* http://cliffrichard.org/biog/index.cfm, accessed January 9, 2008.

14. For example, John Lennon referred to "Move It" as such. *The Beatles Anthology* (San Francisco: Chronicle Books, 2000), p. 10.

15. *The Official Marty Wilde Website,* http://www.martywilde.com/life.html, accessed January 10, 2008. Other sources give Wilde's birthplace as Greenwich.

16. In the key of A major (the tonality of "Bad Boy") the I chord consists of A, C-sharp, and E; the IV chord consists of D, F-sharp, and A; and the V chord consists of E, G-sharp, and B.

17. Chris Eley, liner notes for *The Sound of Fury,* CD, Decca 844 990-2, 2000.

18. Colin Escott, liner notes for *Somethin' Else: The Fine Lookin' Hits of Eddie Cochran,* CD, Razor & Tie RE 2162–2, 1998.

19. Colin Escott, liner notes for *Somethin' Else: The Fine Lookin' Hits of Eddie Cochran,* CD, Razor & Tie RE 2162–2, 1998.

20. Spencer Leigh, "Obituary: Adam Faith," *The Independent* March 10, 2003, Available through *The Independent* Online Edition, http://news.independent.co.uk/people/obituaries/article36330.ece, accessed January 14, 2008.

21. Spencer Leigh, "Obituary: Adam Faith," *The Independent* March 10, 2003, available through *The Independent* Online Edition, http://news.independent.co.uk/people/obituaries/article36330.ece, accessed January 14, 2008.

22. Steven D. Stark, *Meet the Beatles: A Cultural History of the Band that Shook Youth, Gender, and the World* (New York: Harper, 2005), p. 136.

23. Hunter S. Thompson, *Hell's Angels* (New York: Ballantine Books, 1967).

24. Stanley Cohen, *Folk Devils and Moral Panics: The Creation of the Mods and Rockers* (New York: St. Martin's Press, 1980).

25. Ringo Starr, in *The Beatles Anthology* (San Francisco: Chronicle Books, 2000), p. 77.

26. Ron Ryan with Peter Dintino, telephone interview with the author, November 12, 2007.

27. Michael Palin, quoted in Graham Chapman, John Cleese, Terry Gilliam, Eric Idle, Terry Jones, and Michael Palin, with Bob McCabe, *The Pythons Autobiography* (New York: Thomas Dunne Books, 2003), p. 36.

CHAPTER 3

1. In this polyphonic (many-voiced) texture, the piano, harmonica, guitars, and bass all play independent lines. The effect is akin to the polyphonic sections of New Orleans–style or Dixieland-style jazz performances.

2. George Harrison, in *The Beatles Anthology*, episode 1, VHS videocassette, Apple Corps 3392V, 1996.

3. Bill Wyman with Richard Havers, *Bill Wyman's Blues Odyssey: A Journey to Music's Heart and Soul* (New York: DK Publishing, 2001), p. 317.

4. Dave Hunter, "Comeback Kink," *The Guitar Player* (January 1999), available online at http://www.davedavies.com/articles/tgm_0199.htm, accessed April 14, 2008.

5. Liner notes for *Unearthed Merseybeat, Vol. 3*, CD, Viper CD 032, 2005.

6. Recording dates for the Beach Boys' songs are from Mark Linett, liner notes for *Surfin' Safari/Surfin' U.S.A.*, CD reissue, Capitol Records 72435-31517-2-0, 2001.

7. Liner notes for *Unearthed Merseybeat, Vol. 1: From the Birth of Merseybeat to Psyche-delia*, CD, The Viper Label CD 016, 2003.

8. Ron Ryan, personal e-mail to the author, February 15, 2008.

9. See, for example, George Harrison, quoted in *The Beatles Anthology* (San Francisco: Chronicle Books, 2000), p. 89.

10. While the Brill Building is an actual building in Manhattan, standing at 1619 Broadway, just north of Times Square, the term "Brill Building" is used in this context to denote the New York–based pop music publishing and recording establishment of the late 1950s and early 1960s.

11. Reproduced in Roy Carr and Tony Tyler, *The Beatles: An Illustrated Record* (New York: Harmony Books, 1975), p. 25.

12. See, for example, John Lennon in *The Beatles Anthology* (San Francisco: Chronicle Books, 2000), p. 185.

13. Ron Ryan with Peter Dintino, telephone interview with the author, October 22, 2007.

14. Adrian Barrett, *Johnny Kidd and the Pirates*, http://www.johnnykidd.co.uk, accessed January 18, 2008.

15. Adrian Barrett, *Johnny Kidd and the Pirates*, http://www.johnnykidd.co.uk, accessed January 21, 2008.

16. At the time of this writing, Vince Taylor and the Playboys televised performance of "Shakin' All Over," as well as several of their other performances from 1961, are widely available on the Internet at YouTube.com.

17. Incidentally, apparently the only surviving film footage of the Beatles performing at the Cavern was of them performing "Some Other Guy," recorded by Granada Television, August 22, 1962.

18. See, for example, Bruce Eder, "Paul Revere and the Raiders," *All Music Guide,* http://allmusic.com/cg/amg.dll?p=amg&sql=11:h9fuxqugld6e~T1, accessed January 21, 2008.

19. Tony Sheridan, liner notes for *The Beatles Featuring Tony Sheridan—In the Beginning,* LP, Polydor 24-4504, 1970. Reissued on CD, Polydor 314 549 268-2, 2000.

20. Recording dates obtained from the liner notes for *The Beatles Featuring Tony Sheridan—In the Beginning,* CD, Polydor 314 549 268-2, 2000.

21. Tony Sheridan, personal e-mail to the author, October 29, 2007.

22. See, for example, discussion in Stanley Cohen, *Folk Devils and Moral Panics: The Creation of the Mods and Rockers* (New York: St. Martin's Press, 1980), pp. 183ff.

23. Tony Copple, "Interview with Roy Young," *The Ottawa Beatles Site,* 2002, http://beatles.ncf.ca/roy.html, accessed January 28, 2008.

24. Ulf Krüger, "Interview with Tony Sheridan," *Genesis Publications: Special Features,* http://www.genesis-publications.com/news/interviews/sheridan.html, accessed January 29, 2008.

25. Ringo Starr and George Harrison, in *The Beatles Anthology* (San Francisco: Chronicle Books, 2000), pp. 58–59.

26. Gerry Marsden with Ray Coleman, *I'll Never Walk Alone: An Autobiography* (London: Bloomsbury, 1993), p. 23.

27. Gerry Marsden with Ray Coleman, *I'll Never Walk Alone: An Autobiography* (London: Bloomsbury, 1993), p. 24.

28. Not to be confused with the keyboardist and lead singer of the Dave Clark Five of the same name.

29. Ron Ryan with Peter Dintino, telephone interview with the author, October 22, 2007. While Ron Ryan is not listed as a cowriter of "No Time to Lose" on the labels of the Dave Clark Five's releases of the song (the *Glad All Over* album, for example, credits Clark and Mike Smith), the American Society of Composers, Authors, and Publishers' ACE Database confirms Ryan's coauthorship of the song. See http://www.ascap.com/ace/search.cfm?requesttimeout=300&mode=results&searchstr=NO%20TIME%20TO%20LOSE&search_in=t&search_type=exact&search_det=t,s,w,p,b,v&pagenum=2&start=11, accessed February 8, 2008.

30. Bobby Graham, "The Hit List," *The Legendary Bobby Graham: England's Greatest Session Drummer,* http://bobbygraham.co.uk/bobbygraham/hits.htm, accessed February 7, 2008.

31. "Backing Groups," Billyfury.com, http://billyfury.com, accessed February 19, 2008.

CHAPTER 4

1. The work of author Lewis Carroll also heavily influenced Lennon.

2. Although by 1963 compositions by either Lennon or McCartney alone or together were listed as "Lennon/McCartney," early compositions, including "You'll Be Mine" and the songs Lennon and McCartney contributed to the Beatles' debut album (*Please Please Me*) were credited "McCartney/Lennon."

3. George Harrison and Paul McCartney, in *The Beatles Anthology* (San Francisco: Chronicle Books, 2000), p. 41

4. John Lennon, in *The Beatles Anthology* (San Francisco: Chronicle Books, 2000), p. 45.

5. Paul McCartney, in *The Beatles Anthology*, episode 1, VHS videocassette, Apple Corps 3392V, 1996.

6. See, for example, Stanley Cohen, *Folk Devils and Moral Panics: The Creation of the Mods and Rockers* (New York: St. Martin's Press, 1980), pp. 149ff.

7. Steven D. Stark, *Meet the Beatles: A Cultural History of the Band That Shook Youth, Gender, and the World* (New York: Harper, 2005), p. 81.

8. Jeff Nuttall, *Bomb Culture* (London: Paladin, 1970), p. 333.

9. Ian Inglis, "'Some Kind of Wonderful': The Creative Legacy of the Brill Building," *American Music* 21, Summer 2003, p. 222.

10. Fred Bronson, *The Billboard Book of Number 1 Hits* (New York: *Billboard* Books, 2003), p. 105.

11. Quoted by Steven D. Stark, *Meet the Beatles: A Cultural History of the Band That Shook Youth, Gender, and the World* (New York: Harper, 2005), p. 5.

12. George Martin with Jeremy Hornsby, *All You Need Is Ears* (New York: St. Martin's Press, 1979).

13. John Lennon, in *The Beatles Anthology* (San Francisco: Chronicle Books, 2000), p. 70.

CHAPTER 5

1. Ron Ryan with Peter Dintino, telephone interview with the author, November 12, 2007.

2. Mick Ryan, personal e-mail to the author, March 6, 2008.

3. Mick Ryan, personal e-mail to the author, March 8, 2008.

4. The ASCAP online database, for example, lists Dave Clark and Ron Ryan as cowriters of "That's What I Said," "Doo Dah," "No Time to Lose," and "Sometimes." See "ACE Title Search," *ASCAP*, http://www.ascap.com/ace/. Ryan also wrote "The Mulberry Bush" for the Dave Clark Five.

5. Ron Ryan with Peter Dintino, telephone interview with the author, October 22, 2007.

6. Patrick Harrington and Bobby Graham, *The Session Man: The Story of Bobby Graham, the U.K.'s Greatest Session Drummer* (Raglan, Monmouthshire, Great Britain: Broom House, 2004).

7. Bobby Graham, "The Hit List," *The Legendary Bobby Graham: England's Greatest Session Drummer,* http://bobbygraham.co.uk/bobbygraham/hits.htm, accessed February 7, 2008.

8. Bobby Graham, "The Hit List," *The Legendary Bobby Graham: England's Greatest Session Drummer,* http://bobbygraham.co.uk/bobbygraham/hits.htm, accessed February 7, 2008.

9. Peter Doggett, liner notes for *The Kinks,* CD reissue, Sanctuary Records SMRCD025, 2004.

10. Ron Ryan's account of the disputed songwriting credits and royalties can be found in the "Biography" section of *Ron Ryan Music,* http://ronryanmusic.com/album1_007.htm, accessed March 7, 2008. Ryan also confirmed his account in telephone interviews with the author, October 22, 2007, November 12, 2007, and February 6, 2008.

11. ACE Database, *American Society of Composers, Authors, and Publishers* (*ASCAP*), http://www.ascap.com/ace/search.cfm?requesttimeout=300&mode=results&searchstr=NO% 20TIME%20TO%20LOSE&search_in=t&search_type=exact&search_det=t,s,w,p,b,v&pagen um=2&start=11, accessed February 8, 2008.

12. Although the official credits list Ron Ryan and Dave Clark as cowriters, Ryan claims on his Web site that the song is entirely his own. See *Ron Ryan Music,* http://ronryanmusic.com. Interestingly, nearly every song every recorded by the Dave Clark Five that was not a cover lists Clark as sole writer or as cowriter.

13. Ron Ryan with Peter Dintino, telephone interview with the author, October 22, 2007. Also see *Ron Ryan Music,* http://ronryanmusic.com.

14. Rick Clark and Richie Unterberger, "The Dave Clark Five," *All Music Guide,* http://www.allmusic.com/cg/amg.dll?p=amg&sql=11:wifpxqw5ldte~T1, accessed March 7, 2008.

CHAPTER 6

1. Richie Unterberger, Review of "The Kinks," *All Music Guide,* http://www.allmusic. com/cg/amg.dll?p=amg&sql=10:h9frxqqdldte, accessed February 11, 2008.

2. Stanley Cohen, *Folk Devils and Moral Panics: The Creation of the Mods and Rockers* (New York: St. Martin's Press, 1980), p. 183.

3. Stanley Cohen, *Folk Devils and Moral Panics: The Creation of the Mods and Rockers* (New York: St. Martin's Press, 1980), p. 183.

4. Odd-numbered phrases are rare in popular music. The other notable British Invasion exception are the seven-measure phrases in the Beatles' "Yesterday."

5. Dave Marsh, *The Heart of Rock and Soul: The 1001 Greatest Singles Ever Made* (New York: Da Capo, 1999), p. 391.

6. Power chords, a staple of the Kinks and the Who, essentially are open perfect fifths (e.g., G-D) that imply a complete major chord (e.g., G-B-D).

7. The tonality of the Kinks recording of "You Really Got Me" sometimes is given as G major, instead of A-flat major as I have indicated here. Comparison of the recording with standard pitch (A = 440 vibrations per second) places the song somewhere in between the keys of G major and A-flat major. This suggests that either the Kinks detuned their instruments, or the recording tempo may have been changed for release.

8. Doug Hinman with Jason Brabazon, *You Really Got Me: An Illustrated World Discography of the Kinks, 1963–1993* (Rumford, RI: Rock 'n' Roll Research Press, 1994); and Doug Hinman, *The Kinks: All Day and All of the Night* (San Francisco: Backbeat Books, 2004).

9. *Amazing Journey: The Story of the Who,* Murray Lerner, director, DVD, Universal Pictures 2003895, 2007.

10. *Amazing Journey: The Story of the Who,* Murray Lerner, director, DVD, Universal Pictures 2003895, 2007.

11. *Amazing Journey: The Story of the Who,* Murray Lerner, director, DVD, Universal Pictures 2003895, 2007.

12. "I'm a Boy" was written by Pete Townshend, and the others were written by the Who's bassist, John Entwistle.

CHAPTER 7

1. Bruce Eder, "Alexis Korner," *All Music Guide,* http://www.allmusic.com/cg/amg. dll?p=amg&sql=11:fifqxq95ld0e~T1, accessed February 29, 2008.

2. Mark Powell, liner notes for *John Mayall Plays John Mayall,* CD, Decca 9841779, 2006.

3. "The *RS* 500 Greatest Songs of All Time," *Rolling Stone,* http://www.rollingstone.com/ news/coverstory/500songs/, posted December 9, 2004, accessed February 24, 2008.

4. Dave Marsh, *The Heart of Rock and Soul: The 1001 Greatest Singles Ever Made* (New York: Da Capo Press, 1999), pp. 64–65.

5. "The *RS* 500 Greatest Songs of All Time," *Rolling Stone,* http://www.rollingstone.com/ news/coverstory/500songs/, posted December 9, 2004, accessed February 24, 2008.

6. Dave Marsh, *The Heart of Rock and Soul: The 1001 Greatest Singles Ever Made* (New York: Da Capo Press, 1999), p. 508.

7. Bobby Graham, "The Hit List," *The Legendary Bobby Graham: England's Greatest Session Drummer,* http://bobbygraham.co.uk/bobbygraham/hits.htm, accessed March 25, 2008.

8. "The *RS* 500 Greatest Songs of All Time," *Rolling Stone,* http://www.rollingstone.com/ news/coverstory/500songs/, posted December 9, 2004, accessed February 24, 2008.

9. Although this title is sometimes given as "Everyday," according to licensing agency B.M.I.'s database, the legal title is "Every Day." See *BMI Repertoire Search,* "Every Day," http:// repertoire.bmi.com/title.asp?blnWriter=True&blnPublisher=True&blnArtist=True&keyID= 387378&ShowNbr=0&ShowSeqNbr=0&querytype=WorkID, accessed March 26, 2008.

10. Chris Welch, liner notes for *Sonny Boy Williamson and the Yardbirds,* CD, Repertoire Records REP 4776, 2007, p. 4.

11. In the mid-twentieth century, there were two American blues musicians known as Sonny Boy Williamson. The first allegedly to take that name was John Lee Curtis Williamson (1914–1948). Although older than the so-called original Sonny Boy Williamson, Aleck "Rice" Miller (ca. 1899–1965) is thought to have taken the same stage name at a slightly later date. Therefore, Miller sometimes is called Sonny Boy Williamson II.

12. Chris Welch, liner notes for *Sonny Boy Williamson and the Yardbirds,* CD, Repertoire Records REP 4776, 2007, p. 6.

CHAPTER 8

1. The band first began billing itself this way during their 1969 concert tour, a tour recorded for the 1969 live album *Get Yer Ya-Yas Out.*

2. Bill Wyman with Ray Coleman, *Stone Alone* (New York: Viking, 1990).

3. Keyboardist Ian Stewart was one of the original members of the Rolling Stones. Manager Andrew Loog Oldham, however, believed that Stewart's looks were not right for the band; therefore,

while Stewart continued to record with the group and performed live with them, he was not an official member.

CHAPTER 9

1. Brian Epstein, *A Cellarful of Noise* (New York: Pyramid Publications, 1965), p. 68.

2. Chad Stuart and Jeremy Clyde, onstage banter at Lock 3 Live concert, Akron, Ohio, August 20, 2005.

3. Bobby Elliott, liner notes for *Finest*, Two CDs, EMI 0946 3 91127 2 2, 2007.

4. Bruce Eder, "Herman's Hermits," *All Music Guide*, http://www.allmusic.com/cg/amg.dll?p=amg&sql=11:kifuxqe5ld0e~T1, accessed February 7, 2008.

5. Freddie Garrity's birth year often was given as 1940 in order to make him appear younger.

CHAPTER 10

1. Ron Ryan with Peter Dintino, telephone interview with the author, November 12, 2007.

2. Bobby Elliott, Liner notes for *Finest*, Two CDs, EMI 0946 3 91127 2 2, 2007.

3. Ron Ryan with Peter Dintino, telephone interview with the author, February 6, 2008.

4. Dave Hunter, "Voxes, Vees and Razorblades: The Kinks Guitar Sound," *The Guitar Player* (January 1999), reprinted at http:www.davedavies.com/articles/tgm_0199–01.htm, accessed February 13, 2008.

5. Paul McCartney and George Harrison, in *The Beatles Anthology* (San Francisco: Chronicle Books, 2000), pp. 80–81.

6. Paul McCartney, in *The Beatles Anthology* (San Francisco: Chronicle Books, 2000), p. 80.

7. Ron Ryan with Peter Dintino, telephone interview with the author, February 6, 2008.

8. Paul McCartney, in *The Beatles Anthology* (San Francisco: Chronicle Books, 2000), p. 80. Incidentally, the iconic nature of McCartney's Hofner violin-shaped bass is confirmed by the fact that after years of playing other basses, he has returned to the Hofner. The instrument, in fact, can be seen in photographs of McCartney from his July 19, 2008 guest appearance with Billy Joel at the final concert at New York's Shea Stadium and his July 20, 2008 performance as part of the 400th anniversary celebrations in Quebec City.

9. "The Vox Story," *Vox Amplification*, http://www.voxamps.co.uk/thevoxstory/, accessed April 22, 2008.

10. Jim Marshall, in Rich Maloof, *Jim Marshall: The Father of Loud* (San Francisco: Backbeat Books, 2004), p. 50.

11. Dave Hunter, "Voxes, Vees and Razorblades: The Kinks Guitar Sound," *The Guitar Player* (January 1999), reprinted at http:www.davedavies.com/articles/tgm_0199–01.htm, accessed February 13, 2008.

12. Quoted in Bill Wyman with Ray Coleman, *Stone Alone* (New York: Viking, 1990), p. 272.

Bibliography

ACE Database. *American Society of Composers, Authors, and Publishers (ASCAP)*, http://www. ascap.com/ace/search.cfm?requesttimeout=300&mode=results&searchstr=NO%20TIME %20TO%20LOSE&search_in=t&search_type=exact&search_det=t,s,w,p,b,v&pagenum =2&start=11. Accessed February 8, 2008.

"ACE Title Search." *ASCAP.* http://www.ascap.com/ace/. Accessed January 26, 2008.

Amazing Journey: The Story of the Who. Murray Lerner, director. Universal Pictures, 2007. Two DVDs. Universal 2003895, 2007.

"Backing Groups," Billyfury.com, http://billyfury.com. Accessed February 19, 2008.

Barker, Paul, and Alan Little. "The Margate Offenders: A Survey." *New Society,* July 30, 1964, pp. 6–10.

Barnes, Richard. *Mods!* London: Plexus, 1991.

Barnes, Richard. *The Who: Maximum R&B.* New York: St. Martin's Press, 1982.

Barrett, Adrian. *Johnny Kidd and the Pirates,* http://www.johnnykidd.co.uk. Accessed January 26, 2008.

Beat Girl. Edmond T. Gréville, director. MGM British Studios, 1960. DVD. Mondo Crash MC-06D, 2003.

The Beatles. *The Beatles Anthology.* San Francisco: Chronicle Books, 2000.

The Beatles Anthology. Goeff Wonfor, director. Eight VHS videocassettes (also issued on DVD). Apple Corps 3392V-3399V, 1996.

The Beatles with Tony Sheridan—The Beginnings in Hamburg: A Documentary. DVD. Universal Records B0001897–9, 2004.

Begler, Lewis. *Rock Theology: Interpreting the Music of the Youth Culture.* New York: Bengizio Press, 1970.

Belz, Carl. "Popular Music and the Folk Tradition." *Journal of American Folklore* 80 (April–June 1967), pp. 130–142.

Belz, Carl. *The Story of Rock* (2nd ed.). New York: Oxford University Press, 1972.

"Biography." Billyfury.com. Accessed November 12, 2007.

"BMI Repertoire Search." *BMI.com*, http://bmi.com. Accessed March 26, 2008.

Bodroghkozy, Aniko. *Groove Tube: Sixties Television and the Youth Rebellion*. Durham, NC: Duke University Press, 2001.

Brokaw, Tom. *The Greatest Generation*. New York: Random House, 1998.

Bronson, Fred. *The Billboard Book of Number 1 Hits*. New York: Billboard Books, 2003.

Brown, Peter and Steven Gaines. *The Love You Make: An Insider's Story of the Beatles*. New York: McGraw-Hill, 1983.

Carr, Roy. *The Rolling Stones: An Illustrated Record*. New York: Crown Publishing Group, 1976.

Carr, Roy and Tony Tyler. *The Beatles: An Illustrated Record*. New York: Harmony Books, 1975.

Chapman, Graham, John Cleese, Terry Gilliam, Eric Idle, Terry Jones, and Michael Palin, with Bob McCabe. *The Pythons Autobiography*. New York: Thomas Dunne Books, 2003.

Clark, Rick and Richie Unterberger. "The Dave Clark Five." *All Music Guide*, http://www.allmusic.com/cg/amg.dll?p=amg&sql=11:wifpxqw5ldte~T1. Accessed March 7, 2008.

Clayson, Alan. *Beat Merchants: The Origins, History, Impact and Rock Legacy of the 1960's British Pop Groups*. London: Blandford, 1995.

Cohen, Stanley. *Folk Devils and Moral Panics: The Creation of the Mods and Rockers*. New York: St. Martin's Press, 1980.

Cohn, Nik. *Rock from the Beginning*. New York: Pocket Books, 1969.

The Concise Beatles Liverpool. Spencer Leigh and Ray O'Brien, hosts. DVD. Arts Magic DVD AWA 067, 2006.

Copple, Tony. "Interview with Roy Young." *The Ottawa Beatles Site* (posted 2002), http://beatles.ncf.ca/roy.html. Accessed January 28, 2008.

Davies, Dave. *Kink: An Autobiography*. New York: Hyperion, 1996.

Davies, Ray. *X-Ray: The Unauthorized Autobiography*. Woodstock, NY: Overlook Press, 1996.

Doggett, Peter. Liner notes for *The Kinks*. CD. Sanctuary Records SMRCD025, 2004.

Eden, Dawn. Liner notes for *The Very Best of Chad and Jeremy*. CD. Varèse Sarabande 302 066 098 2, 2000.

Eder, Bruce. "Alexis Korner." *All Music Guide*, http://www.allmusic.com/cg/amg.dll?p=amg&sql=11:fifqxq95ld0e~T1. Accessed February 29, 2008.

Eder, Bruce. "Buddy Holly." *All Music Guide*, http://wc01.allmusic.com/cg/amg.dll?p=amg&sql=11:fifpxqe5ldae~T1. Accessed January 4, 2008.

Eder, Bruce. "Herman's Hermits." *All Music Guide*, http://www.allmusic.com/cg/amg.dll?p=amg&sql=11:kifuxqe5ld0e~T1. Accessed February 7, 2008.

Eder, Bruce. "Paul Revere and the Raiders." *All Music Guide*, http://allmusic.com/cg/amg.dll?p=amg&sql=11:h9fuxqugld6e~T1. Accessed January 21, 2008.

Eley, Chris. Liner Notes for *The Sound of Fury*. CD. Decca 844 990-2, 2000.

Elliott, Bobby. Liner notes for *Finest*. Two CDs. EMI 0946 3 91127 2 2, 2007.

Epstein, Brian. *A Cellarful of Noise.* New York: Pyramid Publications, 1965.

Erlewine, Michael, ed. *All Music Guide to Rock.* San Francisco: Backbeat Books, 1997.

Escott, Colin. Liner notes for *Somethin' Else: The Fine Lookin' Hits of Eddie Cochran.* CD. Razor & Tie RE 2162-2, 1998.

Graham, Bobby. "The Hit List." *The Legendary Bobby Graham: England's Greatest Session Drummer,* http://bobbygraham.co.uk/bobbygraham/hits.htm. Accessed February 7, 2008.

Greenberg, Bradley S. and Edwin B. Parker, eds. *The Kennedy Assassination and the American Public: Social Communication in Crisis.* Stanford, CA: Stanford University Press, 1965.

Harrington, Patrick and Bobby Graham. *The Session Man: The Story of Bobby Graham, the U.K.'s Greatest Session Drummer.* Raglan, Monmouthshire, Great Britain: Broom House, 2004.

Helander, Brock. *The Rock Who's Who* (2nd ed.). New York: Schirmer Books, 1996.

Hinman, Doug. *The Kinks: All Day and All of the Night.* San Francisco: Backbeat Books, 2004.

Hinman, Doug with Jason Brabazon. *You Really Got Me: An Illustrated World Discography of the Kinks, 1963–1993.* Rumford, RI: Rock 'n' Roll Research Press, 1994.

Hunter, Dave. "Comeback Kink." *The Guitar Magazine,* January 1999. Reprinted at http://www.davedavies.com/articles/tgm_0199.htm. Accessed April 14, 2008.

Hunter, Dave. "Voxes, Vees and Razorblades: The Kinks Guitar Sound." *The Guitar Magazine,* January 1999. Reprinted at http://www.davedavies.com/articles/tgm_0199–01.htm. Accessed February 13, 2008.

Inglis, Ian. "'Some Kind of Wonderful': The Creative Legacy of the Brill Building." *American Music* 21(summer 2003), pp. 214–235.

Krüger, Ulf. "Interview with Tony Sheridan." *Genesis Publications: Special Features,* http://www.genesis-publications.com/news/interviews/sheridan.html. Accessed January 29, 2008.

Laing, Dave. *The Sound of Our Time.* London: Sheed & Ward, 1969.

Leigh, Spencer. "Obituary: Adam Faith." *The Independent,* March 10, 2003. Available through *The Independent* Online Edition, http://news.independent.co.uk/people/obituaries/article36330.ece. Accessed January 14, 2008.

Lewisohn, Mark. *The Beatles Recording Sessions: The Official Abbey Road Studio Session Notes, 1962–1970.* New York: Harmony Books, 1988.

Liner notes for *Unearthed Merseybeat, Vol. 1: From the Birth of Merseybeat to Psychedelia.* CD. The Viper Label CD 016, 2003.

Liner notes for *Unearthed Merseybeat, Vol. 3: The Dawn of a New Era.* CD. The Viper Label CD 032, 2005.

Linett, Mark. Liner notes for *Surfin' Safari/Surfin' U.S.A.* CD. Capitol Records 72435-31517-2-0, 2001.

MacDonald, Ian. *Revolution in the Head: The Beatles' Records and the Sixties.* New York: Random House, 1997.

Maloof, Rich. *Jim Marshall: The Father of Loud.* San Francisco: Backbeat Books, 2004.

Marcus, Greil, ed. *Rock and Roll Will Stand.* Boston: Beacon Press, 1969.

Markowitz, Rhonda. *Folk, Pop, Mods, and Rockers, 1960–1966. Volume 2 of The Greenwood Encyclopedia of Rock History.* Westport, CT: Greenwood Press, 2005.

Marsden, Gerry with Ray Coleman. *I'll Never Walk Alone: An Autobiography.* London: Bloomsbury, 1993.

Marsh, Dave. *The Heart of Rock and Soul: The 1001 Greatest Singles Ever Made.* New York:
Da Capo Press, 1999.

Martin, George, with Jeremy Hornsby. *All You Need Is Ears.* New York: St. Martin's Press, 1979.

Matteo, Steve. *Let It Be.* New York and London: Continuum, 2004.

May, Chris and Tim Phillips. *British Beat.* London: Socion Books, 1974.

McCartney, Paul. Liner notes for *Run Devil Run.* CD. Capitol Records CDP 7243 5 22351
2 4, 1999.

Melly, George. *Revolt into Style: The Pop Arts.* Garden City, NY: Anchor Books, 1971.

Miles, Barry. *Paul McCartney: Many Years from Now.* New York: Henry Holt, 1997.

Morris, Jan. "Britain's Finest Hour." *Rolling Stone* no. 335 (January 22, 1981), p. 22.

Nuttall, Jeff. *Bomb Culture.* London: Paladin, 1970.

The Official Tony Sheridan Homepage, http://tony-sheridan.de.

Paytress, Mark. *The Rolling Stones: Off the Record.* London: Omnibus Press, 2003.

Powell, Mark. Liner notes for *John Mayall Plays John Mayall.* CD. Decca 9841779, 2006.

Rich, Jim. "Patch-Eyed Johnny Kidd Keeps Rock Rolling." *New Musical Express* no. 703, July 1,
1960, p. 8.

"The *RS* 500 Greatest Songs of All Time." *Rolling Stone* (online edition), http://www.rollingstone.
com/news/coverstory/500songs/. Posted December 9, 2004. Accessed February 24, 2008.

Schaffner, Nicholas. *The British Invasion: From the First Wave to the New Wave.* New York:
McGraw-Hill, 1982.

Sheridan, Tony. Liner notes for *The Beatles Featuring Tony Sheridan—In the Beginning.* LP. Polydor 24-4504, 1970. Reissued on CD, Polydor 314 549 268-2, 2000.

Stanley, Fred and Keith George, eds. *The New Dakota Dictionary of Skiffle.* Liverpool, UK:
Merseytime Press, 1999.

Stark, Steven D. *Meet the Beatles: A Cultural History of the Band that Shook Youth, Gender, and
the World.* New York: Harper, 2005.

Strauss, William and Neil Howe. *Generations: The History of America's Future, 1584 to 2069.* New
York: Quill, 1991.

Thompson, Dave. "The Vipers." *All Music Guide,* http://wm07.allmusic.com/cg/amg.dll?p
=amg&sql=11:fnfwxqekldfe~T1. Accessed November 25, 2007.

Thompson, Hunter S. *Hell's Angels.* New York: Ballantine Books, 1966.

Unterberger, Richie. "The Kinks." *All Music Guide,* http://www.allmusic.com/cg/amg.
dll?p=amg&sql=10:h9frxqqdldte. Accessed February 11, 2008.

"The Vox Story." *Vox Amplification,* http://www.voxamps.co.uk/thevoxstory/. Accessed April
22, 2008.

Welch, Chris. Liner notes for *Sonny Boy Williamson and the Yardbirds.* CD. Repertoire Records
REP 4776, 2007.

Whitburn, Joel. *The Billboard Book of Top 40 Hits* (6th ed.). New York: *Billboard* Books, 1996.

Whitburn, Joel. *Top Pop Singles, 1955–1996.* Menomonee Falls, WI: Record Research, 1997.

Wyman, Bill with Ray Coleman. *Stone Alone: The Story of a Rock 'n' Roll Band*. New York: Viking, 1990.

Wyman, Bill with Richard Havers. *Bill Wyman's Blues Odyssey: A Journey to Music's Heart and Soul*. New York: DK Publishing, 2001.

Zanes, Warren. *Dusty in Memphis*. New York: Continuum, 2003.

Zappa, Frank, with Peter Occhiogrosso. *The Real Frank Zappa Book*. New York: Poseidon Press, 1989.

Selected Discography

Because finding the original vinyl releases of various singles, EPs, and albums is difficult in the digital age, I have limited the listings in this discography to material that is available on CD reissues and compilations, and some material that is available more readily in downloadable, compressed audio files from legitimate online sources. Please note that many of the albums for which I have listed information about CD releases are also available as digital audio files. In fact, the listener may prefer this format, because it allows one to be more selective in one's purchases. Note, however, that some record companies and some artists have not licensed their material for download. In the case of artists for whom I have listed more than one album or compilation, I have listed the albums in approximately chronological order based on the original material. Information on the original vinyl (LP) and plastic (45-rpm single) releases of material by these artists can be found in various print publications, official Web sites, and fan-run Web sites.

THE ANIMALS

Retrospective. "House of the Rising Sun," "I'm Crying," "Baby Let Me Take You Home," "Gonna Send You Back to Walker," "Boom Boom," "Don't Let Me Be Misunderstood," "Bring It on Home to Me," "We Gotta Get Out of This Place," "It's My Life," "Don't Bring Me Down," "See See Rider," "Inside, Looking Out," "Hey Gyp," "Help Me Girl," "When I Was Young," A Girl Named Sandoz," "San Franciscan Nights," "Monterey," "Anything," "Sky Pilot," "White Houses," "Spill the Wine." CD. ABKCO 719325, 2004.

THE BEATLES

In the Beginning. (The Beatles featuring Tony Sheridan.) "Ain't She Sweet," "Cry for a Shadow," "Let's Dance," "My Bonnie," "Take Out Some Insurance on Me, Baby," "What'd I Say," "Sweet Georgia Brown," "When the Saints Go Marching In," "Ruby Baby," "Why," "Nobody's Child," "Ya Ya." CD. Polydor 314 549 268-2, 2000.

Please Please Me. "I Saw Her Standing There," "Misery," "Anna (Go to Him)," "Chains," "Boys," "Ask Me Why," "Please Please Me," "Love Me Do," "P.S. I Love You," "Baby It's You," "Do You Want to Know a Secret," "A Taste of Honey," "There's a Place," "Twist and Shout." CD. Parlophone CDP 7 46435 2, 1987. Also issued on Toshiba EMI 51111, 2007.

With the Beatles. "It Won't Be Long," "All I've Got to Do," "All My Loving," "Don't Bother Me," "Little Child," "Till There Was You," "Please Mister Postman," "Roll Over Beethoven," "Hold Me Tight," "You Really Got a Hold on Me," "I Wanna Be Your Man," "Devil in Her Heart," "Not a Second Time," "Money." CD. Capitol C2–46436, 1987. Also issued on Toshiba EMI 51112, 2007.

Past Masters: Volume One. "Love Me Do," "From Me to You," "Thank You Girl," "She Loves You," "I'll Get You," "I Want to Hold Your Hand," "This Boy," "Komm, gib mire deine Hand" ("I Want to Hold Your Hand" in German), "Sie liebt dich" ("She Loves You" in German), "Long Tall Sally," "I Call Your Name," "Slow Down," "Matchbox," "I Feel Fine," "She's a Woman," "Bad Boy," "Yes It Is," "I'm Down." CD. Parlophone CDP 7 90043 2, 1988.

CLIFF BENNETT AND THE REBEL ROUSERS

Cliff Bennett and the Rebel Rousers/Got to Get You into Our Life. "I Can't Stand It," "Sweet and Lovely," "Make Yourself at Home," "You've Really Got a Hold on Me," "Ain't that Lovin' You Baby," "Sha La La," "One Way Love," "Steal Your Heart Away," "It's All Right," "Beautiful Dreamer," "Mercy Mercy," "Talking About My Baby," "The Pick-Up," "It's a Wonder," "Ain't Love Good, Ain't Love Proud," "634–5789," "Roadrunner," "Baby Each Day," "Got to Get You into My Life," "Barefootin'," "See Saw," "I'm Not Tired," "Stop Her on Sight," "You Don't Know Like I Know," "C.C. Rider Blues." CD. EMI 7243 4 73325 2 4, 2004.

THE BIG THREE

Live at the Cavern. "What'd I Say," "Don't Start Running Away," "Zip-a-dee-doo-dah," "Reelin' and Rockin'." EP. Decca 8552, 1963.

Cavern Stomp. "Some Other Guy," "I'm with You," "Let True Love Begin," "By the Way," "Cavern Stomp," "Peanut Butter," "Bring It on Home to Me," "What'd I Say," "Don't Start Running Away," "Zip-a-dee-doo-dah," "Reelin' and Rockin'," "You've Got to Keep Her Under Hand." LP. Deram 844006–2. 1985. Reissued on CD as London 8440062, 1999.

This album is currently available as a made-to-order CD on Universal's music archive series. It includes all of the Big Three's singles and all the material from the *Live at the Cavern* EP. Short of finding a used copy of the EP, however, this may be the only source for recordings of this band.

DAVID BOWIE

I Dig Everything: The 1966 Pye Singles. "I'm Not Losing Sleep," "I Dig Everything," "Can't Help Thinking about Me," "Do Anything You Say," "Good Morning Girl," "And I Say to Myself." CD. Castle Music 06076 81130-2, 2001.

Although the material on this collection of David Bowie's early singles comes from the edge of the time period on which this book focuses, and although Bowie's work from before approximately 1970 was not particularly commercially successful, these self-penned songs illustrate both the influence of Mod rock ("Can't Help Thinking about Me") and hipster, John Barry–style rock ("I Dig Everything") on David Bowie. The song "And I Say to Myself" also exhibits a few musical references to 1964 Merseyside pop.

CHAD AND JEREMY

The Very Best of Chad and Jeremy. "A Summer Song," "From a Window," "No Other Baby," "Yesterday's Gone," "The Truth Often Hurts the Heart," "September in the Rain," "If I Loved You," "My How the Time Goes By," "Only Those in Love," "Like I Love You Today," "Willow Weep for Me," "Too Soon My Love," "What Do You Want with Me?," "Now and Forever," "Before and After," "I Don't Wanna Lose You Baby," "Distant Shores," "Teenage Failure." CD. Varèse Sarabande 302 066 098 2, 2000.

THE DAVE CLARK FIVE

The History of the Dave Clark Five. "Glad All Over," "Bits and Pieces," "Do You Love Me," "Can't You See That She's Mine," "Because," "Don't Let Me Down," "Any Way You Want It," "Everybody Knows (I Still Love You)," "Any Time You Want Love," "Thinking of You Baby," "Whenever You're Around," "Little Bitty Pretty One," "Crying Over You," "Don't Be Taken In," "When," "Reelin' and Rockin'," "Come Home," "Mighty Good Loving," "Hurting Inside," "Having a Wild Weekend," "'Til the Right One Comes Along," "Catch Us If You Can," "I'll Be Yours My Love," "I Am on My Own," "I Need Love," "Try Too Hard," "All Night Long," "Look Before You Leap," "Please Tell Me Why," "Somebody Find a New Love," "Satisfied with You," "At the Scene," "I Miss You," "Do You Still Love Me," "Nineteen Days," "I've Got to Have a Reason," "I Like It Like That," "Over and Over," "You Got What It Takes," "Doctor Rhythm," "Small Talk," "Concentration

Baby," Everybody Knows," "Inside and Out," "At the Place," "Best Day's Work," "Maze of Love," "Here Comes Summer," "Live in the Sky," "Everybody Get Together." Two CDs. Hollywood Records HR-61482-2, 1993.

To date, this is the only CD compilation of Dave Clark Five material authorized by Clark himself. Because this band's recordings have been so tightly controlled over the years, there have been a fair number of twenty-first-century releases of Dave Clark Five material of dubious legitimacy, including a seven-volume Russian release—*Anthology*—that pulls together just about every recording the group ever made. Dave Clark's official Web site, daveclarkfive.com, however, includes a "jukebox" feature that allows one to listen to many of the group's hit songs, as well as songs from Clark's musical show, *Time,* over the Internet in streaming audio format.

PETULA CLARK

Supersounds from the Superstar. "Downtown," "You'd Better Come Home," "Round Every Corner," "Two Rivers," "A Sign of the Times," "Color My World," "My Love," "Who Am I," "Call Me," "I Couldn't Live without Your Love," "You're the One," "I Know a Place," "This Is My Song," "Don't Sleep in the Subway," "Kiss Me Goodbye." CD. Wounded Bird 1765, 2007.

ADAM FAITH

The Very Best of Adam Faith. "What Do You Want?," "Poor Me," "Someone Else's Baby," "Johnny Comes Marching Home," "Made You," How about That," "Lonely Pup (In a Christmas Shop)," "This Is It," "Who Am I," "Easy Going Me," "Don't You Know It," "The Time Has Come," "Lonesome," "As You Like It," "Don't That Beat All," "Baby Take a Bow," "What Now," "Walkin' Tall," "The First Time," "We Are in Love," "If He Tells You," "I Love Being in Love with You," "Message to Martha (Kentucky Bluebird)," "Stop Feeling Sorry for Yourself," "Someone's Taken Maria Away," "Cheryl's Goin' Home." CD. EMI 7243 8 57413 2 6, 1997.

GEORGIE FAME AND THE BLUE FLAMES

20 Beat Classics. "Yeh Yeh," "Getaway," "Do Re Mi," "My Girl," "Sweet Things," "Point of No Return," "Get on the Right Track, Baby," "Ride Your Pony," "Moody's Mood for Love," "Funny How Time Slips Away," "Sunny," "Sitting in the Park," "Green Onions," "In the Meantime," "Papa's Got a Brand New Bag," "Blue Monday," "Pride and Joy," "Pink Champagne," "Let the Sunshine In," "I Love the Life I Live." CD. Polydor 847 810-2, 1980 (date of the original LP compilation—the CD does not include a separate publication date).

This CD compilation provides a fairly broad spectrum of Georgie Fame's work. For a compilation that focuses solely on his 1964–1966 recordings with the Blue Flames, consider *The Very Best of Georgie Fame and the Blue Flames* (Spectrum 550 015-2, 1997).

BILLY FURY

The Sound of Fury (40th anniversary edition). "That's Love," "My Advice," "Phone Call," "You Don't Know," "Turn My Back on You," "Don't Say It's Over," "Since You've Been Gone," "It's You I Need," "Alright, Goodbye," "Don't Leave Me This Way," "Maybe Tomorrow," "My Christmas Prayer," "I Got Someone," "Open Your Arms," "Don't Jump," "Magic Eyes," "Sleepless Nights," "Please Don't Go," "If I Lose You," "I Love You How You Love Me." Two CDs. Decca 844 990-2, 2000.

The 40th anniversary edition of *The Sound of Fury* includes monophonic and stereophonic mixes of the 10 songs on the original album, as well as bonus tracks that were recorded between 1959 and 1962. Listeners who are interested in hearing Fury's 1960–1964 recordings that find him incorporating a little more R&B and touches of British beat group style in his work might consider the CD *The Rocker* (Spectrum Music 981 865-1, 2005). The big band version of "Kansas City" and the beat group style of "Nothin' Shakin' (But the Leaves on the Tree)" are especially interesting, and the latter track is available for individual purchase as an iTunes download.

GERRY AND THE PACEMAKERS

Gerry and the Pacemakers at Abbey Road: 1963–1966. "How Do You Do It?," "Away from You," "I Like It," "You'll Never Walk Alone," "Chills," "A Shot of Rhythm and Blues," "Hello Little Girl," "Summertime," "Slow Down," "I'm the One," "You've Got What I Like," "Don't Let the Sun Catch You Crying," "Show Me That You Care," "It's Gonna Be Alright," "It's Just Because," "Ferry Cross the Mersey," "I'll Wait for You," "Why Oh Why," "I'll Be There," "Reelin' and Rockin'," "Whole Lotta Shakin' Going On," "Rip It Up," "You Win Again," "It'll Be Me," "Walk Hand in Hand," "La La La," "Girl on a Swing," "Big Bright Green Pleasure Machine." CD. EMI 21133, 1997.

HERMAN'S HERMITS

The Very Best of Herman's Hermits. "I'm into Something Good," "Your Hand in Mine," "Show Me Girl," "I Know Why," "Silhouettes," "Can't You Hear My Heartbeat," "Wonderful World," "Dream On, Dream On," "Just a Little Bit Better," "Take Love, Give Love," "A Must to Avoid,"

"The Man with the Cigar," "You Won't Be Leaving," "Listen People," "This Door Swings Both Ways," "For Love," "No Milk Today," "My Reservation's Been Confirmed," "East West," "What Is Wrong, What Is Right," "There's a Kind of Hush," "Gaslite Street," "Museum," "Moonshine Man," "I Can Take or Leave Your Loving," "Marcel's," "Sleepy Joe," "Just One Girl," "Sunshine Girl," "Nobody Needs to Know," "Something's Happening," "The Most Beautiful Thing in My Life," "My Sentimental Friend," "My Lady," "Here Comes the Star," "It's Alright Now," "Years May Come, Years May Go," "Smile Please," "Bet Yer Life I Do," "Searching for the Southern Sun," "Lady Barbara," "Don't' Just Stand There," "Oh You Pretty Thing," "Leaning on a Lamp Post," "Hold On!," "I'm Henry the VIII, I Am," "The End of the World," "Mrs. Brown You've Got a Lovely Daughter," "I Gotta Dream On," "Dandy," "Don't Go Out in the Rain," "Heartbeat," "For Your Love," "Bus Stop," "Wings of Love," "London Look." Two CDs. EMI 477321, 2005.

Because of the fact that the members of Herman's Hermits were so young, had such little prefame professional experience, and had been together for such a relatively short time before they started making hit records, they did not have a huge backload of cover material in their repertoire like bands such the Beatles did. Therefore, the listener does not need to obtain early archival material to hear this band's development. Because of the enormity of this collection, the casual listener might do well to stick with a greatest hits collection on CD or download. Be aware, however, that some hits collections contain rerecorded versions. Some of the rerecorded versions, in fact, come from incarnations of the band that contain only one of the original members. This EMI collection includes extensive program notes and the track listing includes some B-sides that some listeners may find even more interesting than some of the band's biggest hits.

THE HOLLIES

Finest. "Searchin'," "Lucille," "Memphis," "Just One Look," "We're Through," "Nitty Gritty/ Something's Got a Hold on Me," "Too Much Monkey Business," "It's in Her Kiss," "I'm Alive," "When I Come Home to You," "Fortune Teller," "Hard Hard Year," "I've Got a Way of My Own," "I Am a Rock," "Bus Stop," "Tell Me to My Face," "Clown," "On a Carousel," "Schoolgirl," "Carrie Anne," "Have You Ever Loved Somebody," "You Need Love," Heading for a Fall," "Postcard," "Step Inside," "Away, Away, Away," "Man with No Expression (Horses through a Rainstorm)," "Listen to Me," "The Times They Are a-Changin'," "Just Like a Woman," "Soldier's Dilemma," "Gasoline Alley Bred," "Little Girl," "Lady Please," "Long Cool Woman in a Black Dress," "To Do with Love," "Magic Woman Touch," "The Air That I Breathe," "4th July, Asbury Park (Sandy)," "I'm Down," "Star," "Russian Roulette," "Amnesty," "Let Love Pass." Two CDs. EMI Gold 3911272, 2007.

This collection covers a broad spectrum of a long-lasting British Invasion band. Unlike the greatest hits collections that are available, *Finest* contains a number of covers of Chuck Berry, Little Richard, and other American R&B songs ("Lucille," "Memphis,"

"Searchin'," and "Too Much Monkey Business") that make it possible to compare the Hollies' versions with those of other British Invasion bands. These early recordings are especially valuable in exhibiting the influence of the Everly Brothers on the Hollies' approach to vocal harmony. The collection also includes notes on some of the recordings by drummer Bobby Elliott. An inexpensive alternative that includes only the big hit singles is *All-Time Greatest Hits* (Curb Records D2-77377, 1990).

JOHNNY KIDD AND THE PIRATES

25 Greatest Hits. "Shakin' All Over," "Please Don't Touch," "You've Got What It Takes," "Restless," "Linda Lu," "A Shot of Rhythm and Blues," "I'll Never Get Over You," "Hungry for Love," "Always and Ever," "Oh Boy," "The Fool," "Send Me Some Lovin'," "Let's Talk About Us," "Some Other Guy," "Whole Lotta Woman," "Your Cheatin' Heart," "You Can Have Her," "I Just Want to Make Love to You," "I Can Tell," "I Know," "If You Were the Only Girl," "Feelin'," "Yes Sir, That's My Baby," "The Birds and the Bees," "Doctor Feelgood." CD. EMI 7243 4 95480 2 2, 1998.

THE KINKS

3 Classic Albums. "Beautiful Delilah," "So Mystifying," "Just Can't Go to Sleep," "Long Tall Shorty," "I Took My Baby Home," "I'm a Lover Not a Fighter," "You Really Got Me," "Cadillac," "Bald Headed Woman," "Revenge," "Too Much Monkey Business," "I'm Been Driving on Bald Mountain," "Stop Your Sobbin'," "Got Love If You Want It," "Long Tall Sally," "You Still Want Me," "You Do Something to Me," "It's Alright," "All Day and All of the Night," "I Gotta Move," "Louie, Louie," "I Gotta Go Now," "Things Are Getting Better," "I've Got That Feeling," "Too Much Monkey Business," "I Don't Need You Anymore," "Look for Me Baby," "Got My Feet on the Ground," "Nothin' in the World Can Stop Me Worryin' 'bout That Girl," "Naggin' Woman," "Wonder Where My Baby Is Tonight," "Tired of Waiting for You," "Dancing in the Street," "Don't Ever Change," "Come on Now," "So Long," "You Shouldn't Be Sad," "Something Better Beginning," "Everybody's Gonna Be Happy," "Who'll Be the Next in Line," "Set Me Free," "I Need You," "See My Friends," "Never Met a Girl Like You Before," "Wait Till the Summer Comes Along," "Such a Shame," "A Well Respected Man," "Don't You Fret," "I Go to Sleep," "Milk Cow Blues," "Ring the Bells," "Gotta Get the First Plane Home," "When I See That Girl of Mine," "I Am Free," "Till the End of the Day," "The World Keeps Going Round," "I'm on an Island," "Where Have All the Good Times Gone," "It's Too Late," "What's in Store for Me," "You Can't Win," "Dedicated Follower of Fashion," "Sittin' on My Sofa," "When I See That Girl of Mine," "Dedicated Follower of Fashion." Three CD. Castle Music 897899, 2004.

Early Kinks material is difficult, if not impossible, to find for legitimate download, apparently mostly because of the licensing issues that have arisen as a result of record label moves and resulting contractual disputes. For a historical perspective on just where this important band came from and how their early recordings compare with those of their British Invasion contemporaries, this collection is one of the few alternatives. It contains the band's first two albums: *The Kinks* (1964) and *Kinda Kinks* (1965); what some fans consider the band's first classic album: *The Kinks Kontroversy* (1965); as well as alternative mixes and demos. If the listener is not interested in a complete look at the band's work from the earliest part of its career, these albums are also available individually on several reissue labels. For historical information, it generally is best to look for reissues from later dates: the 2004 reissue of *The Kinks* (Sanctuary SMRCD025), for example, includes extensive notes on the recording and release history of the individual tracks, as well as information on studio musicians who participated on the recording sessions. If the listener is primarily interested in the band's best-known material then there are a number of greatest hits packages available on various labels.

ALEXIS KORNER AND BLUES INCORPORATED

R&B from the Marquee (expanded edition). "Gotta Move," "Rain Is Such a Lonesome Sound," "I Got My Brand on You," "Spooky but Nice," "Keep Your Hands Off," "I Wanna Put a Tiger in Your Tank," "I Got My Mojo Working," "Finkle's Café," "Hoochie Coochie," "Down Town," "How Long, How Long Blues," "I Thought I Heard That Train Whistle Blow," "She Fooled Me," "I'm Built for Comfort," "I'm a Hoochie Coochie Man," "Night Time Is the Right Time," "Everything She Needs," "Up-Town," "Blaydon Races." CD. Castle Music 1371, 2006.

British blues bands such as Alexis Korner and Blues Incorporated and John Mayall's Bluesbreakers were perhaps most notable for and influential because of their live work, so it is unfortunate that this album was recorded not at the Marquee, as the title implies, but in a Decca Records studio. It is, however, an important early (1962) document of the development of British blues, and Blues Incorporated's subsequent *Live at the Cavern Club* seems a little too much of a cash-in on the fame of that Liverpool venue, which was not really a blues haven. There are several competing reissues of Korner's *R&B from the Marquee* album. I have listed the Castle Music release because of its broad range of bonus tracks, and because it is available both in CD and downloadable format.

MANFRED MANN

Down the Road Apiece: Their EMI Recordings, 1963–1966. "Why Should We Not," "Brother Jack (Frere Jacques)," "Now You're Needing Me," "Chattering," "Cock-a-Hoop," "5-4-3-2-1," "Without You," "I'm Your Hoochie Coochie Man," "You Got to Take It," "Down the Road Apiece," "Mr. Anello," "Sack O-Woe," "Hubble Bubble (Toil and Trouble)," "I've Got My Mojo Working," "Smokestack Lightning," "I'm Your Kingpin," "Ain't That Love," "Bring It to Jerome," "Sticks and

Stones," "Untie Me," "Don't Ask Me What I Say," "It's Gonna Work out Fine," "What You Gonna Do?," "All Your Love," "Do Wah Diddy Diddy," "Groovin'," "Can't Believe It," "The One in the Middle," "Did You Have to Do That," "A Love Like Yours (Don't Come Knocking Every Day)," "She," "John Hardy," "Sha-La-La," "Watermelon Man," "Dashing Away with the Smoothing Iron," "Come Tomorrow," "What Did I Do Wrong," "I'll Make It up to You," "With God on Our Side," "Look Away," "Sie," "Weine Nicht," "Bare Hugg," "What Am I to Do," "Oh No Not My Baby," "L.S.D.," "I Can't Believe What You Say," "What Am I Doing Wrong?," "Poison Ivy," "The Way You Do the Things You Do," "The Abomidable Snowmann," "Watch Your Step," "Stormy Monday Blues," "I Really Do Believe," "You Don't Know Me," "My Little Red Book," "Since I Don't Have You," "You Gave Me Somebody to Love," "You're for Me," "Hi Lili Hi Lo," "If You Gotta Go, Go Now," "Stay Around," "There's No Living Without Your Loving," "Tired of Trying, Bored with Lying, Scared of Dying," "I Put a Spell on You," "God Rest Ye Merry Gentlemenn," "Let's Go Get Stoned," "That's All I Ever Want from You Baby," "Spirit Feel," "Tennessee Waltz," "When Will I Be Loved," "Tengo Tango," "Still I'm Sad," "I Got You Babe," "My Generation," "(I Can't Get No) Satisfaction," "You're Standing By," "She Needs Company," "Machines," "Driva Men," "It's Getting Late," "Pretty Flamingo," "Come Home Baby." Four CDs. EMI 3972152, 2007.

The listener can find several hits collections from Manfred Mann. I have included only this extensive package because even a perusal of the titles shows the stylistic range of this band.

JOHN MAYALL'S BLUESBREAKERS

John Mayall Plays John Mayall: Live at Klook's Kleek. "Crawling up a Hill" (two versions), "I Wanna Teach You Everything," "When I'm Gone," "I Need Your Love," "The Hoot Owl," "R&B Time: Night Train, Lucille" "Crocodile Walk" (two versions), "What's the Matter with You," "Doreen," "Runaway," "Heartache," "Chicago Line," "Mr. James," "Blues City Shakedown," "My Baby Is Sweeter." CD. Decca 984 177-9, 2006.

Mayall's band's best-known recording is the 1966 album *Bluesbreakers with Eric Clapton,* perhaps one of the greatest British blues albums ever recorded. The problem is that Clapton's debut recording with the group captures the Bluesbreakers after the time period with which we primarily are concerned in this book. The present album was recorded in December 1964 and it provides an especially interesting contrast with recordings of other British blues bands of the time because it focuses on original songs and not covers of the works of American blues masters. The other especially interesting feature of *John Mayall Plays John Mayall* is that the album demonstrates more than any of the later more purely blues-focused recordings Mayall's band made the connections between British blues and blues-based rock. Note that this CD reissue contains extra tracks not included on the original vinyl release.

THE MOODY BLUES

An Introduction to the Moody Blues. "Go Now!," "I'll Go Crazy," "Something You Got," "Can't Nobody Love You," "I Don't Mind," "Stop," "It Ain't Necessarily So," "Bye Bye Bird," "Steal Your Heart Away," "Lose Your Money (But Don't Lose Your Mind)," "I Don't Want to Go on Without You," "Time Is on My Side," "From the Bottom of My Heart (I Love You)," "Everyday," "This Is My House (But Nobody Calls)," "Life's Not Life," "Boulevard be la Madelaine," "People Gotta Go." CD. Fuel 604, 2006.

Because there were essentially two versions of the Moody Blues—the Denny Laine–led R&B band and the Justin Hayward–led album-oriented progressive rock band—and because the second installment of the Moody Blues is so much better known than the first, it may take some looking around to find this collection. However, in addition to being available in CD format, *An Introduction to the Moody Blues* (which includes only recordings from the Denny Laine/Clint Warwick era) is also available for legitimate download on the Internet.

BRIAN POOLE AND THE TREMELOES

The Very Best of Brian Poole and the Tremeloes. "Do You Love Me?," "Candy Man," Someone, Someone," "Twist and Shout," "What Do You Want with My Baby?," "Time Is on My Side," "I Can Dance," "Out of My Mind," Medley: "Don't Ever Change"/"Let's Twist Again"/"The Loco-Motion," "The Three Bells (The Jimmy Brown Song)," "I Want Candy," "Rag Doll," "We Know," "It's All Right," "Mr. Bass Man," "South Street," "Hey Girl," "Well Who's That," Medley: "Twistin' the Night Away"/"Things"/"Return to Sender," "Twelve Steps to Love." CD. Spectrum Music 551 321-2, 1996.

CLIFF RICHARD

Complete Hits. "I Only Live to Love," "Legata ad un Granello di Sabbia," "A Matter of Moments," "The Young Ones," "Living Doll," "Magic Is the Moonlight," "Outsider," "It's Not for Me to Say," "Don't Talk to Him," "How Wonderful to Know," "Fall in Love with You," "Please Don't Tease," "On the Beach," "The Next Time," "I Love You," "When the Girl in Your Arms Is the Girl in Your Heart," "I'm Looking out the Window," "It's All in the Game," "Do You Wanna Dance," "Lucky Lips," "The Minute You're Gone," "Again," "Kiss," "Summer Holiday," "Sway (Quien Sera)," "All My Love (Solo Tu)," "Constantly," "Theme for a Dream," "Do You Remember," "This Day," "The Twelfth of Never," "Nine Times out of Ten," "I'll Walk Alone," "I Could Easily Fall (In Love with You)," "Amor, Amor, Amor," "In the Country," "A Voice in the Wilderness," "Love Letters," "That's My Desire," "Wonderful Life," "Gee Whiz It's You," "It'll Be Me," "Bachelor Boy," "Move It," "Blue Moon," "Blame It on the Bossa Nova," "Quizas, Quizas,

Quizas (Perhaps, Perhaps, Perhaps)," "It's All Over," "Visions," "Congratulations," "We Don't Talk Anymore," "I Just Don't Have the Heart," "Ocean Deep," "Miss You Nights." Two CDs. EMI 0094638398929, 2006.

THE ROLLING STONES

England's Newest Hit Makers. "Not Fade Away," "Route 66," "I Just Want to Make Love to You," "Honest I Do," "Now I've Got a Witness," "Little by Little," "I'm a King Bee," "Carol," "Tell Me," "Can I Get a Witness," "You Can Make It If You Try," "Walking the Dog." CD. ABKCO 93752, 2002.

More Hot Rocks (Big Hits and Fazed Cookies). "Tell Me," "Not Fade Away," "The Last Time," "It's All Over Now," "Good Times Bad Times," "I'm Free," "Out of Time," "Lady Jane," "Sittin' on a Fence," "Have You Seen Your Mother Baby, Standing in the Shadow?," "Dandelion," "We Love You," "She's a Rainbow," "2000 Light Years from Home," "Child of the Moon," "No Expectations," "Let It Bleed," "What to Do," "Money," "Come On," "Fortune Teller," "Poison Ivy," "Bye Bye Johnny," "I Can't Be Satisfied," "Long Long While." Two CDs. ABKCO CD 627, 1990.

One of the challenges faced in trying to find the earliest recordings of the Rolling Stones is that material such as "Come On," "Fortune Teller," "Poison Ivy," "Bye Bye Johnnie," "I Can't Be Satisfied," "Money," "What to Do," and "Long Long While," which appeared on EPs and singles before the band's first album was recorded, tended for many years only to be available on compilations such as *More Hot Rocks.* This collection is recommended for the listener who wants to put some of the early recordings into historical perspective by comparing them to the group's later recordings; however, recent releases such as *Singles 1963–1965* (ABKCO 711219, 2004) provide more complete coverage of the Rolling Stones' early work. The disadvantage of *Singles 1963–1965* is that the 33 tracks are spread over 12 CDs, in order to mimic the original 45-rpm singles. In addition to the original CD reissue of *More Hot Rocks,* there is a 2002 version of the collection that includes several additional early bonus tracks.

THE SEARCHERS

Meet the Searchers. "Sweets for My Sweet," "Alright," "Love Portion Number Nine," "Farmer John," "Stand by Me," "Money (That's What I Want)," "Da Doo Ron Ron," "Ain't Gonna Kiss Ya," "Since You Broke My Heart," "Tricky Dicky," "Where Have All the Flowers Gone," "Twist and Shout," "It's All Been a Dream," "Liebe" ("Money" in German), "Farmer John" (in German), "Mais c'etait un reve" ("It's All Been a Dream" in French). CD. Castle Music CMRCD 155, 2001.

This CD reissue of the Searchers' 1963 debut album includes monophonic and stereophonic mixes of the original album's tracks, as well as bonus material in the form of the German and French overdubs. While *Greatest Hits* provides for wider historical coverage of this Liverpool band, *Meet the Searchers* is a particularly important collection because of the comparisons it provides (e.g., the Searchers' recording of "Money" versus the Beatles' and the Rolling Stones' contemporary recordings of the song, or the Searchers' version of "Twist and Shout" versus recordings by the Beatles and Brian Poole and the Tremeloes).

Greatest Hits. "Sweets for My Sweet," "Love Potion Number Nine," Sugar and Spice," "Ain't That Just Like Me," "Needles and Pins," "Don't Throw Your Love Away," "Someday We're Gonna Love Again," "When You Walk in the Room," "What Have They Done to the Rain," "Goodbye My Love," "Bumble Bee," "He's Got No Love," "When I Get Home," "Take Me for What I'm Worth," "Each Time," "Everybody Come Clap Your Hands," "Have You Ever Loved Somebody," "Secondhand Dealer." CD. Rhino R2 75773, 1988.

THE SHADOWS

The Shadows' Greatest Hits. "Apache," "Man of Mystery," "The Stranger," "F.B.I.," "Midnight," "The Frightened City," "Kon-Tiki," "36–24–36," "The Savage," "Peace Pipe," "Wonderful Land," "Stars Fell on Stockton," "Guitar Tango," "The Boys," "Dance On!," "Quatermassters Stores." CD. EMI 7243 578198 2 4, 2004.

This CD reissue of the original 1963 album contains both stereophonic and monophonic versions of all the tracks. The selection "Quatermassters Stores" (yes, the spelling is correct) is a bonus track. Some listeners may want to consider a single CD release (EMI CDP 7 95732 2, 1991) that combines the band's first two albums: *The Shadows* and *Out of the Shadows*. While perhaps not essential, the Shadows' first two albums illustrate their ties to jazz and middle-of-the-road pop better than their greatest hits collection.

TONY SHERIDAN

In the Beginning. "Ain't She Sweet," "Cry for a Shadow," "Let's Dance," "My Bonnie," "Take out Some Insurance on Me, Baby," "What'd I Say," "Sweet Georgia Brown," "When the Saints Go Marching In," "Ruby Baby," "Why," "Nobody's Child," "Ya Ya." CD. Polydor 314 549 268-2, 2000.

Although the 1961 and 1962 recordings of the Beatles and Tony Sheridan are available in several CD reissues (some with different versions of "Sweet Georgia Brown" and some with additional tracks by Sheridan backed by other musicians) the sound quality and liner notes make this the preferable reissue. Unlike material that the Beatles later released variously on Parlophone, EMI, Capitol, and Apple, the material on this album is widely available for legitimate digital download. Note that the Beatles perform only on "Ain't She Sweet," "Cry for a Shadow," "My Bonnie," "Take out Some Insurance on Me, Baby," "When the Saints Go Marching In," "Why," and "Nobody's Child." Tony Sheridan does not appear on "Ain't She Sweet" and "Cry for a Shadow."

TOMMY STEELE

The Decca Years: 1956–1963. "Rock with the Caveman," "Rock Around the Town," "Doomsday Rock," "Elevator Rock," Singing the Blues," "Rebel Rock," "Knee Deep in the Blues," "Teenage Party," "Butterfingers," "Cannibal Pot," "Shiralee," "Grandad's Rock," "Butterfly," "Water, Water," "A Handful of Songs," "Hey You!," "Plant a Kiss," "Nairobi," "Neon Sign," "Happy Guitar," "Princess," "It's All Happening," "What Do You Do," "The Only Man on the Island," "I Puts the Lightie On," "Come On, Let's Go," "Put a Ring on Her Finger," "A Lovely Night," "Marriage Type Love," "Hiawatha," "The Trial," "Tallahassee Lassie," "Give! Give! Give!," "You Were Mine," "Young Ideas," "Little White Bull," "Singing Time," "What a Mouth (What a North and South)," "Kookaburra," "Happy-Go-Lucky Blues," "(The Girl with the) Long Black Hair," "Must Be Santa," "Boys and Girls," "The Dit-Dit Song," "My Big Best Shoes," "The Writing on the Wall," "Drunken Guitar," "Hit Record," "What a Little Darlin'," "He's Got Love," "Green Eye," "Butter Wouldn't Melt in Your Mouth," "Where Have All the Flowers Gone," "Flash, Bang, Wallop!," "She's Too Far above Me," "Half a Sixpence," "Giddy-up-a-Ding Dong," "Kaw-Liga," "Young Love," "Take Me Back Baby," "Build Up," "Time to Kill," "Hair-Down Hoe-Down," "Sweet Georgia Brown," "Tommy the Toreador," "Hollerin' and Screamin'," "Lonesome Traveller" (*sic*), "So Long (It's Been Good to Know Yuh)." Two CDs. Decca 466 409-2, 1999.

THE SWINGING BLUE JEANS

25 Greatest Hits. "Hippy Hippy Shake," "It's Too Late Now," "Three Little Fishes," "Good Golly Miss Molly," "Lawdy Miss Clawdy," "Long Tall Sally," "Shakin' All Over," "Tutti Frutti," "Don't Make Me Over," "Crazy 'bout My Baby," "Shake, Rattle, and Roll," "Don't You Worry About Me," "I've Got a Girl," "You're No Good," "Angie," "I'm Gonna Sit Right Down and Cry (Over You)," "It's All Over Now," "Make Me Know You're Mine," "Promise You'll Tell Her," "That's the Way It Goes," "Do You Know," "Now the Summer's Gone," "It Isn't There," "Tremblin'," "Shaking Feeling." EMI Gold 4954832, 1998.

There are several compilations available for the Swinging Blue Jeans. I have listed this one, because at the time of this writing, it is available through several online merchants at attractive prices. Note that below, in the Various Artists section, the Swinging Blue Jeans appear on the *Unearthed Merseybeat* series, in live and otherwise rare recordings.

VINCE TAYLOR AND HIS PLAYBOYS

Le Rock c'est ça. "20 Flight Rock," "Sweet Little Sixteen," "Don't Leave Me Now," "C'mon Everybody," "Shaking All Over," "Long Tall Sally," "Love Me," "Lovin' up a Storm," "So Glad You're Mine," "Baby Let's Play House." CD. Universal 0760852, 2003.

VARIOUS ARTISTS

Unearthed Merseybeat, Vol. 1: From the Birth of Merseybeat to Psychedelia. The Merseys: "Sorrow"; Johnny Guitar and Paul Murphy: "She's Got It"; Denny Seyton and the Sabres: "House of Bamboo"; the Kirkbys: "Don't You Want Me No More"; the Bo-Weevils: "I'm a Lover, Not a Fighter"; King Size Taylor and the Dominoes: "Good Golly Miss Molly"; the Remo Four: "Trambone"; Gerry and the Pacemakers: "What'd I Say"; the Merseybeats: "The Things I Want to Hear (Pretty Words)"; the Four Just Men: untitled instrumental; the Dennisons: "Tutti Frutti"; the Newtowns: "Tomorrow"; Denny Seyton and the Sabres: "I'm Gonna Love You Too"; the Eyes: "She"; Jason Eddie: "Mr. Busdriver"; the Remo Four: "Walk Don't Run"; the Kirkbys: "Dreaming"; King Size Taylor and the Dominoes: "Fortune Teller"; the Swinging Blue Jeans: "Keep Me Warm ('til the Sun Shines)"; Wimple Winch: "Rumble on Mersey Square South." CD. The Viper Label CD 016, 2003.

Unearthed Merseybeat, Vol. 2: The Golden Age. The Kirkbys: "Penny in My Pocket"; Denny Seyton and the Sabres: "Karen"; Gerry and the Pacemakers: "Whole Lotta Skakin' Goin' On"; the Four Just Men: "Friday Night"; the Swinging Blue Jeans: "40 Miles of Bad Road"; the Merseybeats: "All I Have to Do Is Dream"; the Delmonts: "Before You Accuse Me"; the Newtowns: "Please Stay"; the Bo-Weevils: "Keep Your Hands Off Her"; the Four Just Men: "La Bamba"; the Pathfinders: "I'm Ashamed of You Baby"; Denny Seyton and the Sabres: "Big River"; Rory Storm and the Hurricanes: "Lend Me Your Comb"; the Swinging Blue Jeans: "Walk Don't Run"; the Cordes: "Clarabella"; Gerry and the Pacemakers: "Why Oh Why"; Earl Preston and the TTs: "Bony Moronie"; the Merseybeats: "So How Come (No One Loves Me)"; the Kirkbys: "Bless You"; the Newtowns: "Over the Rainbow." CD. The Viper Label CD 027, 2004.

Unearthed Merseybeat, Vol. 3: The Dawn of a New Era. The Kinsleys: "Do Me a Favour"; Lance Fortune and the Firecrests: "Come Go With Me"; the Merseybeats: "Soldier of Love"; the Connoisseurs: "Make Up Your Mind"; the Swinging Blue Jeans: "Once in a While"; Earl Preston and the TTs: "Betty Jean"; Dale Roberts and the Jaywalkers: "Daydream"; Earl Royce and the Olympics: "Shake Your Tail Feathers"; Lance Fortune and the Firecrests: "That'll Be the Day"; Gerry and the Pacemakers: "Pretend"; Jimmy Campbell/23rd Turn Off: "Flowers Are Flowering"; the Connoisseurs: "I'm Looking Through You"; the Four Just Men: "Sticks and Stones"; the Four Originals: "You Won't Be Leaving"; Chris Curtis: "Baby, You Don't Have to Tell Me"; the Merseys: "Nothing Can Change This Love"; the Swinging Blue Jeans: "Ain't What You Do"; Steve Day and the Syndicate: "The Last Bus Home"; Focal Point: "Sycamore Sid"; Jimmy Campbell: "Michaelangelo." CD. The Viper Label CD 032, 2005.

Although this series of three CDs from a small independent Liverpool record label may be difficult to find, these valuable and rare recordings are easily available as legitimate downloads from iTunes and eMusic.com. Some of these tracks are among the oldest Liverpool rock and roll recordings, dating from as early as the late 1950s.

THE VIPERS SKIFFLE GROUP

The Very Best of the Vipers Skiffle Group. "Cumberland," "If I Had a Hammer," "Don't You Rock Me Daddy-O," "Pick a Bale of Cotton," "Hey Liley, Liley Lo," "Easy Rider," "10,000 Years Ago," "It Takes a Worried Man to Sing a Worried Song," "Skiffle Party Medley," "I Saw the Light," "Railroad Steamboat," "Wanderin'," "Pay Me My Money Down," "Jim Dandy," "Streamline Train," "Skiffle Party Medley No. 2," "John B. Sails," "Horning Bird," "Gloryland," "Maggie May," "I Know the Lord Laid His Hands on Me." CD. EMI 584078, 2003.

There is a more complete collection of recordings available (the multidisc set *10,000 Years Ago Today,* Bear Family 15954, 1996); however, it is quite expensive. *The Very Best of the Vipers Skiffle Group* is considerably more affordable and still provides a sense of the importance of the group in the development of British rock music.

MARTY WILDE

The Best of Marty Wilde. "A Teenager in Love," "Donna," "Sea of Love," "Endless Sleep," "Bad Boy," "Rubber Ball," "Put Me Down," "Danny," "Johnny Rocco," "Ever Since You Said Goodbye," "Don't Pity Me," "Splish Splash," "High School Confidential," "Wild Cat," "Blue Moon of Kentucky," "Teenage Tears," "Tomorrow's Clown," "Little Girl," "Are You Sincere," "The Fight," "Hide and Seek," "Jezebel," "Honeycomb," "Dream Lover." CD. Spectrum 551 794-2, 1995.

THE YARDBIRDS

Sonny Boy Williamson and the Yardbirds. "Bye Bye Bird," "Mister Downchild," "23 Hours Too Long," "Out of the Water Coast," "Baby Don't Worry," "Pontiac Blues," "Take It Easy Baby" (two versions), "I Don't Care No More," "Do the Weston," "The River Rhine," "A Lost Care," "Western Arizona," "Slow Walk," "Highway 69," "Hey Little Cabin." CD. Repertoire Records REP 4776, 2007.

Five Live Yardbirds. "Too Much Monkey Business," "Got Love If You Want It," "Smokestack Lightning," "Good Morning Little Schoolgirl," "Respectable," "Five Long Years," "Pretty Girl," "Louise," "I'm a Man," "Here 'Tis." CD. JVC Japan 61097, 2000.

Index

About the Author

JAMES E. PERONE is Professor of Music at Mount Union College, where he teaches American music and music theory, and chairs the Department of Music. He is the series editor for The Praeger Singer-Songwriter Collection, for which he has also written four volumes: *The Sound of Stevie Wonder* (2006), *The Words and Music of Carole King* (2006), *The Words and Music of David Bowie* (2007), and *The Words and Music of Prince* (2008). He is also the author of several Greenwood Press books, including *Music of the Counterculture Era* (2004) and *Woodstock: An Encyclopedia of the Music and Art Fair* (2005).